£2-00

D1493259

4/QC82C37

THE STRANGE LIFE OF
CHARLES WATERTON

BY THE SAME AUTHOR

The Nondescript

The Nondescript was the skin of a Red Howler monkey from British Guiana, manipulated by Squire Waterton with such skill that it appeared to be a stuffed specimen of a Georgian gentleman.

The Strange Life of
CHARLES WATERTON
1782≶1865

by

Richard Aldington

LONDON
EVANS BROTHERS LIMITED

First Published 1949

PRINTED AND BOUND IN ENGLAND BY
HAZELL WATSON & VINEY Ltd
AYLESBURY AND LONDON

Acknowledgment

I am indebted to my friends, William Dibben for books on Waterton, and Alister Kershaw for help and always valuable criticism, and offer them these inadequate thanks.

Contents

Illustrations

I

Then thus: I have from Port le Blanc, a bay
In Brittany, receiv'd intelligence
That Harry Duke of Hereford, Renald Lord Cobham,
That late broke from the Duke of Exeter,
His brother, Archbishop late of Canterbury,
Sir Thomas Erpingham, Sir John Ramston,
Sir John Norbery, SIR ROBERT WATERTON. . . .

(Richard II, Act II, Sc. i.)

CHARLES WATERTON, twenty-seventh Lord of Walton Hall, in the county of Yorkshire, was known to his friends and familiars as "the Squire," just as, during the same epoch, Wellington was known to all the world as "the Duke." Both were men of strong individuality, robust humour, pungent expressions, opinionated, without self-consciousness, detesters of humbug and contemners of idleness, and both belonged to the upper class. But there our parallel must abruptly cease, for, while Arthur Welles-ley's practical genius made him the hero of his age and country, Charles Waterton, by whimsical quirks of character developed by education, became one of its strangest freaks, a holy clown, a kind of ornithological Brother Juniper.

One who knew Charles Waterton and loved him well—and none comes to know the Squire without learning to love him—has re-corded that he paid little attention to most of the attacks made on his veracity as a traveller and naturalist. But he was "deeply stung" when a writer casually remarked that the Squire was "eccentric." He "never forgot it," and in all seriousness would protest that he was "the most commonplace of men." If he should emphasise the justness of his protest by "scratching the back of his head with the big toe of his right foot," or by clambering with ape-like agility barefoot to the "top of a noble oak," what could his listener do but agree?

A character so artless, a career so grotesque, an eccentric so unique form an irresistible combination.

Human society in its evolving institutions tends alternately to stress and to cultivate individualism and collectivism. Whether, as is claimed, this is "a law of progress," or whether, as some suspect, it is merely the result of our tendency to do one thing because our fathers did the opposite, is a matter of opinion. What is germane to our purpose is that Charles Waterton was educated by priests of the Society of Jesus—men who carried the sacrifice of selfhood to the collectivist claims of their Society farther than the most extreme of modern political theorists—and that he grew up to be one of the most uncompromising individualists in the most individualist epoch of once individualist England.

Clearly, it is in the individualist phases of society that the eccentric flourishes. In other epochs he becomes a heretic and goes up in flames, or is marked down as politically undesirable and is liquidated. If he manages to exist in periods of tyranny, it is as precariously as François Villon during a hard winter or Rabelais under a monk's cowl.

But in an age when the average, the general, the commonplace in human character and personality are earnestly put forward as the ideal, the *summum bonum* of humanity, it is difficult to agree with the Squire in his resentment against the title of "eccentric." The English eccentric, though now as extinct as the moa and the passenger pigeon, was a most interesting and valuable contribution to the world's human fauna. But what do we mean by an "eccentric"? We must not apply this proud title to people who are merely among the enormous crowds of the feeble-minded or have gone cracked for some reason or other. No; eccentricity is the comedy-farce of individualism unconsciously carried to absurdity, but not to insanity. Perhaps it is unfair to liken the Squire to Saint Francis of Assisi's brother Juniper, in whom the saint is said to have taken so much delight, for he shows a mediæval grossness and tastelessness which it is impossible to admire. Most of his pranks are loutish, and others hardly rise above the repulsive mischances of the cretin. The Squire, at least, was a gentleman.

By origin he belonged, and his family belonged for centuries, to the upper squirearchy, the "County" as they used to say. But the claims of this illustrious house went far beyond mere English aristocracy, and it seems most appropriate that a personage so extraordinary should have extraordinary origins. True, the craft or mystery of the genealogist is a difficult and abstruse one, much exercised with bridging gaps and discovering missing links; and the lay reader, carried into the abyss of time, may suspect in this impressive pedigree a touch of that over-willingness to believe so characteristic of the Squire.

Yet the fact that he believed in it so implicitly is more important than its authenticity, even if that were sanctioned by Norroy and Clarenceux. In view of the Squire's ascetic practices and almost saintly reputation in his later years, we may surely see significance in the fact that he was—or believed he was—descended from seven or eight canonised persons. With so many saints in the family, piety becomes hereditary. Nothing is more characteristic of the later Watertons in general, and of the Squire in particular, than an obstinate loyalty to the faith of their fathers, even in the darkest days of unpopularity and persecution.

Perhaps it is worth noting that nearly all these saintly ancestors were royal. The most remote of these in place and time was Vladimir I of Russia (956–1015), a "heathen hound" who was converted to Christianity by hearing of the splendours of Byzantine ritual, and who married Basil II's sister, Anna, presumably the "St Anne of Russia" of Waterton tradition. But these two, if ever regularly canonised, were Greek Orthodox saints, and therefore heretical. Then there is a "Queen of Germany," St Matilda; and that St Margaret (1045–1093), Queen of Scotland, who rebuilt the monastic buildings on Iona. St Humbert of Savoy, another ancestor, was the third Duke of that name, and died in 1189. Ferdinand III (1199–1252) fought the Moors, massacred the Albigensians, married his daughter Eleanor to Edward I of England, and was canonised in 1671. Finally, there is St Louis (1214–1270), Crusader and ascetic, who certainly had a touch of the Squire about him, since of him it is recorded that "he had a sense of humour but gave hair-shirts to his friends."

On the profane side the earliest recorded direct ancestor sounds an even more curious and remarkable person than the saints. This was "Norman of Normandy," whose son Reiner became Lord of Waterton in 1159. He, we are told, was "a Saxon," though why a Saxon should have been called Norman of Normandy baffles conjecture. Our Waterton was not of the main line of this Saxo-Norman, but descended from a second son—the Watertons of Waterton dying out in the male line in the fifteenth century. The Watertons of Walton were the progeny of John Waterton, who acquired the Walton estates by marriage in 1453.

These feudal Watertons played their part in the national and civil wars of the Middle Ages, and are said to have fought at Crécy and Azincourt. The Sir Robert Waterton mentioned by Shakespeare joined that Harry Hereford who dethroned Richard II; and among the payments received he and his son, John, were made Masters of the Horse successively to Henry IV and Henry V. An ancestor who was "Master of the Horse at Agincourt" was certainly a family legend to treasure and "be in our flowing cups freshly remember'd" —even though the Squire was a teetotaller.

The Watertons survived the Wars of the Roses which obliterated so many noble English families, but troubles began for them at the Reformation. Contrary to the will of our Sovereign Lord the King (in Watertonian phraseology, "Harry the Eighth, our *royal goat*"), the Watertons obstinately remained loyal to the old form of religion, and consequently became recusants and were deprived of much of their extensive property. According to the Squire, the Reformation occurred because our royal goat "fell scandalously in love with a buxom lass," but he never condescended to explain just how that interesting fact influenced the innumerable Protestants of Germany, France, the Low Countries and other lands. But whatever the causes, there was the Reformation, and there were the Watertons on the wrong side of the religious fence. During the brief reign of "good" or "bloody" Mary Tudor, a Waterton was made High Sheriff of Yorkshire, but thereafter nothing official of "a genteel and confidential nature" was offered by Government to any member of this ancient family. They consoled themselves for fines, sequestrations and humiliations by dwelling on the inevitable and eternal damnation of their enemies, and by piously handing on certain—possibly authentic?—relics of their ancestor, Sir Thomas More, who undoubtedly was judicially murdered for refusing to support the King's marriage to Anne Boleyn.

Insensibly the Watertons sank into the thoughts and prejudices of rustic sporting squires, but it is hardly necessary to add that there was a Waterton at Marston Moor, and that his lady had to stand a siege of Walton Hall "by Oliver Cromwell." Now whatever the Squire and others of his mind have advanced against the Lord Protector of the Commonwealth of England, they can scarcely deny him a miraculous power of ubiquity. It was Sir Roche Boyle who told the Speaker that "not being a bird, I could not be in two places at once"; but Oliver was clearly an advance on the bird. There is scarcely a ruined castle, old mansion or decayed manor-house in the realm, from Cornwall to Berwick-on-Tweed, which was not besieged (simultaneously one must suppose) by Oliver in person.

Often the crop-eared usurper was repulsed from these sieges, and invariably by the ladies of deceased or wandering cavaliers, who also invariably combined (*mem-sahibs* to the last) martial valour with stately courtesy and piquant invective. As it was elsewhere, so —according to the Waterton tradition—it was at Walton Hall. Abandoning all minor concerns, such as ruling England, building a fleet, baffling the Pope and swaying the European balance of power, the dictator of three kingdoms and commander-in-chief of the Parliamentary armies came along with a troop of horse, an infantry company and no artillery to storm an old country house. That he was "not able to get in," as the Squire exultantly boasted, is one of those unsolved mysteries of the past over which it is hopeless to brood and to wrangle. It seems not unfair that the Lord Protector should console himself for this bitter disappointment by carrying off "every thing in the shape of horses and cattle that his men could lay their hands on."

The evidence for this picturesque story was family tradition— handed down of course with the most scrupulous exactitude as such traditions always are—the presence of "musket balls" (instantly labelled "Oliver Cromwell's") in an old oak door, and a small iron cannon-ball discovered by the Squire's father, supposed to have been fired from "an iron swivel-gun" from a (destroyed) third storey of the gate when it (the cannon-ball) "fractured the leg" of one of the besieging soldiery. Judge of the Squire's exultant feelings when, on dredging the lake in 1855, they brought up a small culverin (Wood gives a picture of it) and—"the little iron ball mentioned above, seems to have been cast to fit this gun." It proved the truth of the whole story. "I have no doubt, in my own mind, but that this is the gun and this the ball which were used at the period of the defence."

The disabilities suffered by Roman Catholics in England during the seventeenth and eighteenth centuries were not so strenuous as the rack and faggot reserved for Lutheran heretics in Catholic countries, but they were disagreeable enough. A Catholic had to pay double land taxes and a fine of twenty pounds a month for not attending Church. In comparison, the fact that he could not be a Member of Parliament or Justice of the Peace seems a minor calamity. It is not surprising that high-spirited people chafed against such arrangements, or that the Waterton family contemplated the arrival of "Dutch William" with disgust, and blindly attached themselves to hopes for the restoration of the exiled Stuarts.

When Prince Charles invaded England with his rabble of Scots, Jacobites and Continental adventurers, the Squire's grandfather was promptly arrested and sent a prisoner to York. When, after Culloden, he was released, he found that his horses had been impounded, though being maintained at his expense, while he was not allowed to keep any horse worth more than five pounds—nothing being so galling to a fiery Cavalier as a bad horse. At this time, according to family tradition, "our plate was put under water." Imagine then the Squire's delight, when, along with the culverin mentioned, he recovered from the lake this lost treasure, consisting of "many coins, three or four keys of very ancient shape, a silver spur, and two silver plates."

After the splendid if distant kinship with royal saints noticed above, it seems almost an anti-climax to note that through his grandmother the Squire claimed descent from Sir (now Saint) Thomas More, whose clock with a particularly loud chime the Watertons owned. He was also related to such County families as the Swinburnes of Capheaton, the Charletons of Hazelside and the Bedingfields of Oxburg. Anne Waterton, the Squire's mother, was a Bedingfield, and a near relative of that Sir John Bedingfield who, in 1796, despite his political prejudices, saved King George III from an angry mob outside Drury Lane.

Charles Waterton, "the" Squire, was born on the 3rd June, 1782, at Walton Hall, the eldest son of Thomas and Anne Waterton. It is an unfortunate fact that the Squire, who has written of himself with such entertaining frankness, has left us with practically no information about his parents and his brothers and sisters. We are not even told (for example) when his mother died. It is recorded, though not by her son, that she was "a lady of more than ordinary dignity and judgment" who "early and successfully taught her children high principles and scrupulous conduct." Unluckily, none of the biographers has recorded any of the things which her eldest son said when he discoursed of "her and her deeds with affectionate reverence."

I find but one example recorded of this lady's "judgment" and "scrupulous conduct," and that in connection with an event which fittingly and dramatically opens that long chapter of accidents which distinguished her son's life. At an early but unspecified age, young Squire was much attached to one of his sisters, and liked to rush about the park with her. These "merry children," as the biographer indulgently calls them, found a lark's nest; whereupon the young Squire, "overflowing with fun" and a precocious love of experimental biology, swallowed one of the eggs whole. Little sister tearfully reported this to Mamma, who with excellent "judgment" instantly gave the boy "a mustard emetic," with the result (among others) that "he could never afterwards endure the taste of mustard."

A little more, though not much, is recorded of the Squire's father. His Yorkshire rusticity had been tempered by an education abroad under English Jesuits, who contrived at least to teach him Latin and to give him a taste for the Latin poets. The family traditions which he implicitly believed and passed on to an equally credulous son show at any rate that he was not "corroded by modern scepticism and infidelity." When his heir wished to ride to hounds, old Mr Waterton "liberally and spiritedly" (why "spiritedly"?) bought him a couple of hunters. Later on, alarmed by the dissipations of the hunting set, he desired his son to stop hunting, in a conversation where the two made speeches to each other like the heroes in the *Iliad*. Clearly, he was not a man to be trifled with, for when one of the deer on the Walton Hall island attacked somebody, Mr Thomas Waterton caused them all to be "discarded." He was also a "great sportsman," one of those lovers of animals who show their love for wild life by destroying it.

Although the Squire gives so little information about his parents in his Autobiography, and his intimates forgot to record nearly all his reminiscences of them, there is one anecdote of his father which must not be neglected, if only because of the valuable light it throws on the type of humour fashionable among the County families of aristocratic eighteenth-century England. Strangely—but yet how characteristically!—the Squire omitted this story from his Autobiography, but remembered it when he was penning one of his whimsical essays:

"It was gravely reported that my father baited a hook attached to a long line in one of his stew ponds. An eel swallowed the bait, and whilst the eel was floundering in the water, a heron waded in and swallowed the eel. The heron being of a lax habit of body, the eel glided swiftly downwards from the stomach, and came into the world again through the heron's inferior aperture. Another and another heron played the same game, till at last no less than twelve herons were found there, all strung together on the same line, with the eel still fast to the hook in its native element, in lieu of remaining to be dissolved by the gastric juice of the heron. The report added that my father carried all the twelve herons home in triumph . . . ."

Mr Thomas Waterton was fond of relating this, his "grouse-in-the-gun-room" story, for his son has recorded that "when he told it, I have seen the moisture ooze out at the corners of his eyes, whilst his whole frame was convulsed with laughter." As the Squire's friend and earliest biographer, Dr Hobson, so truly says, he had a "never-failing, enduring and affectionate veneration for the memory of his late parents," and especially "evidenced" this "devoted and reverential esteem" by relating "anecdotes and dubiously-chronicled legends relative to his father," of which far too few unfortunately have been preserved.

II

AMONG the grievances of Roman Catholics in the days before Emancipation was education. How could they send a boy to Oxford, for example, since matriculation involved signing the Thirty-nine Articles of Belief of the Church of England? Only a foreign university could meet the case, and younger Catholic boys were sent to the Jesuit Fathers who established themselves at St Omer in the sixteenth century, and on the suppression of the Order in France moved to Bruges, and eventually to Liége. But, at one time, boys known to be going to or returning from this school were liable to summary arrest, and their parents to severe penalties. Such persecution naturally bred reaction in high-spirited boys, who acquired and even exaggerated the religious and political prejudices of their parents and teachers.

By 1792, when our young Squire was ten and held ripe for the beginning of his education, matters had improved sufficiently for young Catholic children at any rate to be birched by priests of their own faith. The small school to which Charles Waterton was sent has since become famous as having furnished the founders of Ushaw. But when he was first despatched from Walton Hall to Tudhoe, near Durham, the school was a small private affair run by a couple of priests, described by the Squire some sixty years later as "holy and benevolent." They certainly needed to be both in order to deal with the incorrigible imp they had so thoughtlessly accepted, though the benevolence seems to have been displayed chiefly in a more than Scriptural zeal for the rod.

Charles Waterton was now launched on his life of adventure and accident. His infant experience with the swallowed lark's egg and the mustard emetic was, so to say, his baptism of fire into a seventy years' campaign. His fascinating mixture of intrepidity and folly, of physical dexterity and clumsiness, of obstinate bigotry and warm-hearted kindliness, of absurd credulity and genuine knowledge, throughout life involved him in extraordinary situations and calamities. Among the numerous elements which went to produce this genial eccentric we must include the particular brand of education he received.

He very nearly did not live to receive any education at all. At the age of eight, he tells us with his usual cheerfulness, he "managed to climb upon the roof of an out-house," trying to get a starling's nest. "Had my foot slipped . . ." well, most probably his story would have ended prematurely. Let us praise the "ancient house-keeper" who lured his young mastership down safely with a bit of gingerbread, and then—how understandably!—"seized me as though I had been a malefactor."

No doubt that means the "ancient" lady lined his breech with the heartiest smacks she could muster. Certainly this was the method adopted by the "holy and benevolent" priests as it dawned upon them what they had to deal with. As the stories of the lark's egg and the starling's nest go to prove, the Squire at the tenderest age had, in his own words, "made vast proficiency in the art of finding birds' nests." But this and other pranks did not meet with the approval of that "very correct disciplinarian," the Reverend Joseph Shepherd, who undertook to eliminate both the devil and this precocious love of natural science from his pupil by means of "the birch-rod." He knew not with whom he was dealing. In those days priests wore breeches and worsted stockings, and these were no defence against the Squire:

". . . Whilst he was treating me to the unwelcome application of the birch-rod, I flew at the calf of his leg, and made him remember the sharpness of my teeth. I wish I had them now. . . ."

To bite another priest? Probably not, though it must be recorded that the Squire retained this habit of biting people's legs even when he was an octogenarian. It was his habit "to show his playful" levity by creeping "on all fours, like a dog" under the hall table when he saw Dr Hobson coming to the house. While the long-winded doctor was taking off his coat the hidden Squire "commenced to growl like a savage dog . . . and seized my legs in such a practically canine manner that"—in short, Dr Hobson actually thought for a moment it was a dog, and his nerves suffered accordingly.

If holy Mr Shepherd's idea was that he could flog the love of natural history out of his pupil, he was completely mistaken. In commenting on this failure the Squire in later life hit out a happy metaphor. The "bright colours in crockeryware," he said, "are made permanent by the action of fire"; and in a similar way "the warm application of the birch-rod did but tend to render my ruling passion more distinct and clear."

Nor was the birch-rod more successful in curing the young Squire of his propensity for extraordinary, and from the point of view of his teachers unnecessary, and annoying pranks. Even the aid of holy Mr Storey in this judicious flogging only succeeded in teaching the pupil to distinguish between his wigs—the ornate and highly powdered one meant he would be out all day, so there would be no floggings that day from him at any rate.

But there were plenty on other occasions. Our friend was discovered by Mr Storey making an unauthorised exit from the schoolroom window, whereupon in his panic the young Squire got stuck between the bars and put his foot through the pane. With ready wit Mr Storey exclaimed "angrily": "So there you are, Master Charles, are you?" By way of ingratiating himself with this disciplinarian, "Master Charles" went after his hens' nests, and being yapped at by the schoolmaster's favourite "little black and white bitch," tactfully "knocked it head over heels with half a brick." He then got himself severely bitten by the tom-cat, tried to ride one of Mr Storey's cows, and had a fight with a gander—"whilst he was hissing defiance . . . I struck him on the neck and killed him outright." Finally, having launched himself on a pond in an old tub with a couple of stakes as oars, he contrived to upset it at the moment the schoolmaster appeared—"down I went to the bottom, and rose again covered with mud and dirt."

There seems to have been a touch of Dotheboys Hall about this school. Four young men—the very ones who afterwards founded Ushaw—came to complete their studies, but having "giant appetites" found the food inadequate. Our pious young Squire came to the rescue of these good young men—"I stormed the larder and filled my pockets full of bread and cheese, &c."

"And thus," he reflects in old age, "I went on month after month, in sadness and in sunshine, in pleasure and in pain." Month after month! Poor Mr Storey, poor Mr Shepherd!

Meanwhile, an event had occurred in Europe which was to have its influence on the young Squire's life as on everybody's. The French Revolutionary Government had sent its *demi-brigades* storming across the Low Countries. As they approached Liége the English Jesuits had to ask themselves what they should do with themselves and their pupils. Wisely, they decided not to let themselves be captured by rabid anti-clericals. But where were they to go? In England, religious acerbity had weakened; it was no longer believed that a good Catholic must necessarily be a bad subject, and the penal laws were no longer rigorously enforced. The exile of the Jesuits had become an anachronism, and they courageously took refuge in the lion's mouth. A Catholic, Mr Weld of Lulworth Castle (a personal friend of George III, by the way), presented them with a large, old and ruinous country house—and thus Stonyhurst College came into existence. Mr Thomas Waterton decided that Charles should be moved from Tudhoe to Stony-hurst, and therefore brought him and his collection of birds' eggs back to Walton Hall. Even more sensibly, he decided to give the boy "several months' holiday"—almost a lifetime at fourteen—and we can imagine with what ecstasy the young Squire took this respite from the birch-rods of the two holy men and how happy he was to have the freedom of the fields and lanes. It was the foundation of the remarkable field naturalist he became.

Yet even these "halcyon days"—as the Squire, with Ovid in mind, would have called them—could not pass without at least one almost fatal accident to Charles and palpitating excitement for the rest of the family. As behoved an English Catholic gentleman of ancient lineage, Mr Thomas Waterton maintained "a foreign Mass Priest," Monsieur Raquedel, to say Mass in the private chapel and to shrive the family consciences. One night M. Raquedel heard an unusual sound in the room next to his bedroom, jumped up to investigate, and was just in time to prevent the young Squire from walking out the window in his sleep. "As soon as he caught hold of me, I gave a loud shriek." Questioned the next day, Charles confessed he had dreamed he was on the way "to a neighbouring wood, in which I knew of a crow's nest." Once more, the ruling passion.

There was one valuable advantage for the young Squire in this transfer from Tudhoe to Stonyhurst. The Fathers were as "holy and benevolent" as the Tudhoe masters, but though the Squire claims that Mr Storey was "a profound Latin scholar," this was probably truer of the Stonyhurst men. But the difference and the advantage lay in the fact that the Fathers were wise practical psychologists. They soon realised that there was no evil in the boy and that, on the contrary, he had an attractive personality. His innumerable scrapes at Tudhoe were due chiefly to high spirits, courage and unwise attempts to frustrate his "irresistible propensity to natural history." The innumerable floggings at Tudhoe could not have been considered as anything but an injustice as well as an outrage by the victim, and might have soured and brutalised a naturally cheerful nature. Clearly no educational or moral end was served by treating the collecting of birds' eggs as a crime.

On the other hand, as the Squire himself handsomely admits, his "predominant propensity" was a nuisance to the community, since it caused him constantly to break bounds and rules. The Fathers solved the problem thus:

"By a mutual understanding, I was considered rat-catcher to the establishment, and also fox-taker, foumart-killer and crossbow-charger at the time when the young rooks were fledged. Moreover, I fulfilled the duties of organ-blower and football-maker with entire satisfaction to the public."

Mr Edmund Selous, the naturalist, condemns this solution as "a body- and soul-killing one," not only because to fall from a naturalist to a rat-catcher is a "derogation," but also because the rat-catching became associated with ideas and symbols which stimulated Waterton's political and religious prejudices. It is not known who invented the myth that the brown or "Hanoverian" rat was introduced into England by the same ship that brought King George I and an end to the hopes of a Catholic dynasty; nor can anyone say that Waterton was taught by the Jesuits to believe this myth, or to identify the destruction of these alleged Hanoverian vermin symbolically with the destruction of Protestant bipeds. Still, throughout his life Waterton continued a relentless war on "Hanoverian rats"—in marked contrast to his protection of other wild life—and the countless, not to say wearisome, references to "Hanoverian rats" in his writings certainly were not without religious and political intent, and were not intended to further that tolerance for others which Waterton claimed so fractiously for his own sect.

The encouragement of science and biology and natural history to the detriment of other studies is never to be observed in classical scholars and not often then in religious bodies. "Science had its place," no doubt, but what was that place? It does not seem that the Stonyhurst Fathers thought of young Waterton as a possible luminary of natural science. On the contrary, their solution seems to hint that they not unnaturally considered him the usual British Nimrod type, overflowing with physical energy (which should be usefully employed instead of frustrated into a series of scrapes) and interested in wild animals only to the extent of killing them; so let the young barbarian be trained to slay those definitely noxious to man or required for the table. The fact that the tasks of organ-blower and football-maker were added to that of rat-catcher would seem to indicate that what the Fathers chiefly had in mind was the harmless diversion of excessive physical activity.

In spite of Mr Selous, I do not see how they could have done better, considering the epoch. Did Eton and Harrow encourage nature study, biology and kindness to animals in 1796? There is absolutely no evidence that the Jesuits suggested to him the "Hanoverian rat" symbolism—Waterton might equally well have picked this up from his Jacobite parent or, had it been undiscovered before,[1] could easily have evolved it from that fertile White Knight inventiveness of his. At any rate, the good Fathers succeeded in obtaining complete influence over their pupil, and turned a rebellious boy into a docile and happy one:

"I followed up my calling with great success. The vermin disappeared by the dozen; the books were moderately well thumbed; and according to my notion of things, all went on perfectly right . . . *Poteras jam, Cadme, videri felix.*"

The fact that Waterton declares that, on leaving Stonyhurst, he spent a year with his father, *"Gaudens equis canibusque et aprici gramine campi"* (i.e. enjoying field sports), goes to show that the Fathers were right in their "frustrated Nimrod" diagnosis of him. So complete was their influence over him that he remained a Stonyhurst boy all his life. It is not quite true to say that he "always wore" the school uniform of a blue-tailed coat with gold buttons and a check waistcoat. True, as Dr Hobson obligingly tells us, the Squire "pertinaciously adhered" to this costume, but only on "extraordinary occasions." His usual dress at home was "a brown jacket without skirts, very wide trousers and worsted stockings." It is perhaps unnecessary to add that the Squire, who went barefoot in the jungles of Guiana, at Walton Hall wore shoes so loose that he could "by giving his leg a sudden jerk, throw them a considerable distance in any direction he might desire," which he was apt to do at any moment until an advanced age "when in happy harmony with all around him." His hat usually had "a half-detached crown or a few air holes" in it.

Still, wearing the school uniform as his *"robe de parade"* is significant, especially when we add that for many years towards

[1] "Hanoverian rat" was a commonplace of Jacobite propaganda.

the end of his life he always spent Christmas at Stonyhurst. But the most remarkable and valuable example of the Jesuits' influence has yet to be told. When Waterton was in the "class of Poetry" (about equivalent to the Lower Sixth), his form-master was Father Clifford, "a first cousin of the noble Lord of that name" who, "after educating those intrusted to his charge with a care and affection truly paternal, burst a blood-vessel, and retired to Palermo. . . ." One day, before that unfortunate occurrence, Father Clifford sent for young Waterton to come to his room, and "in a tone of voice perfectly irresistible," made the following speech:

"Charles, I have been long studying your disposition, and I clearly foresee that nothing will keep you at home. You will journey into far-distant countries, where you will be exposed to many dangers. There is only one way for you to escape them. Promise me that, from this day forward, you will never put your lips to wine, or to spirituous liquors. The sacrifice is nothing, but, in the end, it will prove of incalculable advantage to you."

That the promise was instantly given goes without saying. What is extraordinary and shows at once the influence of the teacher and the integrity of the pupil is that it was never once broken in over sixty years. (Beer, which was tacitly allowed, was discarded when, on returning from a long absence abroad, the Squire found it unpleasantly bitter.) There can be no doubt that the exaction of this promise was a stroke of genius, and shows how completely and wisely Father Clifford had come to understand the young man's character. With all his perspicacity, Father Clifford could scarcely have foreseen the perilous "wanderings" of the Squire in Guiana. But he knew, of course, that in peace the eldest son of such a family would make the grand tour, and perhaps assumed that if the war continued, so high-spirited a young man would join the Forces. (In spite of the Squire's life-long protestations and complaints that "nothing genteel or confidential" was offered him by Government, many Catholic gentlemen did serve in the Army, though the highest ranks may have been closed to them—the Duke of Wellington once told the House of Lords that nearly half his officers in the Peninsular War were Catholics.) Father Clifford's insight was not so much prophetic as psychological. He saw this queer, good-hearted, impulsive, blundering fellow might by judicious control be restrained at any rate from criminal violence to others or himself, but that if he began to lose his self-control under the influence of drink, he would probably become an habitual drunkard and certainly involve himself in a series of disastrous actions and freaks. Without restraint he might have become another Jack Mytton or "Hellgate" Barrymore. The Charles Waterton we have come to know and delight in was to an incalculable degree the work of Father Clifford. However, we must not attribute too much even to such intelligent handling, for Waterton's son, Edmund, who was educated in a similar way, turned out a very different and disappointing character. But the Squire was himself convinced that he was eternally indebted to the Jesuits, as the following tribute shows:

"The day I left the Jesuits' college was one of heartfelt sorrow to me. Under Almighty God and my parents I owe everything to the Fathers of the Order of St Ignatius. Their attention to my welfare was unceasing, whilst their solicitude for my advancement in virtue and in literature knew no bounds. . . . To the latest hour of my life I shall acknowledge, with feelings of gratitude, the many acts of parental kindness which I so often received at the hands of the learned and generous Fathers of Stonyhurst College, 'Præsidium et dulce decus meum.' "

III

Such was the young Squire when he returned home from Stonyhurst, bringing with him a credulousness which would have been surprising in an unlettered Saxon hind, and a habit of perpetually quoting Latin tags which gives an extra touch of quaintness to his articles on natural history, but must have grown very wearisome in familiar conversation. Even Dr Hobson is "sorry to acknowledge" that "Mr Waterton had an inordinate and . . . injudicious amount of credulity in his composition," for which the doctor is inclined to blame "the Romish Church." He says nothing about the Latin tags, no doubt because he had the same pernicious habit himself.

The credulity had its advantages for Mr Thomas Waterton (himself no mean practitioner in that line, if we may judge by the tales he told his son), inasmuch as it went hand in hand with instant obedience. Now that the young Squire was home for good, his "education completed" even to the point of his being able to climb trees barefoot with the agility of an ape, the question must often have come up: What was he to do in life? Obviously, the most important duty of wealthy English landowners is to protect their tenants from the fearful depredations of the fox. The young Squire must ride to hounds.

Whereupon, as already noted, old Mr Waterton "spiritedly" bought his son a couple of hunters and sent him to hunt with the pack of Lord Darlington, of whom it is recorded that he had an "elegant seat on horseback and cool intrepidity in charging fences," for which or other services to the State he was created Duke of Cleveland. With his temperament and such a master, the young Squire very soon made himself conspicuous on the hunting field by his reckless riding. Even among the hard-drinking, hard-riding Yorkshire squires of the year 1800, he was a sensation. "Zounds! Mr Waterton, what a jump!" shouted one Baronet, staggered into loquacity by the sight of horse and rider plunging over a hedge and into a quarry on the other side—a reckless leap which would have killed nine men out of ten. As the two families were not even on speaking terms at the time, the Baronet's surprise must indeed have been great. Nor was his admiration less, for "they talked together, the feud was at an end, and they rode home friends."

The Squire was always proud of having ridden to hounds with Lord Darlington, for he mentions it more than once in his writings as a sort of knock-down blow to critics of his riding prowess. He was also extremely proud of the fact that his horsemanship (or shall we say, his luck on horseback?) was praised by this great Lord Darlington. Evidently he must have boasted of this at home, for Mr Thomas Waterton suddenly reversed himself on the subject of hunting. He was "scared," we are told. True, he knew Charles did not drink, but who could guarantee that he might not be seduced into drinking or, what was far worse, into the debts and bankruptcy which had befallen several members of this celebrated Hunt, though (according to the Squire) "from reasons totally unconnected with hunting." Whereupon, if we may believe the Squire's recollection and Dr Hobson's reporting, the following remarkable dialogue took place:

"*Mr Thomas Waterton* (scared): Charles, I fear this hunting may ultimately lead you into similarly disgraceful difficulties, now that I frequently hear of your jumping five-barred gates, and being so highly complimented by Lord Darlington for your bold riding. Praise from an old and acknowledged thoroughly good sportsman, and more especially from one of the 'right sort,' and with a sprig of nobility attached to his name, glibly glides into the brains of young men, and, now and then, turns them upside down, and it would greatly distress me if you should slip the cable and come to grief. You obliged me by commencing to hunt—will you still further oblige me by giving it up?"

"*Charles* (instantaneously): Yes, Father, I will do whatever you desire me to do, but I am satisfied that hunting has nothing whatever to do with the failure of the parties to whom you have alluded. On the contrary, I believe that hunting has been of material service to them, in warding off the evil day for a certain period. The hunting field substantially invigorated the physical energies of these men, and, whilst in it, they were neither guzzling champagne, throwing the dice, nor transgressing the bounds of morality, all of which habits extracted infinitely more guineas from their breeches pockets than ever the most extravagantly priced hunters did; and, as to moral comparison, we will let that pass, but from this day, agreeably to your wishes, I shall never again appear in crimson, nor risk my neck over a five-barred gate."

It seems probable that neither debauchery nor bankruptcy was the real fear. What worried old Mr Waterton (and doubtless even more, Mrs Waterton) were the five-barred gates and the reckless leaps into quarries. They had visions of their eldest son being carried home on one of these five-barred gates, for by this time they must have been fully and painfully aware of his infinite capacity for getting himself into weird accidents. It must have seemed a miracle to them that they had been able to rear him to manhood. But, now that fox-hunting was abandoned, here was the young Squire just come of age and without an occupation—for a passionate devotion to natural history could hardly be counted as anything more than a hobby. His father would refer to it with a "significant smile" as a *"studium inutile,"* while Mrs Waterton—eagerly hoping no doubt that some other interest would crop up to divert him from the incessant climbing of trees, which she must have feared would end up in broken limbs and neck—was "very anxious that I should see the world."

The Peace of Amiens had come to interrupt for a time the long struggle between France and Europe which had been going on for most of the young Squire's life, and was to continue (though without his active participation) until he was thirty-three. Mothers are often anxious that sons should travel—it may put off the evil hour of marriage. At any event it was decided that Charles should pay a visit to Malaga, where two of his Bedingfield uncles had established themselves, since their "great parts" and "brilliant education" were inadequately recognised at home.

If Mrs Waterton really thought she was "keeping Charles out of mischief" by sending him to reside with her brothers in Spain, she was reckoning without her young Cæsar and his fortune. At first, all went well. The Squire and his younger brother ("poor fellow! he died afterwards of the yellow fever") set sail in November 1802; and, after no more than the usual delays, vexations and miseries of navigation in the old romantic sailing days, they safely reached Cadiz, which they found *en fête* "in honour of royal nuptials."

Mr Duff, the British Consul, took the boys to a bull-fight. He particularly warned them not to lose sight of him in the scrimmage and confusion of leaving the crowded arena, as they did not know their way about Cadiz. Will it be credited? Although the Consul "was dressed in a brilliant scarlet uniform" or livery, Charles, gaping at "a thousand objects," contrived to lose sight of him.

Unluckily, there were "hundreds of Spaniards in scarlet cloaks" (a picturesque touch, this), and the young Squire wandered about Cadiz until nearly midnight, when a French gentleman "most kindly took me to the Consul's house, which was a long way off."

The next stage of the journey was, strange to say, accomplished without untoward incident, and Charles was united to his Malaga uncles, who "had a pleasant country house at the foot of the adjacent mountains," and "many were the days of rural amusement which I passed at it."

Andalusia in 1803 must have been picturesque and interesting, still intact and unrobbed by Napoleon's "liberating" troops, still with the wealth of its vast colonial empire, with customs and costumes inherited from the Middle Ages and the Renaissance, and the accumulation of centuries of art. The churches and cathedrals, which are still the art museums of Spain, were then in all their unpillaged splendour. But the young Squire's notions of "rural amusements" were almost wholly sporting and ornithological. This is what he has chiefly recorded of "more than a year of my life" spent "in Malaga and its vicinity without misfortune, without care, and without annoyance":

"The red-legged partridges abounded . . . and the vultures were remarkably large; whilst goldfinches appeared to be much more common than sparrows in this country. During the evening, the quails and bee-eaters arrived in vast numbers. . . . Once when I was rambling on the sea-shore, a flock of a dozen flamingoes passed nearly within gunshot of me."

During this year Waterton made an excursion with a friend to Gibraltar, where he was fortunate enough to see the usually invisible baboons changing quarters from one part of the Rock to another. Years afterwards, in his epoch-making work, *The Monkey Family*, the Squire excogitated a theory to account for the presence of these "Barbary apes." They had been cut off by a catastrophe of appalling dimensions which let the Atlantic into the Mediterranean, and as there were no trees on the Rock, they had to live on the ground. Strange as such a theory sounds coming from a creationist who thought he was descended from Adam and Eve, there was in it this amount of truth—there probably was such a catastrophe, but in the Pleiocene, long before Adam. And then, the "Barbary apes" did not live in trees, but on the ground, as they still do on the other side of the African straits. The presence of these animals on Gibraltar is now accounted for, not by desertion from occupying armies, but by the fondness of the Romans and Moors for such animals as pets.

The Squire's chief gain from his residence in Andalusia, apart of course from remarks on its ornithology, was the considerable one of learning Spanish well enough to read and to quote Don Quixote in the original. "*El hombre pone, y Dios dispone,*" as he remarks so originally. Just as the Squire was preparing, with extreme regret, to leave Malaga for Malta, the whisper went round that the "black vomit" had broken out.

What was the "black vomit"? It is a curious fact that, although the Squire had a "passionate Attachment to the Medical Profession," which was reciprocated by more than one of them writing his life, not one of them has condescended to tell us what is meant by the "black vomit." The Rev J. G. Wood, following the Squire, tells us that this visitation of the "black vomit" in Malaga was "accompanied with cholera and yellow fever." But the "vomitò negro" is a well-known form of yellow fever, and there is nothing except Waterton's vague statement to indicate that the epidemic was accompanied by cholera. Yellow fever is an African disease, transmitted by the mosquito, *Aëdes egyptii,* and transferred to the West Indies and South America by the slave trade. Ships became infested by the mosquito—"Monk" Lewis died through being infected on board ship after escaping from Jamaica—and thus transferred the disease to Portugal, Italy, Spain, and even at times to England and the Eastern States of America.

The Malaga epidemic of 1803 was evidently a pretty bad one. One evening, in an alley near the house, the young Squire saw "a mattress of most suspicious appearance hung out to dry." Almost immediately afterwards a Maltese captain who had dined with them was taken ill, and died before "sunrise the next morning." A few days later Waterton himself was attacked. "I had the most dreadful spasms, and it was supposed that I could not last out till noon the next day." An attack of "Yellow Jack" was no joke, and the mortality rates were very high—in the old days the losses of the British garrisons in Jamaica averaged 185 men per thousand every year. But such was the strength of the Squire's constitution, or the reluctance of "whatever gods may be" to destroy so rare a piece of entertainment, that he recovered.

Why he did not instantly leave the town he has omitted to tell us. "Multitudes" of other people did so, and then within about a month Malaga was officially labelled as a plague city, so that none of those remaining could leave. The Bedingfields and the Squire had meanwhile retired to the country house, and it would have been well for them to stay there. "Pressure of business" called the elder uncle to Malaga, and there he was informed of the sickness of a former benefactor, a monk with the name of Bustamante, whom Mr Bedingfield felt obliged to visit. "Father Bustamante breathed his last before midnight; my uncle took to his bed and never rose more."

The uncle was a big man, six feet four, and they took him in a "kind of coffin" to be buried in one of the plague pits dug by the galley-slaves on the outskirts of the town. "But they could not spare room for the coffin; so the body was taken out of it, and thrown upon the heap which already occupied the pit. A Spanish marquess lay just below him." A pleasant experience for a young man, enjoying his first trip abroad in most Catholic Spain! Thousands of people died in this epidemic, and "it was sad in the extreme to see the bodies placed in the streets at close of day to be ready for the dead-carts." The very dogs "howled fearfully during the night"; "all was gloom and horror in every street"; and Waterton saw and characteristically noted "the vultures tugging at the bodies which were washed ashore."

You would think this was about as unpleasant as any holiday resort could be, but Malaga had another surprise in reserve. One evening the Squire suddenly heard a noise "as though a thousand carriages had dashed against each other," and the town "was shaken with earthquakes, shock succeeding shock," until the wretched inhabitants felt they were about to share the dreadful fate of Lisbon in 1753. The Squire went to bed at midnight, but was awakened at about five by his bed shaking from side to side as if it were moving under him. Leaping out of bed and into his "unmentionables," he rushed for the Alameda, where he found "multitudes of both sexes, some nearly in a state of nudity, and others sick at stomach, huddled together, not knowing which way to turn or what to do."

The Squire, always quick in sizing up a situation, now "began to think it high time to fly"; but everyone was subject to quarantine, every ship under an absolute embargo. Naturally, this sort of bureaucratic repression had no least influence with the Squire, who soon made the acquaintance of a Swedish captain, Bolin, "a most excellent man," "of surprising intrepidity and coolness," who also was "anxious to depart." Secretly the Squire took passages for

THE STRANGE LIFE OF CHARLES WATERTON 33

himself and his brother on this ship, but the acute question was: How were they to get away?

They could of course get no clearance papers from the Spaniards, and the most the British Consul did for them was to give them a certificate that Malaga was now free from sickness (which, strangely enough, it now was), remarking with official pessimism:

"My young friend, I shall either have to see you sunk by the cannon of the fort, or hear of your being sent prisoner for life to the fortress of Ceuta."

Captain Bolin was no such snivelling poltroon. Threatening his crew into secrecy, he waited patiently for a strong easterly wind, while forging himself false papers. When the wind at last came, he waited until the harbour-master had made his daily inspection of the forty ships anchored in Malaga harbour, watched the governor go off "for an airing in his carriage" and the Spanish naval officers of the patrol ships go ashore. Instantly this energetic Swede then "worked his vessel clear of the rest" and crowded on "a cloud of canvas." His countenance, says the Squire, "was very manly" and "exhibited a portrait of cool intrepidity." Recognising a kindred spirit, he adds enthusiastically: "Had I possessed the power, I would have made him an admiral on the spot." By the time the slack Spanish warships got under weigh, it was too late, and the fugitives passed Gibraltar "at the rate of nearly eleven knots an hour."

This, one would have thought, all told, made up excitement enough for the Squire's first pleasure "sauntering" in Europe. But their speed passing Gibraltar did not last, and they had to beat up against "cold and stormy weather" for nearly a month before they reached the Channel. With his usual foresight the young Squire had omitted to provide himself with warmer clothes, so that, thinly clad in the wintry Channel and with a constitution shaken by yellow fever, "I caught a cold, which attacked the lungs, and reduced me to the brink of the grave."

In this pitiable condition and with these appalling tales to tell, the young Squire returned with his brother to Walton Hall. What his mother thought of it all, including the death of her brother (soon to be followed by the second), is not recorded. But Charles brought some consolation in the shape of those authentic relics he believed in so cheerfully. The deceased Mr Bedingfield for some reason had received these valuable relics from the Duchess of Alva

c.w.—3

—no doubt the "identical Duchess" who posed for Goya. One of the relics, which Waterton piously presented to his mother, was "a beautiful ivory crucifix" which had been "taken away from Rome by a French general in 1796." The other, which was despatched to Sir Richard Bedingfield, Bart., had an even more fascinating history—it was "a superbly-mounted Spanish gun, the identical one which the famous Duke of Alva had with him in the Low Countries."

The Squire brushes off very lightly his return from "the brink of the grave" and recovery from the "pulmonary mischief"—which Dr Hobson takes for granted was pneumonia. "I must have sunk," the Squire writes, "had it not been for the skill of the late celebrated surgeon Mr Hay of Leeds: he set me on my legs again; and I again hunted with Lord Darlington."

These terse sentences suggest at least two topics of interest. Taking the last first—as is appropriate: "I again hunted with Lord Darlington." But as Dr Hobson relates with such circumstantial prolixity, including the Homeric father-and-son dialogue already quoted, the Squire asserted that he had already pledged himself never to hunt again! "So far I have kept my promise," he told Dr Hobson forty or fifty years later, "and a pledge to my father was recognised by him in as sacred a light as if it had been made to the Pope himself." How then could the Squire have "again hunted with Lord Darlington"? We could suppose that the pledge to his father was made, not before the saunter to Malaga, but at some time in between the return from Malaga at the end of 1803 and departure for Demerara in November 1804. But another difficulty instantly confronts us. According to Norman Moore (who, like Dr Hobson, had these stories direct from the Squire), Waterton met Lord Darlington and his fox-hounds just as he was leaving for Demerara.

"Where are you going?" asked his lordship.

"To South America."

"That's no place for a young man like you," said Lord Darlington contemptuously. "You'd better get down and come with us. We shall have a splendid season."

"No, my lord," the Squire retorted with his usual sparkling wit, "I'll go to South America."

So, evidently, according to another of his veracious stories, he had been riding to hounds up till the day of his departure for Guiana. And it was impossible for him to make the pledge at any later date, since before the young Squire returned from the West Indies his father was dead. The contradictions are insoluble.

The second point concerns the cure of his pneumonia. Mr Hay of Leeds, it will be remembered, was not a physician, but a surgeon. Unluckily, neither the Squire nor Dr Hobson nor Sir Norman Moore has told how the surgeon dealt with pneumonia; but we can perhaps infer it from the wordy labyrinths of Dr Hobson's memories. It was, he says, "about the year 1800" that the Squire "being predisposed to pulmonary disease," was "encouraged under medical advice to largely deplete by venesection." What this means in plain or non-Hobsonian English is that the Squire was "let blood" with lancet and bowl, in the old fashion of barber-surgeons and such contemporary practitioners of his later days as Mr Bob Sawyer and Mr Benjamin Allen.

Weird as it sounds to us with the different type of prejudice we have picked up from a different type of doctor, there was nothing remarkable in such a treatment of "pulmonary mischief" at that time. The remarkable and characteristic thing is that the Squire was so much taken with the bloody treatment that he learned to bleed himself from "a professional proficient, the late Dr Marshall." Towards the end of his life the Squire told an awe-struck listener that he had "blooded himself one hundred and thirty-six times." His average was from sixteen to twenty ounces, though Dr Hobson reports that even in his eightieth year the Squire thought nothing of drawing off twenty-four fluid ounces of his blood. "Tapping my claret," he called it, and made nothing of it. He not only wielded the lancet himself, using right or left hand "without the least difficulty," but usually held the bowl himself, applied his own "compress and fillets," and "tidily bound up his arm with one hand and his teeth."

Dr Hobson "over and over, again and again" remonstrated with the Squire, "entreated" him to tap the claret "less extravagantly" but to no avail. Though not disapproving wholly of phlebotomy (or venesection), Dr Hobson thought it should not be carried so far. He did not, as we should now expect, also remonstrate with the Squire on the careless and insanitary way he treated the lancet when not in use. It is a marvel to me that he never gave himself some form of infection. Listen to this:

One evening Dr Hobson found the Squire "suffering very acute pain" (where?—in the stomach probably, from over-eating after too prolonged a fast), and "repeatedly puncturing the arm but always ineffectually." Examining the lancet, Dr Hobson found it so blunt that though it pierced the skin painfully it always missed the vein. Dr Hobson set the lancet "on a common slate-stone" and the Squire then "used it with the utmost precision." To the doctor's remonstrances on "the danger of such bungling operative practice" the Squire instantly and after his "humorous fashion" replied in these words:

"Teach your grandmother to suck eggs. How could any mortal readily open a vein with an instrument that had been from under his care for the three previous months, and, during that period, had been the common corn-cutting hack for the servant girls of the establishment?"

IV

WHETHER it was experience of the hotter sunshine of Andalusia, or the result of having yellow fever and pneumonia, or the "depletion" caused by these profuse bloodings, or merely "a frame naturally chilly"; at any rate, the young Squire had not been long back at Walton Hall when he found the "wind of England . . . bleak and wintry" and "longed to bask in a warmer sun." How it was that Demerara in British Guiana was selected is quite a little story.

Towards the end of the eighteenth century, a Demerara planter, named Daly, came to England for a holiday; and when walking in the streets of Wakefield saw a "remarkably handsome" woman with whom he "fell desperately in love." This was the Squire's Aunt Anne, one of his father's sisters. The Waterton family were not very much in favour of this match, but eventually Mr Daly succeeded and carried off his bride to his plantation in Guiana. Later on her brother Christopher "wandered" out in that direction, and married a much-widowed lady, Mrs Anne Waddell, with whom he acquired two plantations. Later on Mr and Mrs Christopher Waterton returned to England, and Mr Thomas Waterton bought a plantation (instantly named of course "Walton Hall") as some sort of provision for his younger children when Charles inherited the English estates.

Thus, at the age of twenty-two, without the faintest experience, the Squire boldly set forth to "manage" three large plantations, growing coffee, sugar and cotton, and between them owning at least a thousand negro slaves. On his way through London he called on his uncle, the "intrepid Sir John Bedingfield," who was supposed to have saved the King's life, and was introduced by him to Sir Joseph Banks, at that time President of the Royal Society. Sir Joseph gave the young man this excellent but rather ominous advice:

"You may stay in them" (i.e. low and swampy countries) "for three years or so, and not suffer much. After that period, fever and ague, and probably a liver disease will attack you, and you will die at last, worn out, unless you remove in time to a more favoured climate."

There were several reasons why the tropics in general and the West Indies in particular were at that time so "very insalubrious and fatal to European constitutions." In the first place the revolutionary discovery that yellow fever and malaria are transmitted by mosquitoes had not been made, and mosquito bites were simply considered a minor nuisance. Malaria, as the name implies, was supposed to come from "bad air" exhaled in some unspecified manner from marshes and stagnant water—the breeding-places, of course, of the fatal mosquitoes. The origin of yellow fever was held to be even more mysterious. Then, the presence of so many slaves huddled together in less than sanitary huts close to the plantation house, must have often resulted in the pollution of water, with resultant typhoid. (It is often impossible to know whether the "touch of fever" so airily referred to was malaria or typhoid.) And then, habits of diet and clothing not too sensible even in a cold climate were often persisted in by new-comers in spite of the advice and more rational practice of the old-established families.

Another deadly enemy of the single young man coming out from England to "manage" a plantation was rum. The modern visitor who goes to the West Indies in the winter months, when all is sparkling and sociable, and drinks the "planter's punch" of rum and fruit juices and ice, can hardly conceive of any "danger" from it. But we have to think back to the days of slavery, when solitary men, with no intellectual interests and no family ties, cut off from social intercourse by the heavy tropical rains of the rainy season, sat drinking very strong raw spirit night after night amid the incessant din of stridulating insects, croaking frogs, unearthly sudden screams as a snake seized some small animal or toad, and the dismal laments of night-birds like the Poor-Will's-widow. They probably formed associations with one or more of the slave women, and began to believe in "duppies." Even if they failed to succumb to D.Ts., they so lowered their health and resistance that they quickly died of illnesses such as malaria, from which they might otherwise have recovered.

It was here that the Squire owed so much to his religious training and above all to Father Clifford, for the promise never to drink wines or spirits. Fortunately, too, instead of trying to dress like a Yorkshire gentleman, the Squire rushed to the opposite extreme, and often went barefoot and bareheaded, wearing only a shirt and a pair of trousers. He was also fortunate in having the household of his Aunt Anne to visit, and in the close friendship he formed with a man a good deal older than himself, Charles Edmonstone. What was the bond between these two the Squire never reveals, though he speaks of Edmonstone as "the most valued friend I ever had in the world." Edmonstone had a plantation on the Mibiri Creek, where Waterton always went to recover from "the fever and ague" which "would at times assault me with great obstinacy."

These illnesses, of course, were the result of drinking infected water (if by "fever" is meant typhoid) or from the mosquitoes which swarmed in the marshy canal country where the Squire spent much of his time watching and pursuing the innumerable tropical water-birds. The Squire was obstinately of the opinion that these "fevers and agues" were caused by "remaining in my wet clothes until the sun had dried them"; but if he contracted any fever in such a way, it would not be malarial but rheumatic. He must have been possessed of the most tenacious vitality and strength to survive the treatment he inflicted on himself during what were evidently severe bouts of malaria, in accordance with the lancet lessons received from the late celebrated Dr Marshall. Just as his "most guarded sobriety and abstinence" were no protection from malarial mosquitoes, so they would not have saved him from accidental self-slaughter by "venesection" and relentless purgings if he had not been naturally of a more than metallic strength of constitution.

In any case, his first stay in the country near Georgetown cannot have been a very long one, since his father died in 1805, and the young Squire—now the Squire—returned home to collect his inheritance. How long he stayed in England and what he did there he has omitted to tell us. Characteristically, instead of launching into society and conviviality as was the wont of young gentlemen who had just inherited an estate and become thereby objects of the most flattering interest to families with daughters to marry, the Squire preferred to return to Guiana, fever and ornithology. By now he must have made some progress in his favourite art of taxidermy, though he had not yet fully excogitated his own peculiar and most successful method of preserving both birds and mammals.

The next certain date we have is the 17th September, 1807—on which day, as the Squire tells us with some consequence, he received his commission as lieutenant in the 2nd Regiment of the Demerara Militia. In recording this piece of military news the Squire launches into one of his frequent diatribes against Protestant persecution and "the cruel enactments of our would-be seducers."

He accepted the commission, he protests, only because he was not required to deny transubstantiation or to accept the Thirty-nine Articles; yet, if he had chosen, he could have had a commission at home and even have done some fighting on the same easy terms.

Here Waterton profited by the knowledge of Spanish he had acquired among the perils of plague and earthquake in Malaga. Some citizens of Demerara, with more haste than sense, went out in a small ship to capture a Spanish privateer; and were themselves captured. As they were operating on the high seas without a commission from any Government, it was apprehended that they "ran a risk of being tucked up for pirates" in the Orinoco. Waterton, as the person best acquainted with Spanish, volunteered to try to save them. This expedition turned into a sleeveless errand. The Squire sailed for Barbados to look for Admiral Cochrane, sleeping with "Daniel's life-preserver" under his pillow, as the vessel was so leaky it went down at anchor just after arrival. Admiral Cochrane was not at Bridgetown, and Waterton having spent some time "in one perpetual round of gaiety" caused by the presence of "our troops and tars," eventually "left with regret," having accomplished nothing. The amateur pirates—all but one—had managed to overpower the Spanish crew on their ship and just reached Tobago before expiring of thirst.

As Waterton is said to have returned home "several times" between 1804 and 1812, it may well be that from Barbados he proceeded to England. He was back at the plantation next year, for in August 1808, he was sent off on a small official errand— that of carrying despatches from Admiral Collingwood to Don Felipe de Ynciarte, at Angostura, on the Spanish Main. Waterton was extremely proud at having received this "genteel and confidential" commission. He refers to it twice at least in the *Essays*, to Don Felipe at length in the *Wanderings*, and writes a full account of the important transaction in the *Autobiography*. How many times the Squire's friends in England must have heard the exordium: "When in 1808 I carried Admiral Collingwood's despatches to the Orinoco . . .!" Many an ambassador plenipotentiary and envoy extraordinary has accomplished his diplomatic errand with fewer consequential flourishes.

In company with his friend, Edmonstone, and another unnamed but elderly person "who ill requited the favour," the despatch-bearer duly set forth, and at Barrancas, on the Orinoco, changed into a Spanish boat. But the Squire would not have been the Squire if he had not occupied most of this official journey with ornithology, and if he had not contrived to involve himself in one of his innumerable fantastic adventures.

As they warped their way slowly along the banks of the great tropical river, where "it was quite charming to observe the immense quantities of parrots and scarlet aras" (i.e. macaws) and "waterfowl innumerable," the Squire suddenly noticed "coiled up in a bush" a large "labarri snake"—"evidently," says the Rev J. G. Wood—and in this the reader will probably instantly concur—"a *Craspedocephalus*." The Squire coveted the reptile, shot at and wounded it, and "being wishful to dissect it," reached out to grab the still living and very venomous snake by the throat. He had forgotten the nervous Spaniard at the tiller, who instantly turned the boat into the stream, leaving the Squire hanging on the bush "with the snake close to me." Three times the water went over his head, and then luckily another man put the helm hard over and brought the boat back. "As they were pulling me back"— the Squire could not resist his treasure, and pulled the dying snake in with him—"to the horror and surprise of the crew." "It measured eight feet in length," and lucky it was for the Squire that there was lurking under the bush no "thirty-foot long cayman," such as they saw next day—a remarkable occurrence, since no known species of New World Crocodilia ever exceeds twenty feet.

The delivery of these momentous despatches does not seem to have been followed by any particular result except official convivialities. Don Felipe set down the British envoys to a feast with no fewer than forty different dishes of meat and fish. In tropical heat he came to the feast dressed in a hot and heavy uniform. Observing his host, Waterton murmured to himself the old and elegant saying: "How I sweat! said the mutton chop to the gridiron." "Don Carlos," said the Governor, perhaps reading his guest's thoughts, "this is more than man can bear. *No puedo sufrir tanto*. Pray pull off your coat, and tell your companions to do the same; and I'll show them the example."

This, together with a veracious anecdote from Don Felipe about a murderous cayman (afterwards related in the *Wanderings*), was about all that came of this expedition. After returning to Georgetown, Waterton sent "this courteous governor" an expensive telescope, which was surely a handsome acknowledgment of hospitality in a country where "beef was only a penny a pound, and the finest fish could be had almost for nothing."

And here, for a period of almost four years, we come upon another gap in Waterton's life. Certainly some of the natural history observations recorded in the *Wanderings* must have occurred at this epoch and possibly some of the adventures, but there is no way of telling. In his writings, autobiographical and otherwise, the Squire jumps from topic to topic, like a bird hopping from twig to twig and back again, and is none too accurate or even generous with dates. Perhaps he made one of his trips to England—and incidentally, if he made these cross-Atlantic trips as often as his biographers imply, he must, in those slow-sailing days, have wasted an enormous amount of time at sea.

I find only one incident recorded between the genteel and confidential mission to Don Felipe in 1808 and the beginning of the great curare poison "wandering" in 1812. That great and good man, Governor Ross, afflicted by an unspecified tropical disease, was compelled to retire from the scene of Guiana. In accordance with the hearty customs of those days (which our own colonial administrators would doubtless be very glad to see revived) the citizens of Demerara sent the retiring Governor an address of "warmest gratitude," together with a little gift of fifteen hundred (gold) guineas. Nor was this all. Modestly waiting until the day after Governor Ross had sailed, the Squire, having summoned up his Stonyhurst Latin, published in the local newspaper the following remarkable sapphics:

> *Tristis heu nobis, nimiumque durus*
> *Ordo Parcarum est! Demerara damnum*
> *Flet repentinum, lacrymasque fundet,*
> > *Tempus in omne.*

> *Ille, qui justis manibus regebat*
> *Lora, jam currum, medio reliquit*
> *Cursu, et invitis pedibus remota*
> > *Gramina quærit.*

> *Tempore æstivo, rutilans ut agri*
> *Ros fovet gramen sitientis—Ille*
> *Sic opem nobis, tulit, et levamen*
> > *Auxiliumque.*

Hac die pectus, rigidum dolorem
Sentit, et luctum lacrymæ sequuntur,
Dum Ducem nostrum, Demeraræ ab oris
        Cedere cerno.

Te, procellosos pelagi tridenti
Qui regis fluctus, precor O secundo
Numine adsis, dum liquido carina
        Æquore fertur.

Let us hope that the *"Ille sic opem nobis tulit"* was not a
reference to the fifteen hundred guineas. The Governor apparently
left on the 31st March, 1809, so the poem appropriately appeared
next day.

In 1812 Waterton handed over the plantations "to those concerned in them, and never more put foot in them." "Those concerned" were presumably his father's younger children, and as the
Squire seldom (so far as is recorded) mentions any one of them again,
it would appear from the phrase about never setting foot in the
estates again that they parted on something less than good terms.
It is unlucky that the Squire has recorded so little of his life as a
Demerara planter. He had such a natural sympathy with the
grotesque, so magnetic an attraction for absurd accidents that he
might easily have entertained us with many strange anecdotes of
colonial life in the old days of slavery. But no! except for passing
references the Squire is mum, or has incorporated his memories in
accounts of other periods of his life. The references to "Daddy
Quashi" all seem to belong to a later time; but the Squire has left
a characteristic little diatribe on slavery, embedded in one of the
Wanderings between commercial statistics and a description of the
kit he took as an explorer:

"Slavery can never be defended. He whose heart is not of iron
can never wish to be able to defend it: while he heaves a sigh for
the poor negro in captivity, he wishes from his soul that the traffic
had been stifled in its birth; but unfortunately the Governments of
Europe nourished it, and now that they are exerting themselves to
do away with the evil, and ensure liberty to the sons of Africa, the
situation of plantation-slaves is depicted as truly deplorable and their
condition wretched. It is not so. A Briton's heart, proverbially kind
and generous, is not changed by climate or its streams of compassion dried up by the scorching heat of the Demerara sun; he cheers

his negroes in labour, comforts them in sickness, is kind to them in old age, and never forgets that they are his fellow-creatures."

It is true that the "Governments of Europe nourished" the slave trade from the sixteenth to the eighteenth centuries, with the "kind and generous" Britons doing at least their fair share of the business; but the Squire, with his love and knowledge of Church history, might have recollected that the carrying of negro slaves to the New World was suggested, not by Governments, but by "a holy and benevolent" prelate, Las Casas, Bishop of the Indies, because the aborigines perversely insisted on committing race suicide rather than submit to Spanish tyranny. As for the life of the slaves in Demerara, apart from the above generalised and meaningless rant, the Squire gives only one characteristic scene. And this, as we might expect, is concerned with fleas—those chigoes or jiggers which burrow under the skin, breed there, and if not extirpated soon cause ulcers:

"In the plantations of Guiana there is generally an old negress known by the name of Granny, a kind of *Junonis anus,* who loiters about the negro yard, and is supposed to take charge of the little negroes who are too young to work. Towards the close of day you will sometimes hear the most dismal cries of woe coming from that quarter. Old Granny is then at work grubbing the Chigoe nests out of the feet of the sable urchins, and filling the holes with lime-juice and cayenne pepper. This searching compound has two duties to perform; firstly, it causes death to any remaining Chigoe in the hole; and secondly, it acts as a kind of a birch-rod to the unruly brats, by which they are warned, to their cost, not to conceal their Chigoes in future; for, afraid of encountering old Granny's toma-hawk, many of them prefer to let the Chigoes riot in their flesh rather than come under her dissecting hand."

Inspired by this Stephen Foster memory of the dear old planta-tion days, the Squire lets us have one or two of his own experiences with this burrowing flea, whose first onset, by the way, he describes as "a pleasant and agreeable kind of itching." On one occasion, on his last sailing from Guiana, the Squire intentionally allowed one of these insects to burrow into his skin. "In three days" it had formed under the skin a "spot somewhat like a blue pea," and "by the time we were in the latitude of Antigua my guest had become insupportable." Whereupon the Squire operated on himself and "poured spirits of turpentine into the cavity."

Plantation ticks, incidentally, should never be allowed to worry you—just "make a large fire and stand close to it, and if you be covered with ticks they will all fall off."

In 1812, when Waterton finally abandoned life as a planter, Demerara had a new Governor. This was one General Carmichael, a bit of an eccentric also in his way, and therefore a man after the Squire's own heart. The General was a little man, "shrivelled and weatherbeaten," but "wonderfully active" in spite of his great age. He was "generous," but "exceedingly fiery," though his "ire soon subsided"; and he had such a reverence for royalty, even Hanoverian, that "he would have sent his own brother out of the house had he heard him speak with levity of the Prince Regent of England." Evidently:

> A fiery etter-cap, a fractious chiel,
> As het as ginger and as stieve as steel.

Knowing he intended going into the interior (where he would need a Government passport), the Squire judiciously neglected to call on this gentleman, and—to cut short a long, rambling, and not very interesting tale—got himself further into the Governor's good books by thwarting and resisting the police when they came to arrest an "absconding gentleman" who was "skulking up the river sorely afflicted with a liver complaint" for which he had most unwisely sought the Squire's ruthless medical attention. Now it happened that General Carmichael was so anxious for the arrest of this interesting outlaw that he had offered as much as five hundred pounds as a reward. Judge then of his delight when he learned that the Squire had not only defied and opposed by force the Demerara police officers, but had connived at the outlaw's successful escape! Naturally, a warrant arrived, commanding the Squire's instant appearance at Government House.

Whether the Squire had any qualms as he obeyed this tremendous summons he does not say; but he certainly handled the situation with cool impudence and turned an awkward scrape into a triumph. This is what happened. As soon as the Squire's name was announced, the Governor came into the hall and, "looking at me full in the face," exclaimed severely:

"And so, Sir, you have dared to thwart the law, and to put my late proclamation at defiance?"

The Squire's defence is both so irrelevant and so memorable as to deserve the closest attention:

"General, you have judged rightly; and I throw myself on your well-known generosity. I had eaten the fugitive's bread of hospitality, when fortune smiled upon him; and I could not find it in my heart to refuse him help in his hour of need. Pity to the unfortunate prevailed over obedience to your edict; and had General Carmichael himself stood in the shoes of the deserted outlaw, I would have stepped forward in his defence, and have dealt many a sturdy blow around me, before foreign bloodhounds should have fixed their crooked fangs in the British uniform."

The General must have been a man of quick perception, for he instantly appreciated the Squire's fantastic genius [1] and saw there was fun to be had here. Instead of whistling up his sleuths to arrest this declaimer of fustian, as the average official would have done, he instantly exclaimed:

"That's brave!"

He then advanced and shook the Squire's hand, and entered upon a conversation which lasted for two hours.

The main topic of this talk, which was also the chief reason for the Squire's determination to explore the then unknown inland regions of British Guiana as far as the borders of Brazil, was a truly Watertonian one. It was and is a matter of common knowledge that the South American Indians hunted with the blow-gun, which fired small arrows tipped with poison. The Macusi Indians of the Guiana uplands manufactured a particularly powerful poison which they exchanged with the tribes nearer the coast. This is the drug which Waterton writes "wourali," Dr Hobson and Miss Sitwell "woorali," and the rest of the world "curare" or "urari." Now, the drug was hard to obtain on the coast in any but small quantities, and, being very susceptible to damp, had often lost its potency and thus disappointed European experimenters. Waterton's plan was to penetrate to the unknown interior, make contact with the tribe which gathered and compounded the poison, and bring back a sufficient quantity for numerous experiments.

Moreover, the Squire was not animated solely by the wish to conduct experimental poisonings of dogs, chickens and donkeys. He hoped to discover an antidote, for those recommended in the coastal regions he had found by experiment to be totally useless. Curare has some curious properties. One is that animals killed by it are nevertheless quite wholesome for human food. Another is that it acts by rapid paralysis of the nervous system and muscles,

[1] Tipped off, perhaps, beforehand by some of the Squire's friends?

and Waterton's friend, Sewell, head of the London Veterinary College, had suggested that since tetanus and hydrophobia were marked by "frightful spasms," appropriate doses of curare poison might act as a remedy. Except that it didn't work, this was a reasonable idea. We should remember that the action of quinine (or "quassia bark") on malaria must have seemed actually more mysterious and improbable. As a side issue to this important errand, Waterton also hoped to clear up the mystery of Lake Parima and the mythical city of El Dorado, which had eluded Sir Walter Raleigh.

"Old Hercules," as General Carmichael was called from his strenuous though not always successful efforts to root out corruption and peculation in the colony, naturally listened to all this with delight and amusement. The Squire volunteered the information that he had complied with the bureaucratic regulations needed for leaving the settled parts, whereupon the General instantly gave him permission to explore any part of the interior he wished, and added a passport, signed and dated April 16th, 1812.

Waterton was now poised for his departure for the interior; yet, in the last few days before he left, he contrived by another display of reckless anti-Government generosity to risk, not only his expedition, but—in view of the offence he had just been forgiven—possibly his liberty, certainly the friendship of Governor Carmichael. Another of Waterton's Georgetown friends, fancying that "Old Hercules" had marked him down for investigation, decided not to risk it and to abscond from the colony without notice. Waterton did not think the Governor's suspicions had been aroused. By way of proving this, he hid the fugitive under some troely palm leaves at the bottom of his canoe, and then paddled along in company with the Governor's boat on its way to visit Edmonstone at Mibiri Creek, turning the conversation on to the hidden man. From what the Governor said, Waterton and his friend could both perceive that the fugitive was flying only from his own conscience and not from any official investigation. All was well that ended well—but where would the Squire have been supposing the Governor *had* intended to arrest the man and *had* discovered him under the palm leaves?

In view of the large and sometimes perhaps immoderate equipment of modern expeditions, there may be some interest in noting how this intrepid pioneer prepared himself for that formidable unknown country. Of course, since much of his journey was to be made—could only be made—by water, he had a canoe and several Indian paddlers. He must also have taken a shot-gun and ammunition and fishing tackle, for he "depended on the skill of an Indian," or his own, "for fish and game"; and some means of preserving and bringing away skins of animals and birds. His personal equipment was of the simplest. First, he had a large waterproof sheet about twelve by ten feet to "suspend in betwixt two trees in the shape of a roof," because "under it in your hammock you may defy the pelting shower." "A hat, a shirt and a light pair of trousers" were all "the raiment" he required. In one of the later "Wanderings" he thus addresses the "gentle reader" more at length on the same topic, and in rather more detail:

"I would here, gentle reader, wish to draw thy attention, for a few minutes, to physic, raiment and diet. Shouldst thou ever wander through these remote and dreary wilds, forget not to carry with thee bark, laudanum, calomel and jalap, and the lancet. There are no druggist shops here, nor sons of Galen to apply to in time of need. I never go encumbered with many clothes. A thin flannel waistcoat under a check shirt, a pair of trousers and a hat were all my wardrobe: shoes and stockings I seldom had on. In dry weather they would have irritated the feet and retarded me in the chase of wild beasts; and in the rainy season they would have kept me in a perpetual state of damp and moisture. I eat moderately, and never drink wine, spirits, or fermented liquors in any climate."

Later in this narrative I shall have occasion "to draw the gentle reader's attention" to some of the consequences of going barefoot in the jungle (and elsewhere), of "plying the lancet" so unsparingly and of fearful doses of jalap and calomel.

Waterton started on this adventurous search for curare about the end of April 1812, a little before his thirtieth birthday, and was absent about four months, having thus judiciously and characteristically chosen the rainy season for his explorations. His plan was to paddle up the Demerara River to a point a little below the falls; have his canoe portaged by Indians to the Essequibo River, a four-day journey overland; proceed up the Essequibo and into a tributary he calls the "Apoura-poura." This would eventually bring him to the territory of the Macusi Indians. Leaving the canoe, he hoped to make his way on foot to the Portuguese frontier fort of São Joachim. On the map this looks not far short of four hundred miles in a direct line; so that, with the devious route followed, and a detour Waterton had to make owing to the flooding of the upland

Charles Waterton

Reproduction of a sketch which appeared in the issue of the Illustrated London News, *dated August 28th, 1844.*

Walton Hall

savanna country, he must in his four months have travelled considerably over a thousand miles by water and land in an almost unexplored country—a great achievement for a solitary white man with a few Indians.

Like many amateur writers, the Squire had not much art or method in the arrangement of his thoughts and impressions, memories and opinions, and practically no sense of form. He even went far beyond the usual vagaries of his type of writer, and was content to pour out a farrago of natural history, prejudices, personal adventures, Latin tags, exhortations to the reader, private crochets, excellent pieces of description and observation, forming such an eccentric muddle that even his muddle-headed friend, Dr Hobson, hardly outdoes him, while it is scarcely surprising that scientific pedants who had never seen a jungle refused to believe Waterton's reports—which in some cases were both original and true. This is particularly unfortunate, since the *Wanderings* are the work of a man who genuinely loved wild nature and had gifts as a writer. As a naturalist Waterton belonged to the old-fashioned "virtuoso" type, something between the sportsman, the collector and the æsthete, despising as pedantic the severe and often arid but necessary disciplines of biological science. His merits lie in his first-hand acquaintance with the scenes and creatures and plants he describes, in the curious skill he developed as a taxidermist, and in the fact that he evolved from a collector and hence killer of wild life to be the most successful of pioneers in its systematic protection.

Another difficulty encountered by the modern reader of the *Wanderings* is Waterton's insistence on rejecting all scientific Latin names and using only the names he picked up from settlers and the Indians. As most of these popular names have changed, it is often impossible to make out what animals or birds or trees he is talking about. The Rev J. G. Wood, who published an annotated edition of the *Wanderings* in 1880, has fortunately cleared up many of these mysteries, but there are still a number of names which even he was unable to identify. What Waterton calls a "hou-tou" seems to be the bird now called "mot-mot"; the bird Wood figures as a Great Jacamar is quite unlike the birds now called "jacamars"; while Selous identifies this metallic jacamar with a "water-hen"; and Waterton's "pi-pi-yo" bird has not been identified any more than his "pataca." But the reader who can be patient with all these confusions will find a good deal that is rewarding in the literary productions of the eccentric "wanderer."

There can be no doubt that Waterton immensely enjoyed the first part of his journey up the Demerara River from Georgetown to the falls. Doubtless the lower reaches must have been familiar to him from his long residence, and he is evidently drawing on accumulated observations as well as on vivid new impressions when he tries to give his reader some idea of the abounding wild life and colour of the tropical forest. "Here," he exclaims emphatically, "the finest precious stones are far surpassed by the vivid tints which adorn the birds." And if in his descriptions he mixes up trees and animals and birds and snakes and insects in a marvellous confusion, still, after all, that rather adds to the effect of picturesque profusion and variety. Here is a good passage:

"Every now and then the maam or tinamou sends forth one long and plaintive whistle from the depth of the forest, and then stops; whilst the yelping of the toucan and the shrill voice of the bird called pi-pi-yo is heard during the interval. The campanero never fails to attract the attention of the passenger; at a distance of nearly three miles you may hear this snow-white bird tolling every four or five minutes, like the distant convent-bell. From six to nine in the morning the forests resound with the mingled cries and strains of the feathered race; after this they gradually die away. From eleven to three all nature is hushed as in a midnight silence, and scarce a note is heard, saving that of the campanero and the pi-pi-yo; it is then that, oppressed by the solar heat, the birds retire to the thickest shade and wait for the refreshing cool of evening."

The tinamou, Wood thinks, is *Tinamotis elegans,* "about the size of a grouse" with "rather a lumpish appearance." I suggest that the "pi-pi-yo" may be a native name for the "kes-ka-dee," or the hawk called "How-are-you." Waterton proceeds with his description:

"At sundown the vampires, bats and goat-suckers dart from their lonely retreat and skim along the trees on the river's bank. The different kinds of frogs almost stun the ear with their hoarse and hollow-sounding croaking, while the owls and goat-suckers lament and mourn all night.

"About two hours before daybreak you will hear the red monkey moaning as though in deep distress; the houtou, a solitary bird, and only found in the thickest recesses of the forest, distinctly articulates 'houtou, houtou,' in a low and plaintive tone an hour before sunrise; the maam whistles about the same hour; the hannaquoi, pataca and maroudi announce his near approach to the eastern horizon, and the parrots and parroquets confirm his arrival there. The crickets chirp from sunset to sunrise, and often during the day when the weather is cloudy. . . ."

Taken as a whole, that is a vivid and accurate presentation. Of course we have had almost numberless such descriptions since and are perhaps a little *blasés,* but we must recollect that Waterton was a genuine pioneer in this respect. Nothing is more odd (and irritating) than the lack of curiosity and elementary scientific knowledge of the Conquistadores and other early explorers, who seem to have noticed nothing, while their artists could not even use their eyes—they make an alligator look like a scaly bear and give some squalid Indian the ideal proportions of the Apollo Belvedere. Even a comparatively recent writer, Chateaubriand, gives so fantastic a description of the Mississippi that many people are convinced he never saw it.

Yet Waterton has many omissions. In his account of this first "Wandering" he does not tell us, for instance, whether he collected any specimens of birds or even whether he did any of his barefoot climbing of trees. Presumably he did both; but we can only infer this from slight hints and because we know both were lifelong habits. But whatever else he forgot to put down, and however whimsically he mixes the information in with quite irrelevant matter, he did not forget his curare poison. He found an Indian in a hut just below the falls who sold him some "wourali poison" in a little gourd. Eager to test his deadly new toy, the Squire purchased a "middle-sized dog" and, rather cruelly, experimented by stabbing it in the thigh with a poisoned arrow. He watched and recorded the result most carefully:

"In three or four minutes he began to be affected, smelt at every little thing on the ground around him, and looked wistfully at the wounded part. Soon after this he staggered, laid himself down and never rose more. He barked once, though not as if in pain. His voice was low and weak; and in a second attempt it quite failed him. He now put his head betwixt his fore-legs, and raising it slowly again he fell over on his side. His eye immediately became fixed, and though his extremities every now and then shot convulsively, he never showed the least desire to raise up his head. His heart fluttered much from the time he laid down, and at intervals beat very strong; then stopped for a moment or two, and then beat again; and continued faintly beating several minutes after every other part of his body seemed dead.

"In a quarter of an hour after he had received the poison he was quite motionless."

So much for the wretched dog, which the Squire's narrative abruptly quits at that point in order to describe the falls. Presumably the lethal experiment was undertaken chiefly to see that the poison purchased was genuine. Before leaving the Demerara for the Essequibo, the Squire noted that at midnight on the 1st May he was startled and the Indians terrified by "a most strange and unaccountable noise" which "seemed as though several regiments were engaged and musketry firing with great rapidity." On returning he found that this was caused by a sudden eruption on the distant island of St Vincent.

The "accidental traveller," as he calls himself with unconscious but accurate humour, now proceeded across-country to the Essequibo. Here indeed, for once, he gives a hint of tree-climbing, for addressing the reader, he says:

"Ascend the loftiest mountain, climb the loftiest tree, as far as the eye can extend, whichever way it directs itself, all is luxuriant and unbroken forest."

If only he had condescended to tell us something of his tropical tree-climbing, and to describe what he saw as vividly as the river scenery! He does tell us that the flooded river was very difficult to navigate in May 1812, thereby pointing out his own mistake in choosing to travel in the rainy season. But the rapids were passed; and five days further travel brought the party to a "noble range of hills." Here they were really launched on country virtually unknown to white men, where "there are no huts," where "you must bring your own cassava bread, hunt in the forest for your meat and make the night's shelter for yourself." At this point the narrative becomes encumbered with digressions which had better had been put elsewhere, and the chronology is so vague that its computation is very difficult. This is what I make out:

From the point of launching on the Essequibo to the "Indian habitation of three huts" took "about nine or ten hours"—say one day. Passage of the rapids "five days." "Seven hours" after leaving the rapids, "you enter the River Apoura-poura." "On the third day" "you come to a little hill"; and "two days after leaving this" "you get to . . . a little hut," and are "now within the borders of Macoushia." Here "the Indians are uncommonly dexterous in the use of the blow-pipe and famous for their skill in preparing the deadly . . . wourali."

Here, one would imagine, would have been the place to lay in a stock of curare. Perhaps the Squire did. But after a rambling digression on parakeets, rubber trees, the "elegant crest bird called cock-of-the-rock," crystal mountains, macaws and the weapons of the Indians (all this by the way in less than forty lines), we suddenly find we have gone on two more days and have reached "a place where once a white man lived." One day later, with startling abruptness we are told "to drag the canoe up into the forest, and leave it there."

A toilsome journey on foot now lay ahead, but—how characteristic of Waterton!—in spite of much tedious minuteness about other matters, he does not tell us precisely if he bought any curare here.

The journey to the Brazilian (then, of course, Portuguese) frontier lay through forest and savanna country, much of the latter knee-deep in stagnant rain-water. The water became so deep that a long detour through foot-hills was needed in order to reach "four Indian huts"; and here he certainly did buy curare.

"The wourali poison procured in these last-mentioned huts seemed very good, and proved afterwards to be very strong."

The wording of that seems to imply that he had bought other samples and that they turned out to be less powerful. Perhaps it was the Indians in these "four huts" who allowed him to see how the drug was collected and compounded. The "vine" which Waterton's Indian gathered is the real source of the poison, and is now known as *Strychnos toxifera*. To this the Indian added "a root of a very bitter taste" and "two kinds of bulbous plants which contain a green and glutinous juice." After some search he found two species of ants, "one very large and black, and so venomous that its sting produces a fever" and "the other a little red ant which stings like a nettle." Finally, he collected "a quantity of the strongest Indian pepper" and the "fangs of the labarri and counacouchi snakes." All these were pounded up and reduced by boiling "to a thick syrup of a deep brown colour." The "glutinous juice" may perhaps be needed to make the poison adhere to the arrow heads, but as Waterton rightly infers, all the other ingredients were useless, and added only for purposes of sympathetic magic. A considerable number of taboos surrounded the making of this poison. For example, no women or young girls might be present; the shed in which it was made must be abandoned for ever; the operator must fast throughout the whole process; and finally, the pot used must be a completely new one.

This description of the manufacture of curare was a genuine contribution to scientific knowledge, and formed the basis of all subsequent descriptions—almost invariably without acknowledgment to Waterton. But, although he threw it out only as a "conjecture," his explanation of the legend of Lake Parima was also most probably correct. On his way to the "four huts" he had been struck by the sight of "an immense plain which appears to the eye . . . as level as a bowling green." Much of it was flooded by the summer rains and "put on somewhat the appearance of a lake." From this, Waterton inferred, had come the Indian stories of a vast inland lake; and later geologists are inclined to think that indeed this plain actually was the bed of a great lake which, owing to some earthquake or change of elevation, lost its water. Since old Mexico City stood on an inland lake, it was natural for the Conquistadores to infer a similar city built on this delusive "Lake Parima," which city their imaginative cupidity labelled "El Dorado." Waterton certainly deserves credit for suggesting a plausible explanation of this curious myth.

But now Waterton's good luck on this "wandering" deserted him. As he approached the Brazilian frontier he went down with a very severe attack of malaria, and of course proceeded to make it worse by his fearful remedies (of which more later), consisting of profuse blood-letting and violent purges. Luckily for him the commander of the fort was a humane man, not fettered by rules and commands. His orders indeed forbade him to bring in any foreigner, but a letter from Waterton, written in very creditable Spanish, brought the commander at once to see the stranger. He was a tall and thin man, shrivelled up by many years in the tropics. Coming to Waterton's hammock, he felt the patient's pulse and then said:

"I am sorry, Sir, to see that the fever has taken such hold on you. You shall go directly with me to the fort; and though we have no doctor there, I trust we shall soon bring you about again. The orders I have received forbidding the admission of strangers were never intended to be put in force against a sick English gentleman."

Excellent "Portuguese officer," whose name Waterton has forgotten to tell us! The bullying type of official would certainly have refused to receive him and would have left him to die in the damp forest.

A week's treatment at the fort with "good nourishment" and rest restored Waterton sufficiently for him to start on his way back. He took practically the same route, but though weak from illness, decided to shoot the rapids.

"The roaring of the water was dreadful; it foamed and dashed over the rocks with a tremendous spray, like breakers on a lee-shore. . . . You would have thought, by the confusion it caused in the river and the whirlpools it made, that Scylla and Charybdis, and their whole progeny had left the Mediterranean and come and settled here. . . . It was in vain to speak. The sound was lost in the roar of waters. . . . The canoe drove down the torrent with inconceivable rapidity. It did not touch the rocks once all the way. The Indian proved to a nicety: '*medio tutissimus ibis.*' "

How characteristic all that is, down to the little Latin tag at the end! The reader must recollect that Waterton had just recovered from one very bad attack of malaria and was about to succumb to another. There was absolutely no need to make this very dangerous descent, except for the devil of it. And he tells it all so casually, with such an air of its being all in the day's work, that we are likely to underestimate the fantastic recklessness and to forget that there was an excellent chance of the Squire and all his habits vanishing for ever in the roaring Essequibo cataract. It is by no means an infallible rule, for the Squire drags in classical references at any moment, but he is particularly fond of them in all moments of danger and when working up for an attack on hostile closet naturalists. "Scylla and Charybdis" possibly implies that on this shooting of the rapids the Squire more than once thought the game was up.

"The fever returned, and pressed so heavy on him that to all appearance his last day's march was over." And at this point came a little episode which the Squire forgot when writing the "Remarks" at the end of the first "Wandering," but which he recollected many years later when, in the quiet of Walton Hall, he penned his celebrated essay on "The Chegoe or West Indian Flea." Exhausted by fever, he lay down in the hut of an Indian. He had been so ill for days that he was "quite unconscious that there were nine thriving nests of chegoes" in his back. They were noticed by an old negro, whereupon, "I handed him my penknife and told him to start the intruders." Something in the situation and the operation awoke the Squire's sense of the picturesque:

"Sick as I was, I wished an artist were present at the operation. The Indian's hut, with its scanty furniture, and bows and arrows hanging round; the deep verdure of the adjoining forest; the river flowing rapidly by; myself wasted to a shadow; and the negro grinning with exultation, as he showed me the chegoes' nests which he had grubbed out, would have formed a scene of no ordinary variety."

"A scene of no ordinary variety!" It seems the appropriate one with which to close the drama of the Squire's first tropical "Wandering."

V

VERY naturally Waterton's achievement as an explorer made a stir in Georgetown and among the Guiana planters. The feat would have been talked about if it had been performed by some scientific stranger from England or Germany, with a string of learned letters after his name and "requests and requirements" from distant but formidable authorities to the local government for aid. If we may judge from the Squire's very poor record as an agriculturist at home in England, his work as a planter must have been of a perfunctory sort, and was probably done through overseers; but from the point of view of the Demerara planters he was no stranger and ranked as one of themselves. His reckless defence of the two absconding gentlemen from Georgetown showed moreover that he was no Government toady or respecter of police spies, and this must have acquired for him considerable popularity. The planters, by their first-hand knowledge of the dangers and difficulties overcome, were the best judges of what he had accomplished.

Chief among these was the Squire's friend, Charles Edmonstone of Mibiri Creek, to whom the Squire went for a time in the hope of shaking off his repeated attacks of malaria with a battery of too much blood-letting and purging and too little quinine. Edmonstone knew the jungle country well, for during his life in Demerara he led fifteen expeditions against the roving or stationary bands of runaway negroes who were a menace to the outlying white properties. We may be quite sure that Edmonstone took care to publicise the adventures of his admiring and eccentric young friend. And by this time the Squire's oddities, embryonic though they were in comparison with later luxuriant developments, must have made him well-known as a "character" and well-liked by those who had a taste for freaks.

Most important among Waterton's Demerara admirers and very far from the least enthusiastic was Governor Carmichael. Waterton had made the expedition at his own expense (always an important recommendation to authority), and with no help beyond an official passport which cost nothing. The curare drug he had brought back was naturally of no interest to a civilised power which had more expeditious and complicated methods of killing its enemies, but Waterton had also brought back first-hand information of the real condition of the interior, and had blazed a pioneer trail right across the newly acquired colony to its uncertain frontier with Brazil.

Before Waterton departed for England in search of the health which obstinately refused to return in the tropics, he was the guest of Government House at a "brilliant ball." Governor Carmichael introduced him to the naval captain who was to command their convoy (it was still war-time, and American privateers had joined the old French enemies), and entrusted Waterton with "the colonial despatches to be delivered to Lord Bathurst," then Secretary for the Colonies, together with "a warm letter of introduction to his lordship."

Some time in the spring of 1813—the exact date seems to have gone unrecorded—the vessel *Fame,* so appropriate in the circumstances, landed the explorer and his despatches at Liverpool. According to Waterton, "the voyage to Europe did not recruit" his health, and therefore he did not carry the despatches direct to London, but sent them by mail with a letter of apology to the Colonial Secretary. Now, the point of entrusting the despatches to a private gentleman was to give him the chance of a personal interview with a member of the Cabinet, which might lead to something "genteel and confidential," such as Waterton so plainly hankered for all his life. That Governor Carmichael's recommendations had been sincere and successful is proved by the fact that "his lordship returned a very kind answer" and "requested that I would repair to London *when I had got the better of the tertian ague,* as he wished me to explore Madagascar."

I have italicised the words "when I had got the better of the tertian ague" because they mark the crux of Waterton's self-willed and fatal blunder which lost him all chance of Government employment for life. What that meant was that Lord Bathurst believed he was really ill as a result of his daring exploits in Guiana, and therefore wished him not to come to London until he was well enough to discuss and to undertake the important mission to Madagascar. A desperate war, it will be remembered, was still being waged, and gentlemen of courage were needed as officers by land and sea. Hundreds of Catholic gentlemen had volunteered to serve, and had been able to take with a clear conscience whatever oath was then required of an officer. But Bathurst implied that the Government was willing to respect Waterton's excessive scruples, and to offer him an important official job on his own chosen lines, involving no oath-taking or risk to his soul.

In due course Waterton journeyed to London (May 1813), and was courteously received by the Colonial Secretary, who explained the proposal. Waterton was to go out in October in a man-of-war (an extraordinary privilege for a civilian who was not a peer) with permission to visit Monomotapa and the Seychelles Islands, and instructions to explore and report on the interior of the great and then practically unknown island of Madagascar. What more could he have asked? And what did the silly fellow do? He went away and wrote a stiff note saying "the ague was still annoying me cruelly" and "begged to resign the commission"! Of course, after such a snub he was officially ignored for the rest of his life.

Waterton himself realised and owned his mistake. The commission, he admits, "was a star of the first magnitude" which had appeared "after a long night of political darkness, which had prevented the family journeying onward for the space of nearly three centuries." Why then did he refuse so handsome an offer made in so decent a spirit? Surely, as Lord Bathurst instantly inferred, the ague was only an excuse; for by the very terms of the original proposal Waterton was not to call until he "had got the better of the tertian ague." If, then, he refused the offer, it must have been for another motive.

What was that motive? It is obvious to anybody who considers Waterton's upbringing and the absurd religious and political prejudices he was always reiterating in and out of season. The people who had trained him by acquiring so complete an influence over him did not wish him to serve their enemies, and whether there was actually any intervention or whether the docile pupil had learned his lesson so well that no intervention was needed, the fact is that he did petulantly refuse this offer from Government because they were Protestants and he was a Catholic. Look at his own positive statements:

"We" (i.e. the Catholic Watertons) "were declared totally incapable of serving our country; we were held up to the scorn of a deluded multitude, as damnable idolaters; and we were unceremoniously ousted out of our tenements; our only crime being a conscientious adherence to the creed of our ancestors, professed by England for nine long centuries before the Reformation."

And here again:

"I would rather run the risk of going to hell with St Edward the Confessor, Venerable Bede, and St Thomas of Canterbury, than make a dash at heaven in company with Harry VIII, Queen Bess, and Dutch William."

Later in the century Sir Robert Peel had devised an oath which merely required Catholics to "disclaim, disavow and solemnly abjure any intention to subvert the present Church Establishment within this realm . . ."—surely not a piece of intolerant persecution, but a request to abstain from advocating it? This was not good enough for the Squire:

"In framing that abominable oath, I don't believe that Sir Robert Peel cared one fig's end whether the soul of a Catholic went, after death, to the King of Brightness, or descended to the king of brimstone."

Sir Robert's aim, the Squire maintained, was for the Church of England to keep possession of "the loaves and fishes." But then, "I have a vehement inclination to make a grab at those loaves and fishes," under the time-honoured but specious pretext of "distributing them to the poor." So there the matter remained, and the Squire was left to realise disconsolately that he had by his intransigeance deprived himself for life of any further chance of "genteel and confidential employment."

But though the motives of bigotry and resentment underlying this refusal must be regretted, it is impossible not to feel glad that the Squire did refuse this mission. Had he accepted it and succeeded, other employment would have been found, "Honours" would have been given him, he would have complied with the times and the petty usages of Society, and that magnificent individuality would have been clipped and trimmed and polished into mediocrity. What gain would there be in losing a unique dodo and gaining one more barnyard fowl? Only repulsively fraternal utilitarians would applaud such a transaction.

Having thus successfully dismissed himself from what he most wanted in life, the Squire was now at leisure to attend to his health, his estate, his Hanoverian rats, his poachers, his taxidermy and his sinister new toy, the curare poison.

It may have been at this period or it may have been much earlier—at the time of his return from Malaga—that the Squire, contrary to his other ascetic habits, developed a custom of always having a fire at Walton Hall even in the middle of summer. When he rose in the morning his very first action was to light a fire, and whenever he visited his friends in England they knew that, however uncomfortable to themselves, the Squire must instantly have his fire. He even lighted himself a fire out-of-doors whenever possible, and warmed himself at it while watching birds or trimming his hedges, though he never solved the problem of how to take it to the top of his "favourite oak tree."

"If the Squire came to my house unexpectedly," says Dr Hobson, "even in July or August . . . he would immediately rush into the kitchen until a fire could be prepared . . . and on my return would say, 'How I have enjoyed myself at a roaring fire in your kitchen.'"

The doctor's considered medical opinion is that this "morbid sensibility" was the result of "excessive fasting," too much "tapping the claret" (i.e. blood-letting) and his "prejudicial habit of abstracting an inordinate amount of blood at one time."

The Squire's conduct of his estate in Yorkshire was inevitably after his own fashion, and only by chance and moral training did it turn out on the side of solvency. We must recollect that the confiscations had reduced the Waterton income much below what, at that epoch of aristocracy, was considered adequate to their rank. (Old untitled families, like the Watertons, were often far more considered in good society than newly made viscounts and commercial earls.) Therefore, it might have been foreseen either that he would try to squeeze more out of his land and tenants than his easy-going father had done, or that, like so many young heirs "newly come to their estate," he would cut a dash on borrowed money and try to recoup later by a mercenary marriage.

He did none of these things. When he returned home in 1813, the Squire had been in possession of his inheritance for six or seven years, and it was quite clear that he did not intend to waste or encumber it in any of the innumerable ways young men—and others not so young—devised for getting rid of money they were incapable of earning. Not that he was niggardly with anyone but himself. He liked giving handsome gifts—the telescope to Don Felipe, for instance, or the sixty guineas he gave one of the Demerara fugitives for a watch worth scarcely half that sum. But his personal expenditure was never high, even when he was young. He spent what was needed to maintain his property and to keep up his father's charities and even the hospitality of Walton Hall. He spent nothing on show, and never, for instance, gave balls or dinner-parties.

All this was sensible enough——for when his whims by some odd chance happened to run in the same groove as common sense, nobody could be more common-sensical than the Squire. And perhaps it was common sense on his part to leave "agricultural improvement" alone, for much money had been dropped on that chimera. He certainly carried farmers' conservatism rather far, for even the most "trifling drainage" of his fields "was absolutely coaxed out of him by an agricultural friend." He obstinately maintained the high value of swamp grass when——as Dr Hobson remarks with his usual sagacity——the real reason it was so flourishing was because it was too coarse for his cattle to eat. Never mind! the grass "afforded an agreeable lounge and fertile feeding resort for the herons"——and even in those early days the Squire was inclined to use his land more for natural history than for crops. One addition to agricultural economy he brought back from the West Indies greatly startled his rural neighbours. He had managed to tame one of the beautiful Demerara wild cats, a marjay, and this engaging animal not only waged fierce war on the "Hanoverian rats" which swarmed at Walton Hall, but (it is said) was trained to accompany the spaniels and behave with all their sagacity on shooting expeditions.

Shooting!——and thereby hang at least a couple of adventure-and-accident stories. Game-preserving, of course, was conducted on Watertonian lines. Thus, when he found his keeper was shooting owls:

"I threatened to strangle him if ever, after this, he molested either the old birds or their young ones. . . ."

But game-preserving, however eccentrically carried out, in those days inevitably invited poachers. Not that the Squire was vindictive, and he was always ready to be merciful if he could work off one of his unhandy jokes.

"If you please, Sir," said the keeper one Sunday morning, "I've catched eight tailors and a half stealing young rooks."

The "half" was an apprentice.

"Well," said the Squire with that terse and ready wit he kept for great occasions, "after all this noise on Sunday morning, you have not managed to bring me a full man, for we all know in Yorkshire that it requires nine tailors to make a man. Send them about their business; I can't prosecute eight-ninths and a half of a man."

So there was another grouse-in-the-gunroom story, which did

duty for half a century. But poachers were not always so amenable
to the authority of the keeper and the genial autocracy of the
Squire. Though undated, the following perilous encounter seems
to have occurred about this time, though it is mentioned in an
essay on the not very zoological topic of "Tight Shoes, Tight
Stays, and Cravats":

"One night, on going my rounds alone," and, by the way, it
was essentially prudent for the Squire to go entirely alone whenever he might meet armed and ferocious poachers, "in an adjacent
wood I came up with two poachers: fortunately one of them fled,
and I saw no more of him. I engaged the other; wrenched the knife
out of his hand, after I had parried his blow, and then closed with
him. We soon came to the ground together, he uppermost. In the
struggle, he contrived to get his hand into my cravat, and twisted
it until I was within an ace of being strangled. Just as all was
apparently over with me, I made one last convulsive effort, and I
sent my knees, as he lay upon me, full against his stomach, and
threw him off. Away he went, carrying with him my hat, and leaving with me his own, together with his knife and twenty wire snares."

Naturally, the moral drawn by the Squire from this dangerous
encounter bore no reference to poachers or the possible unwisdom
of hunting them alone and unarmed. On the contrary, it was a
fierce diatribe against cravats. Why, the Squire asks, are we "strong
and healthy men . . . doomed by fashion to bind up our necks
like sheaves of corn?" "Why"—and this is quite in the style of
Webster or Tourneur—"do we keep our jugular veins in everlast-
ing jeopardy?" There is a "philosopher in Sheffield" who "sets
this execrable fashion nobly at defiance." "How I revere him for
this; and how I condemn myself for not having sufficient fortitude
to follow his example!" For consider, the armadillo and land tortoise (those experts in dress reform), "although encased in a nearly
impenetrable armour, have their necks free." And even now, after
a century of progress, civilised man has not wholly learned to
follow the armadillo and the Sheffield philosopher. The wiser
female has abandoned "tight stays," and so no longer do "thousands of young females lose their health and symmetry" and "sink
into the cold and dreary grave long before their time."

Poachers and cravats were not the only dangers the Squire had
to reckon with in carrying on his Yorkshire sports. As always, one
of the most formidable menaces to his own life and limbs was
himself.

It was in 1814, in fine autumn weather, and the Squire was out shooting with his brother-in-law; and ". . . my gun went off accidentally." He had "just rammed the paper down upon the powder," when somehow or other in his inimitable way he contrived to fire his gun and shoot the ramrod "through my fore-finger, between the knuckle and the first joint, without breaking the bone." The powder, of course, at that close range, made the finger "black as soot." Here was a priceless opportunity for appallingly vigorous self-doctoring. He poured warm water "plentifully through the wound" until the powder was gone, then collected and replaced "the ruptured tendons," "not forgetting" (as he easily might) "to give to the finger its original shape as nearly as possible."

And what next? Rest, to recuperate from the shock? "After this, I opened a vein with the other hand, and took away to the extent of two and twenty ounces of blood." Follows a discourse on his many self-inflicted treatments. And then: "On reaching home, I applied a very large poultice, which was renewed every day."

In spite of which, he recovered; one cannot say why, but he did. "Inflammation" he considered "the root and origin of almost all diseases," and his "constant care" was to subdue it "at its early stage." Writing in 1837, he states that beginning at the age of twenty-three (i.e. not long after he first reached Guiana) he had been "blooded" more than a hundred and ten times, eighty of them "with my own hand."

"This, with calomel and jalap mixed together, as a purgative, with the use of rhubarb in occasional cases of dysentery, and with vast and often repeated potations of powdered Peruvian bark as a restorative, has enabled me to grapple successfully with sickness when I was far away from medical aid."

By way of compensation for this accident Waterton could contemplate with satisfaction his splendid triumph in the resuscitation of the Ass Wouralia. The curare poison he had collected in the wilderness, carried successfully through damp jungles and tropic rivers enclosed in balls of wax, had proved to be of uncommonly good quality and potency. Already, before leaving Demerara, the Squire had used it in a series of somewhat gruesome "scientific" experiments, describing with minute care the deaths of the various creatures with the record of the time between "stabbing with the poison" and complete extinction.

Experiments with rattlesnakes at Leeds

The Sepulchral Resting-place of the late Mr. Waterton at Walton Hall

"A healthy full-grown" fowl died in five minutes after passing through various stages of dissolution which are best left unrepeated, but may be traced by the curious in the pages of the *Wanderings*. Sixteen hours later, in a damp tropic climate, this fowl was still perfectly fresh—thereby establishing the fact that curare does not in any way corrupt game or birds shot for food. Other fowls were sacrificed in further experiments which showed the futility of the popularly supposed antidotes to the poison. The next victim was a three-toed sloth. By this time Waterton seems to have felt that he was in danger of incurring the reputation of a Borgia or Brinvillers to animals, and tries to hide the real poisoner of the sloth behind the vague description of "a gentleman who was collecting curiosities" and "wished to preserve the skin"—for which purpose this un-Watertonian character naturally "resorted to the wourali poison as the easiest death." The sloth was eleven minutes a-dying. Finally "a large well-fed ox, from nine hundred to a thousand pounds weight" died in "five and twenty minutes." "His flesh was very sweet and savoury at dinner."

There remained one more crucial experiment to perform—that of poisoning a creature and then curing it. The unfortunate fowls mentioned above had been in turn dosed with cane-sugar, intoxicated with rum, and held up to their beaks in water, all without avail. But in the first *Wandering,* written one may surmise during the tedious days of sailing home, Waterton mentioned another "difficult and tedious mode of cure" he had heard of, not very easy for a man struck by a hostile arrow to practise on himself when "wounded in the forest, far away from his friends." It was thought that "wind introduced into the lungs by means of a small pair of bellows would revive the poisoned patient."

With the enlightened encouragement and under the distinguished patronage of "Earl Percy," the third Duke of Northumberland of the Smithson creation, the Squire determined to settle this once for all, and at some unspecified time during the year of victory, 1814, proceeded to London with the Duke, the poison and his stabbing arrows. A London sweep consented to part with his three-year-old female donkey, which was taken to the London Veterinary College and "inoculated with wourali poison by Mr Waterton"—Earl Percy standing by and consenting. In ten minutes the donkey was apparently dead. Then, "under the scientific superintendence of Mr Sewell," the inanimate form received "an incision in the wind-pipe" and "through it the lungs were regularly inflated for two hours with a pair of bellows." For two hours, then, this strange scene was prolonged, and it may well have seemed to most if not all those present that artificial respiration would have to follow rum, cane-sugar and immersion. But suddenly "suspended animation returned," and the ass "held up her head and looked around." Alas, on discontinuance of the bellows, the ass instantly died again, and another anxious two hours of treatment followed before "she rose up and walked about, free from agitation and apparently free from pain."

There at any rate was one case, showing that artificial respiration, if applied within a few minutes of wounding, could save a victim of curare poisoning. But the donkey's constitution was so "severely affected" that for a long time it was doubtful "if ever she would be well again." By the express orders of his grace she was sent down to Walton Hall, where she "looked lean and sickly for above a year," but "began to mend the spring after" and "by midsummer became fat and frisky." Named "Wouralia" by her benefactor, she was "sheltered from the wintry storm" and fed "in the finest pasture" for nearly a quarter of a century. No "burden had been placed on her" and her days were ended in peace. The *St James's Chronicle* published an account of her from an anonymous hand, almost immediately after her death "on Saturday morning, the 15th of February, 1839." This unknown writer displays an astonishing familiarity with the ways of Walton Hall, and winds up by quoting "Mr Waterton's directions," stating positively that Mr Waterton would willingly try the effects of "wourali poison" on any animal suffering from hydrophobia and even on "any one of our own species labouring under a permanently locked jaw or mad from the bite of a rabid animal." Mr Waterton was "ready to do the needful with a steady hand," and should the well-meant effort "prove ineffectual" and he be called "to take his trial at York for a cool and deliberate act of Manslaughter," well, Mr Waterton "would not feel daunted" by the prospect.

VI

INTEREST in the fascinating career of the "ass Wouralia" has led us on ahead in time, and we must return to "the ague-beaten wanderer" at Walton Hall and the years of the abdication at Fontainebleau, the Hundred Days and the end of that particular world war on the Plains of Waterloo. Like many of his contemporaries, Waterton did not fill his writings with the hashed-up journalism and ersatz patriotism so common in the age of the sovereign newspaper. The remark is often made that Jane Austen's characters lived through a terrific war, and never mention it. Only the personal life is a fitting topic for art; and the Squire, an artist in eccentricity, instinctively refrains from boring us with comments on what he had been reading in *The Times* that morning. Only when the war actually touched his own life does he even refer to it. His acquaintance, Captain Peake, R.N., is "cut in two by a cannon ball" in a hopeless but heroic battle with a much heavier American ship. He mourns Captain Peake. Having occasion to recommend himself to the Portuguese commander of a frontier fort, the Squire in his letter communicates the news that "Milord Wellington se ha apoderado de Ciudad Rodrigo." And his one mention of Waterloo is to explain the glumness he found in the inhabitants of French Guiana in 1816.

The guns were silent, and "the Continent open" for the wanderer to become the saunterer—the Squire's distinction between tropical exploration and touristing. Although at other periods of his life the Squire enjoyed "sauntering" in Europe, in 1815 he thought "there was nothing very tempting in a trip across the Channel," while "England had long ceased to be the land for adventures." Perhaps the reason for his distaste was that after the long semi-imprisonment of war, travel on the Continent had become not only possible but very fashionable with the English, rivalled only by tours to the "Walter Scott country." It would scarcely be possible for the Squire to comply with any fashion of the "worldlings" on whom he delighted to exercise his satire.

Having refused to explore Madagascar on an official mission, with all the advantages he admitted came from Government support, the Squire determined early in 1816 to undertake another "wandering" on his own. He planned to go to Brazil, make his way through the interior to the frontier of British Guiana, and thus make a second and even more sensational appearance at Georgetown. Of course, he meant also to collect more specimens, chiefly of the brightly coloured birds he admired, for his museum at Walton Hall. But the plan was ill-considered, and the absence of any precise motive (such as obtaining fresh curare poison from the Indians) made his movements uncertain and capricious, and the second "Wandering" the least interesting.

Sailing from Liverpool on the 19th March, 1816, he reached Pernambuco at some unspecified date in the same year. As so often happens with foreign towns, Pernambuco, which looked so romantic and charming at a distance when seen from on board ship after a tedious voyage, turned out a disappointment on closer acquaintance. The streets, the Squire thought, were laid out haphazard, the houses were often "stained and mouldy," the balconies "dark and gloomy," while the filth underfoot was repulsive—"when the wind begins to blow eyes and nose are too often exposed to a cloud of very unsavoury dust."

But Pernambuco was in the tropics, close to the great tropical garden of Olinda and to country swarming with birds. We are not allowed to reach them, however, until we have listened to a long panegyric on the Jesuit college, and a diatribe against the wicked Portuguese premier, Marquess Pombal, who ordered the suppression and expulsion of the Jesuits—"the college of Pernambuco was plundered, and some time after an elephant was kept there." The Squire was particularly annoyed by the idea of this elephant, from which he passes abruptly to a denunciation of Southey, who had spoken of these Fathers as "Missioners whose zeal the most fanatical was directed by the coolest policy." The Laureate catches it hot and strong, and is told bluntly that as historian he "cuts a sorry figure"; and, this not sufficing outraged piety, the ghost of Father Nobrega is made to "rise from the tomb" and to denounce the "ungrateful Englishman." The reader is not sorry when, by another of his abrupt and unhandy transitions—or rather lack of transition—the Squire drops the Jesuits, and begins his next paragraph:

"The environs of Pernambuco are very pretty."

But nothing much happened in the pretty environs, except that the Squire shot and preserved birds. Still, it would not have been

Waterton if he had not contrived to get himself into a scrape when, as he truly says, "these adventures were near being brought to a speedy and final close." This was another of his snake adventures, though comparatively undramatic for one who could boast that he had "been in the midst of snakes for many years" and whose standard of combat leaves the infant Hercules a poor second.

What happened was this. Waterton saw a number of blackbirds squawking and fluttering wildly in the lower branches of a tree, while in the long grass he saw or fancied he saw "a palegreen grasshopper fluttering." Now it must already be clear to the reader that when the Squire took a notion into that queer noddle of his, he always held on to it with extreme obstinacy. In this instance he saw a pale-green grasshopper of a kind new to him, and instantly set out to collect it. He did not want to risk breaking legs and wings while it fluttered (has anyone else ever seen a grasshopper hovering in one place without settling?), so he stalked it carefully. And then, just as he was about "to make sure of it"—"behold, the head of a large rattlesnake." Only "an instantaneous spring backwards prevented fatal consequences." The supposed grasshopper was in fact the snake's rattle, though how the Squire failed to hear and thrill at that ominous sound will for ever be a mystery to anyone who has heard it. As to the birds:

". . . they flew away on his retiring—one alone left his little life in the air, destined to become a specimen, mute and motionless, for the inspection of the curious in a far-off land."

These little prose elegies in the style of Laurence Sterne, which the Squire occasionally lavishes on his victims, are disconcerting. If he felt that way about the birds, why did he kill them? But it was this sensibility in the Squire, developing with age, which turned him from a bird-killer to a bird-lover; and while he could not wholly abandon the joys of collecting and taxidermy, he atoned for them most handsomely at Walton Hall.

The rainy season came on in Brazil, and instead of seizing this favourable opportunity to catch more chills and fevers in the tropical jungle, the Squire hesitated. The forty days' journey to Maranham, he decided, was too tame for an explorer, too uncivilised for a traveller—a nice distinction. But with the rain, the birds began to moult, and he had already secured "fifty-eight specimens of the handsomest." It was time to leave, and he decided to sail for Cayenne (for no particular purpose that I can discover) on "a Portuguese brig, with poor accommodation," where "the most eligible bed" was "the top of a hen-coop on deck," and even here "an unsavoury little beast, called bug, was neither shy nor deficient in appetite."

Nothing much happened at Cayenne either. The Squire saw and smelled "twenty-two thousand clove-trees in full bearing," but was not moved to any particular comment by so tremendous an olfactory experience. A more interesting phenomenon to his way of thinking (gleaned, by the way, from the *Essays,* which here supplement the *Wanderings* and *Autobiography*) was his meeting with "a naturalist by name Howe." This gentleman showed the greatly interested Squire a box containing sixteen of his own teeth, with the melancholy comment:

"These fine teeth once belonged to my jaws: they all dropped out by my making use of the *savon arsenètique* for preserving the skins of animals."

The Squire used corrosive sublimate, and was always happy to find evidence of the pernicious results of using arsenical soap— whether to the specimens or to the *savant* using it. "I have applied the solution" (of corrosive sublimate) "to my hat," he boasts, "and to the long Indian arrows with complete success."

Another less happy experience off the coast of French Guiana would scarcely be worth mentioning but for its illustration of the Squire's pitiless exposure of himself in the interests of natural history, and his inevitable habit of getting into scrapes and weird maladies. Off the coast of Cayenne there is a huge rock, Le Grand Connêtable, renowned for the vast quantities of sea-fowl which feed and breed there. The Squire had to see this. Starting off at six o'clock in the evening, he began by getting soaked through ("it rained piteously"), and then his canoe missed its way. At ten o'clock next morning they stuck on a mud-bank under a scorching sun, which, however, brought its reward:

"On every side of us were egrettes and herons, scarlet curlews and spoonbills, and other sea fowl, in countless numbers. . . . We counted above five hundred flamingoes, which were ranged in a straight line, putting us in mind of a file of soldiers in the scarlet uniform."

But as evening came and the tide rose, even the Squire could see that its "turbulence and angry aspect" made impossible the trip to the rock. He therefore "reluctantly" returned through another "night of hardship." The two wettings, according to his medical reckoning, were the cause of an "inflammation of the œsophagus" and "the act of deglutition became so exceedingly painful, that I was obliged to live on bread soaked in tea for three succeeding days." (Perhaps he had tonsillitis?) Yet "even with this light food I barely escaped from the lancet."

Just before the Squire left Cayenne, so Norman Moore tells us, "while sitting under a cinnamon tree, a branch fell on his head," cut through by "the insect, which the colonists call a knife-grinder." It is reasonable to suppose that the literate Squire instantly quoted Canning's parody of the anti-Jesuitical Laureate: "Needy knife-grinder, whither art thou going?" He took the branch home to Walton Hall. I wish respect for truth permitted me to say that he also took Mr Howe's teeth, but extensive researches show no evidence for this most probable of freaks.

The next move was to Demerara, by way of Paramaribo and New Amsterdam. Evidently the Squire was kindly remembered and welcomed back to Georgetown, for he addresses its inhabitants in one of his absurd Shandyean apostrophes: "Long may ye flourish, peaceful and liberal inhabitants of Demerara! Your doors are ever open to harbour the harbourless; your purses never shut to the wants of the distressed: many a ruined fugitive from the Oroonoque . . ." and so forth, casting (without acknowledgment to Mr Gray) "a longing, lingering look behind," as we "now, gentle reader, retire from the busy scenes of man and journey towards the wilds in quest of the feathered tribe."

Six months were spent in "the wilds" in the congenial task of shooting and preserving the skins of two hundred specimens of birds, but without any of the usual adventures and accidents. He discourses with enthusiasm of humming birds and cotingas, toucans, campaneros and hou-tous, cassiques, jacamars, aras and whip-poor-wills. He remembers that "eight years ago" (which would have been 1808, that memorable year in which a certain distinguished Englishman carried Admiral Collingwood's despatches to the Orinoco) it was "while eating a boiled toucan" that he suddenly thought of how to preserve the beak without losing its colour. And an eloquent defence of the woodpecker from the charge of destroying sound trees opens the Squire's long series of campaigns on behalf of those he persisted in calling "the feathered tribe."

Towards the end of this second "Wandering" the Squire, as he takes leave "of thee, kind and gentle reader," adds this promise: "The new mode of preserving birds heretofore promised thee shall not be forgotten. The plan is already formed in imagination, and can be penned down during the passage across the Atlantic." This, presumably written before he left Guiana, is dated "April 6, 1817," and brings up a couple of problems in the confused Watertonian chronology.

When did the Squire excogitate his "new method" of preserving skins? According to the passage just cited, it must have been worked out before 1817. But according to another passage in the third "Wandering," it was in 1820, "one night, while I was lying in the hammock," that the Squire devised his method of taxidermy. The apparent contradiction is due to the fact that the Squire omits to say specifically that there were two problems to be solved. One was the problem of preserving birds, which must have been solved early, since Dr Hobson speaks of having seen at Walton Hall birds preserved and exposed intentionally without any protection for "upwards of fifty-five years" without any loss of colour or damage from insects, which puts it back to 1812. The second, and evidently more complex problem, was that of preserving quadrupeds, and that this was the difficulty solved "in the hammock" becomes plain from another passage at the end of the third "Wandering." What was Waterton's famous method of taxidermy, which gave such marvellous results in his hands that eventually he was able to model the skin of a Red Howler Monkey into a very plausible human bust? The most concise and lucid exposition is (perhaps inevitably) not the Squire's. It is Sir Norman Moore's:

"He soaked the skin in corrosive sublimate. The mixture penetrated every pore, and being anti-putrescent, preserved the skin from decay, and being poisonous, secured it from the depredations of insects. As the solution kept the skin moist and flexible for several days, it could all this while be moulded at will. The hollows and protuberances of the animal frame, the play and action of feather and limb, the physiognomy of pain and pleasure, rage or mildness, could be faithfully impressed upon the skin, which once more assumed the shape and gesture its wearer bore in life. Protected from wind, sun and fire, the remodelled skin was dried very slowly, and the corrosive sublimate caused it to stiffen without shrinking, till the form and features given to it by the artist became as firm set as if they had been carved in marble. This is the general principle of Waterton's discovery."

To this we may add that the Rev J. G. Wood (who also visited and examined the collection while it was still at Walton Hall) tells us every preserved creature was "perfectly hollow, so hollow indeed that the hands and faces are translucent as letter-paper—even to the very finger-nails. There is literally nothing in it but air, the skin being hard and elastic as if made of horn. . . . It can be crumpled between the fingers and squeezed like a sponge, returning to its original shape by the strange elastic firmness which the skin has now attained. It can be picked up by a pinch of hair and swung about without damage. . . . It can be kicked downstairs or flung from the top of the Monument, without showing a sign of ill-usage. It may be squeezed flat as a pancake, and, when the pressure is removed, will resume its shape with the elasticity of a hollow india-rubber ball."

The Squire's taxidermic contemporaries spent much energy in sneering at his methods. If we ask why they did not rather imitate a technique which gave such incomparable results, the answer is: Because they couldn't.

The Squire sailed for England, and, the better part of a year having elapsed since he nearly "terminated his adventures" by mistaking a rattle-snake's rattle for a grasshopper, it was obviously high time for him to be involved in some new grapple with Death. He was; but only to the extent of thoughtlessly and foolishly sending another man on an errand from which he barely escaped with his life. Waterton shot a tropic bird while the ship was "going smartly" through the water, and as he badly wanted a specimen for his collection, shouted:

"A guinea for him who will fetch the bird to me!"

A Danish sailor jumped in after it, but when others of the crew ran to lower the jolly-boat, they found it full of stuff and lashed down tightly. On top of this carelessness, they contrived to miss stays as they tacked and—in short, by the time they managed to wear her, "we all expected that the Dane had gone to Davy Jones's locker." At last they found him, "buffeting the waves, with the dead bird in his mouth" and the Squire received it "from the cold and trembling hand of our adventurous Dane." I do not know which is the more remarkable—the recklessness with which Waterton risked a man's life for such a trifle, or the calm *dégagé* way in which he tells the tale. Certainly, if the man had been drowned, the Squire might have had to face a charge of manslaughter.

During what months did Waterton make this voyage? If he had left Demerara on the 6th April, how could it have been "early in the year 1817" that he was in London, asking Sir Joseph Banks to let him volunteer for the exploring expedition to the Congo then planning? Considering the time a transatlantic passage then needed, it is quite impossible that Waterton could have left Demerara after 6th April and yet have been in London before midsummer, let alone "early in the year." The only possible solution of these time difficulties in which the Squire's vagueness involves us is this: Sir Joseph asked him to put his knowledge of the tropics at the disposal of the "scientific gentlemen," after having cancelled his permission for Waterton to accompany them on the ground that "the powers" of the "steam-vessel appointed" were not "adequate to make way against the downward stream of the Congo." (If that were so, why did not the influential President of the Royal Society veto the whole expedition, which he said was "doomed to disappointment and misfortune," and insist on a better boat, instead of allowing the "scientific gentlemen" to perish?) Waterton's text seems to show that he merely talked or lectured to them, giving them the fruits of his experience in Guiana. But a brief note from Sir Joseph, printed both as a footnote and in the Preface to the *Wanderings*, refers in one version to "your manuscript" and in the other to "your journal." Perhaps the date, 6th April, 1817, was that of sending in this document; but the fact that Waterton cannot copy even a brief letter twice without confounding "journal" with "manuscript" shows once more how his *étourderie* was not confined to fantastic adventures. His critics were certainly justified in doubting his exactitude, though at the same time everyone who comes to know the Squire will feel that he never put down anything he did not believe at the moment to be true.

Although Waterton initiated them into his "new method" of taxidermy, impressed on them the necessity for temperance, and gave them the grandmotherly advice "never to sleep in their wet clothes," "several of the gentlemen perished" and the expedition failed. Whether it was because their steamboat was no good, or because they rashly practised the Squire's medical advice by blooding and dosing themselves with calomel and jalap, or for some other reason, does not appear. And the suspicion arises that Sir Joseph's permission to the Squire to join the expedition was withdrawn, not so much because the boat was unsatisfactory, as because he heard of the offence given in high quarters by the Squire's refusal of Lord Bathurst's Madagascar offer in 1813.

There was nothing for him to do but to return to Walton Hall, still nursing his passion for travel and the tropics and—it may be surmised—his disappointment that "nothing genteel and confidential" from Government was to come his way. There he occupied himself with the collections he had brought back from South America, and with guerrilla warfare on the Hanoverian rats which infested his house and on the poachers who stole his game. Perhaps it was at this time that he invented one of his "dodges" for circumventing the midnight marauder who came after his pheasants. Gradually he filled the clumps of wood where his pheasants roosted with cleverly made but simple dummies of the birds. It was impossible for the poacher to know which was a real sleeping bird and which an imitation. Ten to one his shots merely brought down dummies and gave the alarm to the Squire and his retainers, and, as Waterton reflects with complacency: "Six or seven dozen of wooden pheasants, nailed on the branches of trees, in the surrounding woods, cause unutterable vexation and loss of ammunition to these amateurs of nocturnal plunder."

At a later period of life than this the Squire protested that he preserved pheasants only as an ornithologist; their flesh "he heeded not." Perhaps this was not true of the years before 1817, but it is fairly certain that in this year the Squire made up his mind definitely to turn Walton Hall park into a bird sanctuary. This is his greatest achievement, and one for which he has never yet received his due. It must suffice to mention now that he began preparing shelters for the nesting of wild birds, and issued certain orders to his keeper and other retainers. For instance, no boat was to be launched on the lake from late autumn until May, in order to leave the water birds undisturbed; no gun was to be fired; dogs were not to be allowed to run loose, and the keepers were to stay out of the coverts; no wild life was to be destroyed, except of course Hanoverian rats. Even the weasel was to be protected, for the Squire thought its destruction of game more than made up for by its consumption of rats, mice and beetles. Even the fruit-trees and kitchen gardens were not to be defended.

But he became restless. Perhaps the lack of exciting episode during the second wandering had disappointed him; perhaps his "chilly frame" shrank from the prospect of a Yorkshire winter; or perhaps the first flood of British tourists to the Continent having ebbed somewhat, a "saunter" in the direction of Rome now became a Watertonian possibility. At all events, he set

out to spend the winter in Rome with his friend, Captain
Alexander, R.N.

It is much to be lamented that the Squire failed to keep, or at
any rate to publish, a journal of his "doings and dodges" during
this visit to Rome. His account is more laconic and meagre than
his disappointing report on Spain in 1802. Yet Rome in 1817–18
must have had much of interest, especially for so ardent a Catholic,
which we should be glad to know. Above all, how much one longs
for more than a brief paragraph—all he allows—to describe one
of the most famous and most Watertonian of escapades.

In Rome, the Squire tells us, he "fell in with" his "old friend
and schoolfellow," Captain Jones. "Captain" Jones was only a
militiaman, it is true; but that does not seem a reason for omitting
so remarkable a character from the Stonyhurst Centenary Record.
He was not a Waterton, but he was born to be a Waterton crony
and the pictorial recorder of another famous Waterton freak—the
riding of the live cayman. Now, at Stonyhurst, Jones and the
Squire had been almost equally renowned—or disliked—for their
application to the unrecognised science of "tree-climbing." "Many
a tree we had climbed together in the last century," says the
Squire nostalgically of his friend.

Talking over these past delights, they were able to boast to each
other that "their nerves were in excellent trim," and they longed
for something to climb to test their mettle. We do not know for
certain who made the suggestion—but surely the Watertonian
fantasy is here revealed at its ripest?—but they agreed to climb up
the façade of St Peter's. How they escaped the vigilance of the
guards is not reported, but undoubtedly they "mounted to the top
of St Peter's," and, not satisfied with that, "climbed thirteen feet
higher, where we reached the point of the conductor, and left our
gloves on it."

"After this"—was it on the same day, and how did they escape
arrest?—they proceeded to the Castello di Sant' Angelo, the great
papal fortress built on the ruins of the Mausoleum of Hadrian.
The modern name comes from a huge gilded angel which stands
on the summit of the building. Somehow "we contrived to get on
the head of the guardian angel," and, still unsatisfied by this interesting accomplishment, there "we stood on one leg." If ever a
statue of Waterton is erected—and there certainly ought to be
one—he should be shown in this posture, standing on one foot on
the head of an angel.

When his attendants told this story to Pius VII (Chiaramonti), His Holiness, instead of being amused, was very angry. Heavy thunderstorms break over Rome, and the Pope may have been nervous of lightning. He realised that personal sanctity and the prayers of Christendom might not avert a thunder-bolt if (as he perhaps erroneously supposed) the two pairs of gloves on the point had made the lightning-conductor useless. He ordered them instantly to be removed. But the command of the Pontifex Maximus was as inoperative as the "Off with their heads" of the Queen in *Alice*. Nobody dared to make the ascent—or so the legend says. It goes on to claim that the chief culprit himself had to be approached. Instantly, of course, he gladly repeated his fantastic and dangerous feat, this time in the presence of a vast and appreciative audience, who doubtless uttered the "alalagmus of the Roman Legions" when they saw him successfully reach the gloves and descend safely with them.

Immediately after this Mr Waterton of Walton Hall, accompanied by Captain Alexander, R.N., left Rome *en route* to England.

This simple journey was not accomplished without a serious accident—whether as a punishment for this quasi-sacrilegious act or as a natural result of the Squire's heedlessness it is impossible to say. As their travelling carriage was crossing Mont Cenis, the Squire fancied that the baggage on the top was slipping. Instantly, and without reflecting on the danger, he "mounted on the wheel," his knee "as bad luck would have it" smashed the window-pane, and he contrived to stick himself just above the knee-cap with two pieces of glass at least an inch deep. To complete the disaster, he had chosen ten o'clock on a dark night to perform this useful service to himself and his travelling companion.

What was to be done now? Well, the Squire "put my thumb firmly on the wound," and the Captain hastily brought one of the carriage lamps. The "steady not pulsating" flow of blood reassured them. No artery was cut. Plucking out the pieces of glass with his customary unflinching courage, the Squire now bound up the wounds with his cravat, cut the pocket from his coat and called for a poultice—which the Captain managed to procure at the next house. But the journey to Paris was a dismal one. Twice they were held up "on account of the fever" (did the Squire "have recourse to the lancet?" he does not say), and when at last they reached Paris, the "wound was in a deplorable state."

This, it must be remembered, was in 1818, when the allied armies were just about to be withdrawn from France. At that time, Paris was one of the greatest, if not the greatest, of medical centres in Europe. In addition it contained many skilled surgeons of the Grande Armée, who had striven to bind up the wounds of the Emperor's soldiers. The Squire of Walton Hall, either through his embassy or his purse, could easily have called on any or several of these excellent surgeons. But no! "Doctor Marshall, a friend from Demerara," was called in. He "showed exquisite skill" in treating the wound and "would have done marvels," but the Squire insisted on continuing his journey to London—a city also not deficient in medical and surgical talent. But once arrived there, "Father Scott, of the Society of Jesus," was the oracle called in, and he brought to the scene "the celebrated Mr Carpue," to whose "consummate knowledge and incessant attention" the Squire believed he owed the preservation of his limb and even of his life.

VII

THE effects of this severe wound above the knee-cap were tiresome and protracted. "For nearly two years," the Squire tells us, the knee "continued stiff," and was only restored "by constant exercise" and by strenuous refusal to use a walking-stick. The constant exercise must have taken place in the park of Walton Hall, to which the Squire returned as soon as possible. Did it include bare-foot climbing of trees and battles in the dark with poachers? Very likely. The Squire certainly continued the work of turning his paternal acres into a bird sanctuary, but consideration of his many "doings and dodges" as well as of the outside and inside of Walton Hall may conveniently be left to the period when marriage and fatherhood put an end to the Squire's "wanderings."

Scarcely had the knee been restored to a condition when it was "as sound as though it had never been injured" when the Squire was off to Guiana again, and this time not in an aimless manner, but with definite plans. He would complete his collection of tropical birds, add to them snakes and a cayman and various quadrupeds. He intended to investigate the habits of the sloth and of the vampire bat, and also (it appears) he formed the ambition of bringing home a live ant-eater in a commodious glass box. "Natural history headquarters" were to be established at Mibiri Creek, in the now-abandoned home of his friend Edmonstone, who had saved enough money to buy back the paternal estate in Scotland and to resume his life as a laird. And so, in February 1820, the wandering Squire set off from the Clyde on the *Glenbervie*—a starting-point which seems to imply some important business connected with the Edmonstones.

The Squire's narratives, however entertaining, are always rather mixed up and sometimes obscure. Indeed, a good deal of their entertainment derives from the fact that he has more than usually abused the amateur author's privilege of ignoring such literary details as construction, compression, selection and lucidity. One can imagine him sitting down each day to write, and starting on whatever topic or experience of his "Wanderings" he happens to remember, without the slightest concern for what went before or is to follow. This pleasing amateurism is often ludicrous and always rather endearing. Less pleasing is the fact that even in such trivial but essential matters as dates and the duration of journeys, he is liable to forget something. If he tells you the day of starting, ten to one he forgets to say when he arrived; or vice versa. We have seen how he involved us in confusion by his vagueness as to the date of his return to England in 1817. He now confounds us by forgetting to say in what month he reached Georgetown in 1820.

The scene which met him there was anything but cheering and auspicious. A fearful epidemic of yellow fever had swept through the prosperous little colonial capital, carrying off "numbers of the old inhabitants" while daily funerals were still disposing of "the remains of many a newcomer."

Very naturally the Squire did not linger, but made his way to the house at Mibiri Creek as soon as he could collect supplies and servants. It may seem strange that a colonial mansion, which had feasted "generals and governors," should not be sold but simply abandoned. The probable reason is that the peace of 1815 abruptly put an end to the excessive profits of West Indian planters. Here another shock awaited the Squire. Though abandoned only "for some years," the plantation was already in ruins, while the jungle had almost obliterated traces of the cleared land. Frogs, snakes, bats, owls, vampires had made their abode in the once handsomely furnished rooms—much of course to the Squire's delight. However, all but the bats and vampires chose to depart as the roof was repaired and part at least of the house made habitable for the stoical Squire.

And now occurred a third *contretemps*. Since the event took place in June, only four months after the departure from Scotland, it must have been very soon after his arrival at Mibiri Creek that the Squire fell ill of "a severe attack of fever," which he attributed to the dampness following "a deluge of rain." It is instructive to muse over the Squire's minute, almost affectionate, description of his symptoms and the progress of his "ague," and not a little awesome to contemplate the "remedies" he employed.

For two or three days fits of yawning, a feeling of fatigue and unrefreshing sleep ought to have warned the Squire of what was brewing. But even though he had been reading Horace—the lines about the ship being carried out to sea—he omitted all precautionary dosings. And so one night he awoke, thirsty, with a "cruel headache" and "pain in the small of the back." Still he did nothing but doze fitfully, starting awake as he dreamed he was "falling down a precipice," until—strange aubade—"the return of the bats to their diurnal retreat" announced to his weary eyes the dawn. Only then, rising "in languor," did he find his pulse at a hundred and twenty, and begin his medical operations. Calomel, it may be said, is now never given in larger doses than five grains, and jalap is chiefly reserved for cases of dropsy. For his attack of malaria, the Squire led off with ten grains of calomel and "a scruple of jalap." At five that evening, the pulse having risen to one hundred and thirty while "the headache was almost insupportable," the Squire proceeded still further to lower his resistance by making "a large orifice" in his arm, from which "rushed sixteen ounces" of blood. Although he had plenty of quinine, he made no use of it, but "steeped" his feet in warm water, and discovered with unwise satisfaction that the blood-letting had reduced his pulse to ninety.

The night, however, was "very restless," and of course his temperature soon rose, while the pulse again reached a hundred and twenty and "the headache was distressing." He put cold-water compresses to his head but as "the fever ran very high" (as well it might), he further lowered his resistance by taking ten grains of jalap and five more of calomel. His "determination" not to take any more calomel may have been a belated tribute to common sense, but luckily, about two o'clock in the afternoon, the period of violent perspiration of the malaria patient came on, the painful symptoms decreased, and he managed to get some sleep. Next morning he again punished himself with "a large dose of castor oil," but only on the next day did he start taking quinine, which he "continued for a fortnight." "This put all to rights." Perhaps the reader may be reminded that, in the days before atabrine, the standard modern treatment of malaria was thirty grains of quinine a day during the attack, and ten grains a day thereafter for at least two to three months. "Building up the general health and bodily resistance" is now considered of the utmost importance to the patient—a result hardly to be obtained by profuse blood-letting and overdoses of violent purges.

Restored, by the perennial miracle which always prevented him from medicining himself to death, Waterton was able to turn his attention once more to natural history. His industry was great, for in eleven months (which included an excursion to the Essequibo) he collected "rare insects, two hundred and thirty birds, two land-tortoises, five armadillos, two large serpents, a sloth, an ant-bear and cayman," all of which he preserved himself by the Waterton method.

Among mammals the Squire paid particular attention to the ant-eater, the sloth and the vampire bat. His observations of the ant-eater (or "ant-bear" as he calls it) enabled him to correct mistakes then made in drawing and stuffing that animal, as well as in describing it. According to Waterton, nobody before him had noticed and described the large glands which lubricate the ant-eater's tongue when it is sweeping up ants. Moreover, the creature was at that epoch represented in illustrations and museum specimens as standing or walking with its large fore-claws "in the same forward attitude as those of a dog, or a common bear"; whereas in fact the animal folds the claws to a point and "walks on the calloused backs of his paws."

The largest number of pages devoted to one topic in these amusingly scatter-brained "Wanderings" concern the sloth. It seems incredible, but is the fact, that its habits had never been properly observed, and the peculiar structure, which enables it to move fairly rapidly through the forest clinging to the underside of branches, was totally misunderstood. The sloth was considered to have been afflicted with "enormous defects" at the Creation, and Buffon (as the Squire tells us) "was compelled to ask why should not certain animals have been condemned to misery, seeing that nine-tenths of the human race were?" Waterton's account of the animal was the first accurate one to reach Europe, and inspired Sydney Smith (who reviewed the *Wanderings* when they first came out) to his famous description of the sloth as an animal "who moves suspended, rests suspended, sleeps suspended, and passes his whole life in suspense, like a young clergyman distantly related to a bishop." This very clerical jest, added to the highly individual, not to say eccentric, manner in which Waterton reported his discoveries, gives a strange notion of how natural history was studied in pre-Darwinian days.

Waterton's style certainly does provide some excuse for the "closet naturalists" (abhorred by the Squire only less than Hanoverian rats) in their reluctance to believe him. They were ignorant, it is true; but he gave every opening to their scepticism by absence of method, a farrago of disconnected observations, apparently tall tales, obvious prejudices, evident mistakes in small points, and above all by affectations of style. In the case of the

sloth, Waterton was handsomely vindicated when a living specimen was brought safely to England, and the "closet naturalists"
could see for themselves that he had observed correctly and reported accurately. But ever since the founders of the Royal Society
framed their statutes to keep Sir Thomas Browne out, scientists
have favoured a plain, dull, unliterary style, and were then as now
inclined to despise as a mere amateur or even charlatan any writer
on scientific topics who indulged in literary frills. Take, for instance, the Shandyean phraseology and galumphing humour of
this description of a sloth:

"As soon as we got up to him he threw himself upon his back,
and defended himself in gallant style with his fore-legs. 'Come,
poor fellow,' said I to him, 'if thou hast got into a hobble to-day,
thou shalt not suffer for it. I'll take no advantage of thee in misfortune; the forest is large enough both for thee and me to rove
in: go thy ways up above, and enjoy thyself in these endless
wilds; it is more than probable that thou wilt never have another
interview with man. So fare thee well.' On saying this, I took
a long stick which was lying there, held it for him to hook on, and
then conveyed him to a high and stately mora. He ascended with
wonderful rapidity, and in about a minute he was almost at the
top of the tree. He now went off in a side direction, and caught
hold of the branch of a neighbouring tree; and then proceeded to
the heart of the forest. I stood looking on, lost in amazement at
his singular mode of progress. I followed him with my eye till
the intervening branches closed in betwixt us; and then I lost
sight for ever of the two-toed sloth. I was going to add that I never
saw a sloth take to his heels in such earnest; but the expression
will not do, for the sloth has no heels."

It requires no great effort of the imagination to visualise the
amazement, the bewilderment, the anger of somewhat heavy-
witted "closet naturalists" when they read such passages as that.
What, they might well ask themselves, is the scientific reason for
addressing the sloth in the terms of Uncle Toby's apostrophe to
the captive fly? And if this "eccentric amateur" was prepared to
joke about sloths "taking to their heels," might not the whole
description be a joke? The safest and easiest course was to accuse
the Squire of "a propensity to dress fact in the garb of fiction," a
not wholly undeserved charge which needless to say greatly infuriated him.

With the vampire bat the Squire was perhaps less successful, since his great wish was to confute those who denied that these creatures suck blood by himself becoming a victim to their winged phlebotomy. Waterton had been playing around this problem for years in his desultory and capricious way. There was, for instance, the case of Mr Tarbet, the Scotchman. . . .

But the mention of Mr Tarbet inevitably reminded the Squire of another adventure endured by that morose Caledonian, who seemed quite unable to appreciate the gay and humorous side of life. One night Mr Tarbet, having made "a very capital dinner on crabs," awoke "in that state in which Virgil describes Caeleno to have been, viz. 'faedissima ventris proluvies.' " Mr Tarbet therefore made his way in the darkness to the "little temple, dedicated to the goddess Cloacina" and placed himself "in the usual situation which the votaries of the goddess generally take." What happened was described graphically by Mr Tarbet afterwards as being like "a lighted match dropped on a pound of gunpowder," with the result that "up he jumped and forced his way out, roaring for help and a light, for he was worried alive by ten thousand devils." He had, in fact, sat down unclothed upon a large column of venomously stinging ants.

This laughable little incident had its counterpart in Mr Tarbet's experiences with the vampire bat—experiences which, in spite of all the Squire's most humorous sallies, this dense Scot continued to find entirely without a funny side. They had been sleeping in hammocks side by side when Waterton heard Mr Tarbet "letting fall an imprecation or two just about the time he ought to have been saying his morning prayers." The Squire at once scented fun, and asked "softly":

"What is the matter, sir; is anything amiss?"

For some reason Mr Tarbet replied "surlily":

"What's the matter? Why, the vampires have been sucking me to death. There," thrusting his foot out of the hammock, "see how these infernal imps have been drawing my life's blood."

The Squire examined the wound, and being one of the world's experts in blood-letting, was able instantly to compute that Mr Tarbet had lost "from ten to twelve ounces of blood." By way of sympathy the Squire remarked humorously "that a European surgeon would not have been so generous as to have blooded him for nothing." Strangely enough, Mr Tarbet was not convulsed with mirth at this jest on his wound, with its Attic side-glance at Scottish frugality. On the contrary, "I think I put him in a worse humour," for "he looked up in my face, and did not say a word." From which the Squire concluded, not without some probability, that Mr Tarbet thought, "I had better have spared this piece of ill-timed levity."

Then there was the case of the household attached to Mr Walcott from Barbados, who was visited by the Squire at a plantation high up the Demerara River. On arriving the Squire was enchanted to learn that the vampires had "sucked his son (a boy of about ten or eleven years old), some of his fowls, and his jackass." The jackass had suffered most from these "sanguinary imps," and indeed "looked like misery steeped in vinegar." Here was an opportunity for the Squire to get himself bitten and thus discover "how the vampires actually draw the blood." But he failed here, as he failed during the eleven months spent at Mibiri Creek, where "many a night have I slept with my foot out of the hammock to tempt this winged surgeon." But, alas, "the vampire seemed to have taken a personal dislike to me," and "though he would tap the more favoured Indian's toe" in a hammock slung alongside, "the provoking brute would refuse to give my claret one solitary trial." Might this have been due to the callouses developed by going barefoot in the jungle for months on end? But perhaps it was mere bad luck, or perversity on the bat's part.

If the Squire failed to get the vampire to tap the claret from his foot, he certainly succeeded only too well in tapping it himself through one of those accidents which are only outdone in horror by the methods he used to treat his wounds. On this occasion——following close, by the way, on a warm panegyric of the advantages of going barefoot in the Guiana forests——he was pursuing a woodpecker, when, forgetful of all else but the bird, he "trod upon a little hardwood stump." This sharp projection "entered the hollow part of my foot, making a deep and lacerated wound" which "brought me to the ground," where he lay "until a transitory fit of sickness went off." After allowing the wound to bleed freely and probing it ruthlessly, the Squire treated his foot to alternate "steepings" in cold water and hot and nauseous poultices made of boiled cow's dung. "Had there been no cows, I could have made out with boiled grass and leaves." Three weeks later he "sallied forth sound and joyful," chanting to himself his "favourite Horace."

I, pedes quo te rapiunt et aurae
Dum favet sol, et locus, i secundo
Omine, et conto latebras, ut olim,
Rumpe ferarum.[1]

All this, as was natural, was but a Watertonian prelude to the real business of this expedition, those Battles of the Snakes and Cayman which he has described so vividly in English (there is said to be extant a version of the Cayman battle in Latin hexameters) and which caused the Squire so much vexation in later years when his narrative was doubted by stay-at-homes. But before entering on this epic, something must be said of the characters engaged.

First, then, for Daddy Quashi. He was "a faithful, honest negro," belonging to Mr Edmonstone, and "had been an able fellow in his younger days" when he accompanied his master on his numerous expeditions into "the wilds" in pursuit of bands of runaway slaves. His "gallantry" as a young man was recorded by "a large scar over his eyebrow caused by the stroke from a cutlass of another negro while the Daddy was engaged in an intrigue." Mr Edmonstone had sent out orders that Daddy Quashi was to wait upon the Squire, whom he had often entertained with stories of his master's "frays" with "snakes, wild beasts and runaway negroes." But whatever the Daddy's gallantry and ardour for "frays" may have been in the past, his bravery was now purely gastronomic—"he had a brave stomach for heterogeneous food . . . caymen, monkeys, hawks and grubs." His horror of snakes was "beyond description." "I could never get him to face a snake." The Daddy was, in fact, a hopeless coward—a negro Sancho Panza to our Yorkshire Quixote—and, on purely Watertonian grounds, this worse than useless ally was obviously the one person indicated to stand beside him in these perilous encounters.

The other characters in the drama are the Snakes and the Cayman. Little need be said of the Cayman or on the question whether it was an alligator or a crocodile or merely a cayman, as Waterton always asserted. The American species of Crocodilia are said by modern zoologists to be "particularly inoffensive," and there are no records of their having made actual attacks upon man—the veracious Don Felipe to the contrary, he having told Waterton a sensational story of a cayman attacking a man on dry land, carrying him off and (presumably) devouring him, as he appeared no more among his neighbours.

[1] See *Odes,* Book III, xi, 49–52. Considerably altered by pious expurgation.

Those who may be tempted to refer to the *Wanderings* should be warned that though the Squire was certainly justified in his boast that he "had been in the midst of snakes for many years," his prejudice against Latin names and his adoption of vague native names (some now forgotten) make difficult the identification of his victims. Here is a brief tabulation of Waterton's snakes:

Camoudi: The Anaconda, *Eunectes marinus,* the largest American constrictor. Waterton claims they grow to "thirty to forty feet." The largest specimen known to modern science did not exceed twenty-five.

Coulacanara: Another constrictor, possibly the Boa, *Constrictor constrictor.* This snake in South America seldom exceeds twelve feet.

Rattlesnake: The tropical rattlesnake, *Crotalus terrificus,* which in South America grows to seven feet and is more venomous than any other rattlesnake.

Counacouchi: The Bushmaster, *Lachesis muta.* Grows to twelve feet, and is dangerously poisonous.

Labarri: This must be the fer-de-lance, probably *Bothrops atrox,* which grows to a length of eight feet, and is extremely venomous. There are thirty-six recorded species of *Bothrops.*

A glance at that list will show that while Waterton may have overestimated the length and ferocity of the cayman, the snakes he chose to encounter were most formidable customers. They are among the most dangerous in the world, yet the Squire not only "went for" them with complete intrepidity whenever he wanted to capture a live specimen for the Walton Hall museum, but had convinced himself that if "you have self-command" and "never approach a snake abruptly," they will not attack you. He himself, he says, had often softly gone within two yards of a fer-de-lance (labarri), and "sometimes" placed a stick ten feet long on its back. "He would then glide away . . . but when I put the end of the stick abruptly to his head, he immediately opened his mouth, flew at it, and bit it." All this to prove to himself that the most venomous snakes are not vicious if approached gently and fearlessly. But there must have been some special quality in the Squire which enabled him to make friends with these dangerous reptiles. Late in life he demonstrated to the Rev J. G. Wood just how to handle rattlesnakes:

"He said that after that lesson I should be as able to carry living rattlesnakes as he was. Perhaps so, but I should feel rather nervous about trying it."

In Guiana Waterton performed on a fer-de-lance a dangerous operation which, it is true, is a daily occurrence on modern serum-manufacturing snake-farms, but at that time was unheard of. He held a live fer-de-lance (he doesn't say how he captured it) close up to the head, and pressed "a small piece of stick" against the fang, which produced a jet of the deadly poison, "a liquor thick and yellow, like strong camomile tea." On another occasion he made a live fer-de-lance bite itself, thought it was going to die as "it appeared dull and heavy," but found that "in half an hour" it "was as vigorous and brisk as ever." "This subject" (i.e. the snake's immunity to its own poison) the Squire modestly thought "not unworthy of the consideration of the naturalist."

He does not tell us in detail how he captured alive these venomous serpents of Guiana. With a noble simplicity he only says: "I caught a fine labarri." Apparently he would cautiously approach a bushmaster or fer-de-lance, softly slide a caressing hand along its back, firmly clasp it by the neck—and there you are. For the constrictors (who would of course have replied to a firm hand on the neck by instantly throwing coils round the Squire's neck) he adopted a different procedure. Barefooted, dressed in "Russia sheeting trousers" and a check shirt, but apparently with a hat and a "lance" made of "an old bayonet on the end of a long stick," he made light of boas and perhaps even of anacondas.

Thus was he clad on that memorable (but unspecified) day in 1820 when he arrived at Hobbabba Creek, and found himself in the company of Archibald Edmonstone and Mr President Rough. Just as the Squire was apologising for his peculiar "habiliments," an excited negro rushed up to say that "a large snake had just seized a tame Muscovy duck." Snatching up his lance, the Squire rushed in pursuit, only to find that the snake had taken refuge in the shallow water where "a number of trees had been felled in the swamp." Moving from bole to bole and branch to branch, the Squire cautiously followed or "headed" the snake "as he rose and sank." At last, on what he thought "a favourable opportunity," he "made a thrust . . . with the lance." But—who could have imagined this?—the thrust was made "in a bungling manner," and only gave the snake "a slight wound":

". . . he instantly sprung at my left buttock, seized the Russia sheeting trousers with his teeth, and coiled his tail round my right arm. All this was the work of a moment. Thus accoutred, I made my way out of the swamp, while the serpent kept his hold on my arm and trousers with the tenacity of a bulldog."

This snake must have been a young boa, like the "coulacanara" the Squire dealt with in an even less orthodox manner. Seeing this ten-foot snake "slowly moving onwards," he became desirous of capturing it. Instantly therefore he covered his right hand with his felt hat and "laid hold of his tail with the left." When the snake naturally came at him in hissing fury, "as if to ask what business I had to take liberties with his tail," the intrepid wanderer waited until its head was within two feet of his own, and then knocked it out with a Yorkshire punch on the jaw—the only pugilistic encounter with a snake ever recorded. The knock-out was only partial, for the snake was allowed "to coil himself round my body," and thus the Squire "marched off with him" as "my lawful prize." "He pressed me hard, but not alarmingly so." At that moment up came Daddy Quashi, who during the combat had wisely been looking for his umbrella. As soon as he saw "what company" his master was in, Daddy Quashi took to his heels, and ran off home. This was a good opportunity for one of those laughable little jokes, so the Squire instantly "ran after him, shouting to increase his fear."

The third of these encounters was also with a "coulacanara," which, as it turned out to measure fourteen feet, was either a remarkably large boa or a partly grown anaconda. The story begins in that breathless hour of the tropics, just after noon, and the Squire, barefoot, with his spare form clad only in shirt and trousers, his cropped sun-bleached hair, tanned face and hands, was sitting on the steps of the ruined mansion "with a little Horace in his hand." Suddenly another "daddy" negro (not Quashi, who was in Georgetown) came to announce that a bushmaster snake had been discovered.

Picking up his hat and lance, and accompanied by a little dog and two negroes with cutlasses as a bodyguard, the Squire set off, and discovered it was not a "counacouchi" but a "coulacanara." "A thought" struck him. Why not take the snake alive? On communicating this excellent idea to the bodyguard, the Squire was annoyed to find that instead of welcoming the "fray," "they begged and entreated" to be allowed to go for a gun. He made short work of this pusillanimity. "Taking a cutlass" and "ranging both the sable slaves behind," he "told them to follow" and that "if they offered to fly" he "would cut them down" with the cutlass. Upon this they "looked very uneasy," and seemed to feel it "an intolerable act of tyranny" when the Squire insisted on taking away their cutlasses (in case they foolishly damaged this valuable snake) and ordered them once more to follow as he advanced on the victim with the bayonet on a stick he called a lance. It was a splendid combat.

"On pinning him to the ground with the lance he gave a tremendous loud hiss. . . . We had a sharp fray in the den, the rotten sticks flying on all sides, and each party struggling for superiority."

Waterton now found his weight was not sufficient to hold down this writhing monster, and therefore "called to the second negro to throw himself upon" him. At this the snake struck his colours, and while one negro held the lance, and the other helped with the tail, the Squire took off his braces and tied up the snake's mouth. Resenting this familiarity, the boa resumed the struggle, but was cunningly induced to wrap himself round the lance, instead of round the men. In this way the three men carried him slowly home, but the creature was so heavy they had to rest ten times, particularly since the obstinate snake "fought hard" for freedom though "all in vain."

Since there was not time to kill, skin and preserve the creature before dark, and his corpse might begin to go bad during the damp tropical night, they induced him to enter a large bag and "left him to his fate till morning." "I cannot say he allowed me to have a quiet night," the Squire records, though without animosity. "He was very restless and fretful; and had Medusa been my wife, there could not have been more continued and disagreeable hissing in the bedchamber that night." Next morning, with the aid of ten negroes, Waterton got the boa safely out of the bag, and then cut its throat. "He bled like an ox." So large was the snake that when skinned his open jaws easily were large enough to admit a man's head. Need it be said that no sooner had this pleasing thought occurred to him than the Squire instantly put it into practice, reflecting that "the singular formation of the jaws admits of wonderful extension."

One more toil remained for this Hercules of taxidermy, and that of course was the encounter with the cayman—a contest which marks the highest point of his career as a scientific field naturalist. To obtain a specimen of this reptile, unmarred by shot wounds, the Squire once more plunged into the "wilds" and made his way to the River Essequibo. (It was perhaps on this very journey that he stopped at Hobbabba Creek and had his encounter with the snake that stole the Muscovy duck and bit the Squire in the left buttock.) But the baited shark-hook with which he tried to catch his prey proved a failure, and the Squire began to suspect the "coloured man" who had volunteered as a cayman-catcher. The coloured man, although so totally unable to live up to his promises, also began for some reason to "give himself airs." He was therefore instantly dismissed, for "airs" were something (the Squire confides) "I never admit on any expedition where I am commander"—which might almost have been said by the Duke of Wellington.

Having got rid of this impostor, the Waterton expedition then made a long journey to get in touch with some Indians, who were supposed to have the genuine secret of cayman-catching. They fed the wanderer on "boiled ant-bear and red monkey," two dishes, which, the Squire rightly surmised, were unknown "even at Beau-villiers in Paris and at a London city feast." The ant-bear, he adds, "stunk as our venison does in England," but the red monkey "was very good."

The Squire then unfolded his purpose, and persuaded these friendly gastronomes to help him in his last and greatest labour. When showed the shark-hook, the Indian cayman-catcher "shook his head and laughed at it, and said it would not do." He promised that next day he would "make something that would answer." And, as the Squire lay awake that night, he fell into a train of Rousseauesque meditation on civilisation and the natural man. Here, he said to himself, we arrive with everything in the way of tackle, "hooks, lines, baits and patience." "We spend nights watching," but each night the cayman has taken the natural bait and refused the civilised hook. Now we find "this poor wild man of the woods" who will "probably succeed by means of a very simple process," and thus prove "to his civilised brother" the extraordinary proposition that "there is a vast deal of knowledge to be picked up at every step."

Luckily for the reputation of the "poor wild" brother, he succeeded with a hook made of "four pieces of tough hardwood a foot long, and about as thick as your little finger, and barbed at both ends; they were tied round the end of the rope in such a manner that if you conceive the rope to be an arrow, these four sticks would form the arrow's head; so that one end of the four united sticks answered to the point of the arrow head, while the other end of the sticks expanded at equal distances round the rope." Next day they found "a cayman ten feet and a half long fast to the end of the rope." So far, so good; but now "the poor wild man" and his friends refused to pull a live cayman on land, and Daddy Quashi of course wanted to shoot it. "I immediately offered to knock him down for his cowardice, and he shrunk back, begging that I would be cautious"—an obviously impossible thing for Waterton to be, as Daddy Quashi should have discovered long before. "Darting a disdainful eye" on these unsporting but unmoved Indians, and "chasing Daddy Quashi on the sandbank for a quarter of a mile," the Squire returned to the hooked cayman and reflected:

"Hoc res summa loco. Scinditur in contraria vulgus."

What was to be done?

After "revolving a dozen projects" as he walked feverishly up and down, the Squire at last discovered the right Watertonian solution. He picked up the eight-foot mast from the canoe and wrapped the sail round it. He would kneel with this in his hands as a weapon, like a soldier with a fixed bayonet, and thrust it down the cayman's gullet, if, as seemed only too probable, the experience of being suspended for hours on the poor wild man's hook had made it so crusty that "it would come open-mouthed at me." The Squire expounded his strategy to the Indians, and, when they discovered that he intended to place himself between them and the great reptile, they instantly brightened up and agreed to haul it in, confident that if it showed fight they could escape while the Squire fought for his life.

Into action they went (as depicted in Captain Jones's picture) "four South American savages, two negroes from Africa, a creole from Trinidad, and a white man from Yorkshire." When they began hauling the rope, Waterton's thoughts wandered, as any man's would in such a situation, "to Cerberus and the other side of the Styx ferry"; but as the "monstrum horrendum, informe" reached the bank, the Squire instantly perceived—though how you read the expression of emotions on a crocodile's face is hard to say—that "the cayman was in a state of fear and perturbation," rather like de Quincey's German baker when the English amateur floored him in the twenty-third round after announcing the probable value at an annuity office of the fellow's throat. Flinging away the mast:

"I sprung up and jumped on his back, turning half round as I vaulted, so that I gained my seat with my face in the right position. I immediately seized the fore-legs, and by main force twisted them on his back; thus they served me for a bridle."

What next?

Well, the poor wild man and Daddy Quashi and the rest of them set up such a tremendous yelling of triumph that they did not hear the Squire shouting to them to drag the cayman away from the water; for, if the rope had broken, and the now furiously lashing cayman had taken the Squire for a dip in the river, "that would have been more perilous than Arion's morning ride." At last they heard him and dragged the strange steed and his rider forty yards inland. Now came struggles to tie up the creature's jaws and fore-feet and to carry the indignant cayman back to camp. Arrived there at last, "I cut his throat; and after breakfast was over commenced the dissection."

It would seem impossible to make any comment on a contest so stirring but, as ever, the Squire comes up with the true Watertonian line of thought:

"Should it be asked how I managed to keep my seat, I would answer, I hunted some years with Lord Darlington's fox-hounds."

As for the reason which impelled the Squire to this bizarre and useless feat, anybody's guess is valid. In spite of what the Squire said to Dr Hobson many years after, I do not believe he set out to catch a live cayman with the express purpose of riding it. That was clearly a Watertonian afterthought, a flash of non-eccentric genius. It may have had a purpose. It may have been intended, for instance, to restore the prestige of the white man in the eyes of the poor wild brother, who had perhaps been giving himself airs over the failure to catch a cayman on a shark-hook. But it was more probably just exuberance, an ebullience of hard-headed Yorkshire common sense. What is difficult to understand is how the Squire managed to sit that squirming, low, knubbly seat without breaking an ankle or a patella. His vivid account of the episode was to cause him much vexation from the doubts and sneers of closet naturalists who had never seen a live cayman, never ridden to hounds with Lord Darlington, and had never entered the Squire's strange world of whimsy and prejudice put boldly into action.

The rest of this wandering is an anticlimax; with nothing more remarkable than a descent of the rapids during which the canoe half filled with water and nearly carried the Squire and his companions to "the other side of Styx"; and another adventure at sea when they were stranded on a mud-flat, and the Squire was so scorched by the sun that "I could get no sleep during the night, and the next morning my lips were all in blisters." Which only goes to show the advantages of not wearing a hat in the tropics.

VIII

THE Squire made the passage home "in fine trim and good spirits." This wandering had been even more fertile in good results than the first, since he brought back with him as trophies "some rare insects, two hundred and thirty birds, two land-tortoises, five armadillos, two large serpents, a sloth, an ant-bear, and a cayman" packed in ten large boxes, together with "several eggs of curious birds" carefully coated with gum arabic and packed in charcoal "according to a receipt I had seen from the *Edinburgh Philosophical Journal*."[1] The Squire hoped to rear and acclimatise these birds in Yorkshire. His good spirits predisposed him to philanthropy, and he resolved to confer upon humanity, gratis, the immense boon of his discoveries in taxidermy. Three lectures or treatises were to acquaint a grateful world with these invaluable secrets: one on insects and serpents, one on birds ("the feathered tribe") and one on quadrupeds.

This good humour communicated itself to the officers of the West Indiaman *Dee*, on which Waterton made the voyage. "Great was the attention" he received from Captain Grey and "his mate, Mr Spence." It is said (though I do not know on what evidence) that the Squire had already crossed the Atlantic on this ship. In any case by this time he was well known among West Indians as a character. Whether he entertained the "honest tars" by walking about the deck on his hands and similar athletic feats such as he performed in his old age to entertain the Stonyhurst Fathers and their pupils is not stated; though, if the captain had given him leave to climb the rigging, his agility in barefoot climbing would no doubt have beaten most of them. Certain it is that the boxes of specimens were "opened almost every day" during the voyage, for the pleasure and astonishment of the "honest tars." But alas, all these benevolent plans for improving humanity with achievements in

[1] Yet how ineffective the Squire was even as a collector may be judged from the fact that he discovered but one humming-bird unknown to science. W. H. Bates, some forty years later, sent back from Brazil 8,000 species new to science. True, most of these were insects, but the new species included mammals, birds, fish, reptiles and batrachians.

taxidermy and the good fellowship of the voyage were destined to
be soured by the "illiberality" of a Whitehall official.

The *Dee* reached Liverpool early in the spring of 1821 (Norman
Moore's "1825" is obviously a misprint), and a Customs officer
came on board, "a very civil" person who was already acquainted
with the Squire and the strange cargoes he brought with him. They
were looking through some of the boxes when there entered the
cabin "an entire stranger" who "seemed wonderfully aware of his
own consequence." With true Whitehall courtesy he "thrust his
head over" the Squire's shoulder "without preface or apology," and
said they had no business to open the boxes without his permission.
Many of less perception than the wanderer would have augured ill
from this bullying rudeness, though perhaps few would have said
to themselves, as the Squire did, "I shall see that man again at
Philippi."

He did. The boxes were taken on shore, and examined by the
Customs officers on duty in the presence of "several gentlemen who
wished to see the collection" and who, after seeing it, "expressed
themselves highly gratified." A reasonable duty was paid, the
boxes closed and on the point of being removed when the man at
Philippi "stepped in" and "abruptly" announced that he would
detain the whole collection on the ground that he was "dissatisfied
with the valuation." He then took the Squire aside and made the
improbable assertion that he "had a great regard for the arts and
sciences" and "lamented" that what he referred to as his "conscience" obliged him to detain the collection. For once, as the
Squire himself says, the Watertonian face bore "no marks of
credulity." But there was nothing to do except to leave the keys
and make his way to Yorkshire, in a considerable fret and fume,
particularly in view of the fact that the eggs of "curious birds"
would perish under this treatment.

A correspondence with the Treasury—conducted, let us hope,
on the Squire's side with acrimony—the intervention of "titled
personages in London" and the "private and public representations
of the first Customs officer at Liverpool" resulted in the decision
of one, T. R. Lushington, writing on behalf of "The Lords Commissioners of His Majesty's Treasury" that any specimens Mr
Waterton gave to public institutions might enter duty free, but
those he meant to keep "can only be delivered on payment of the
ad valorem duty of 20 per cent."

Now, in the course of hard riding on his hobby-horse of natural

history and taxidermy, the Squire had come to regard these gratifi-
cations of his own tastes as public benefactions. His "chills and
fevers," hardships and battles with snakes and a cayman, his tree-
climbing and going barefoot and "pulling poisonous snakes out of
their lurking-places"—though all undertaken voluntarily and without the slightest hint either from His Majesty or from anyone in a
genteel and confidential position, had come in the Squire's mind to
rank as so many services to his country. And the only official
acknowledgment was that, to adapt Canning's phrase, they
"clapped on a duty of twenty per cent."

The Squire was furious. It was not the money so much as the
insult, the philistine relegating of a man of science to the level of a
shopkeeping importer. But that, after all, was to be expected from
"Lords Commissioners" who, in those days, might easily have been
put in their places by higher authority. But now was seen the error
of rejecting Lord Bathurst's civil advances, above all the incivility
of so much railing against "Hanoverians," whether rats or bipeds.
Had the twenty-seventh lord of Walton Hall been sufficient of a
courtier to recommend himself to the attention of the Prince Regent,
with what princely magnanimity, with what charm and urbanity
of manner would he have waived all claim to anything so vulgar as
a money payment on Mr Waterton's "transcendent" collections!

The Squire's method of revenge is a good example of an angry
man cutting off his nose to spite somebody else's face. He had been
burning to communicate to the tiny public of naturalists his discoveries in taxidermy which, if reasonably and modestly promul-
gated by him in 1821, would have brought him something of the
"genteel and confidential" reputation he yearned for. But no; to
punish Mr Lushington and My Lords Commissioners, the Squire
withheld publication of his methods of preserving skins—a punishment of which they naturally were not aware and for which, if they
had known of it, they would have cared rather less than nothing.

Fuming and sulking, the Squire retired in dudgeon to Walton
Hall, and if we take literally his own words that for three years he
"seldom or never mounted my hobby-horse," he must for that
period have given up taxidermy as well as the desire "to rove" once
more in the tropics. But this tiff with the Treasury, and subsequent
pique, may have been just what was needed to spur on the Squire to
undertake what—after his own character and adventures—is his
greatest claim to the regard of posterity. He decided to turn the
two hundred and fifty-nine acres of Walton Hall's park and lake

into a bird sanctuary by enclosing them in a wall, sufficiently high to keep out foxes and badgers and to intimidate both the poachers of Wakefield and the bargees from the canal which ran along one side of the estate.

Before this, menageries and "volaries" had been formed and certain types of game preserved, but nobody had yet thought of giving protection to the native wild creatures—particularly the birds—of a district, without any wish to destroy them for sport or food or to own them as personal property. The numerous wild life protection societies now functioning under the name of Audubon should, if strict justice were done, be called Waterton Societies. The fight he undertook was a seemingly hopeless one; the prejudices he undertook to combat and remove almost as violent in their way as his own political and religious views. There were no Wild Birds Protection Acts, and, as the caricaturists and journalists of the period show, nothing was so common as "cockney sportsmen" coming out of London and other towns to slaughter indiscriminately any wild birds they could find on the still unenclosed commons. Waterton himself has described in his *Essays* the barbarous and useless slaughter of the sea birds on Flamborough Head:

"Parties of sportsmen," he writes in 1834, "from all parts of the kingdom, visit Flamborough and its vicinity during the summer months, and spread sad devastation all around them. No profit attends the carnage; the poor unfortunate birds serve merely as marks to aim at, and they are generally left where they fall. Did these heartless gunmen reflect, but for one moment, how many innocent birds their shot destroys; how many fall disabled on the wave, there to linger for hours, perhaps for days, in torture and in anguish; did they but consider how many helpless young ones will never see again their parents coming to the rock with their food . . ." the Squire thought they wouldn't shoot, which perhaps only goes to show that he knew more about birds than about sportsmen.

The squires and farmers round Walton Hall would not have cared tuppence about the Flamborough Head gulls—Waterton could preserve them all he wished—and for reasons of their own they detested the "cockney sportsmen" as much as he did. But by turning Walton Hall into a bird sanctuary he was fostering and multiplying birds which the squires thought destroyed precious game, and which the farmers thought damaged their crops and robbed their poultry yards and ravaged their fruit trees. Whether by his practical demonstrations and quaintly laboured *Essays* he ever succeeded in convincing them that they were wrong does not appear and seems unlikely. But it speaks most eloquently for his local popularity that they put up with what must have seemed an eccentric public nuisance without complaint and without retaliation. "I turn loose upon the public, from my park, about threescore carrion crows per annum," he was able to boast in 1837. And they were far from being the only "feathered vermin" he annually fostered.

On making a survey of his land, the Squire discovered that his fortifications would run to a length of three miles—longer than those of many a mediæval and small Roman town—and decided that the minimum height must be eight feet, rising to sixteen opposite the Barnsley Canal, from which formidable irruptions of the bargee barbarians were to be feared. The final cost is variously estimated at from nine to ten thousand pounds, and the circuit was not completed until 1826. Making allowances for the Squire's absence in the United States and Guiana during parts of 1824-5, this gives a period of more than four years for the work. Why did it take so long?

Well, this Watertonian project of walling in the park had to be carried out in a Watertonian way in the matter of finance. Supposing some other country gentleman of substantial though not large means had conceived a project so beyond the limited imagination of such persons, he could have raised the whole money—and thereby concluded his wall in a much shorter time—by means of a bank loan against securities or a mortgage on his land, to be paid off by subsequent economies. But that was not at all the way the Squire did business. As we have already noticed, he was a very poor agriculturist, and quite incapable of adding to his income as a landed gentleman by the improvement of his land. The only way for him to have money, then, was to live with great frugality and regularity.

Fortunately, Dr Hobson discussed the whole transaction many years later with the Squire and, with the Squire's full concurrence, has left us an account of how the wall was built and paid for. Mr Waterton (we learn) was not only "anxiously punctual" in all monetary payments, but had "the greatest horror of being in debt." This put bank loans and mortgages out of the question. Moreover —and this was an additional complication—he had a most understandable mistrust of paper money, whether Government sponsored or otherwise, and a rational preference for what he called "solid tin." Now the Squire had "a favourite deal drawer," in which he kept his "solid tin," and so began to hoard golden guineas in it, keeping "an argus-eyed guard" over the said drawer as the lock "having been manufactured in an age of greater honesty and less roguery" was of "ancient and simple construction."

When "by a laudable and thrifty economy" (not descending, the Squire was certain, "to the cheese-parings system" which he "ever did and ever shall abominate") he had managed to accumulate five hundred gold sovereigns, he "engaged masons" to build the wall. But, before starting, he called them together and made an arrangement with them. He engaged to pay them in gold and not in "flimsy paper" ("which a drunken mason might accidentally use to light his pipe"); but when the store of gold in the drawer was temporarily used up, they must agree to summary dismissal ("even on a Friday") until the "laudable and thrifty" economist had hoarded another five hundred gold pounds. The masons agreed to the bargain; and both sides honourably stuck to it. As long as the gold lasted, payment was regularly and promptly made. When it gave out, the work was instantly suspended until another five hundred was saved. This inevitably meant delays and must have been vexatious to the masons, but it avoided (for the Squire) the "horror of being in debt."

During one of these suspensions of labour (so the Squire informed Dr Hobson) "a professing friend . . . officiously and impertinently censured" the Squire's conduct, adding "remarks unworthy of a gentleman," indeed "of much too coarse a nature to be gratifying or even palatable." The Squire was always enraged by this sort of thing, so immediately asked if he had performed his part of the contract.

"Abstractedly, you have," the professing friend grudgingly admitted.

"Sir," retorted the Squire, who had not read his Boswell without results, "when my father disapproved of anything I was saying in the presence of a third party, he would very audibly whisper, '*tace* is the Latin for a candle,' which was tantamount to saying, hold your tongue and don't make such a fool of yourself. This, sir, is the observation I should have thought it my duty to have made to you, if a third party had been present, which is unfortunately not the case."

While admitting "the extreme severity of the rebuke," Dr Hobson felt that "an overwhelming majority" of his "just, equitable and high-principled readers" would be "induced to concede" its "necessary propriety," for, as the Squire himself pointed out, "it required a giant's blow or something tantamount to steam power to level this gentleman with the ordinary usages of society."

The Squire, as must be abundantly clear by now, was not one to put up tamely with an affront; and in due course we shall see how ingeniously—but, alas, ineffectively and with damage to himself—he strove to avenge himself upon Mr Lushington of the Treasury. Nor did he ever shrink from a contest with man or beast. It was while the wall was building (in 1823, to be precise) that the Squire had an encounter which sounds tame enough after battles with anacondas and with the cayman, but which had its annoyances. He was crossing a common when he was attacked by two dogs, one "an insignificant female cur," the other "a stout, ill-looking uncouth brute . . . half bull, half terrier." These bull-terriers can be dangerous brutes—quite recently the American newspapers reported that a woman had been killed by them in Florida and a baby in Los Angeles, which perhaps explains why the dog is always referred to as "the friend of man."

This particular friend of man came at the Squire, who had just time to take off his hat and use it as a shield, while he gave the brute "a hearty kick under the breast." Meanwhile, "the female cur" attacked from behind and was kept off by back kicks, while the Squire with his hat and forward kicks kept off the repeated attacks of the male. A lucky kick in the muzzle sent the bitch off howling, followed instantly by the dog, just as two masons were coming up to assist the Squire. As he remarks, the encounter was not worth relating except that it goes to show "the advantage of resisting the attack of a dog to the utmost."

There was another quadruped with which the Squire waged unceasing war and refused utterly the protection of his wild life sanctuary. "This was no other than a little grey-coloured short-legged animal. . . . Known to naturalists as"—of course—"the Hanoverian rat." The Squire's father (he tells us) was "always positive" that the rat had come over to England "in the same ship which conveyed the new dynasty to our shores," which was proof positive. So great was its rapacity and prodigious its increase that, if we may believe these two "naturalists of the first order," father and son, the Hanoverian rat had nearly exterminated "the original rat of Great Britain," so that even the Squire never saw but "one single solitary specimen" which he apostrophised thus:

"Poor injured Briton! hard, indeed, has been the fate of thy

family! In another generation at farthest it will probably sink down
to the dust for ever!"

However this may be, there can be no doubt that Walton Hall
was long afflicted by the "baleful presence" of multitudes of these
"insatiate and mischievous little brutes." When the Squire returned
from Guiana in 1813, he found these rats had "gnawed through
thirty-two doors, and many of the oaken window-frames were irre-
parably injured." This state of affairs (as we have seen) had been
met by the typically Watertonian solution of loosing on the enemy
a tamed South American tiger-cat. But by the 1820s either this
interesting animal had died or it had ceased to function efficiently;
and the cats, dogs and owls on or about the premises were not up
to the job. As the Squire sat at night in his favourite sitting-room,
he "many a time wished the ship at Jericho, which first brought
their ancestors to these shores," for the rats had "formed a run
behind the plinth" and "their clatter was unceasing." Meanwhile,
study of the habits and phobias of the beasts suggested a most
curious form of attack, which is vouched for by the Squire as well
as by Dr Hobson.

Having caught "a fine old rat" in a box trap, the Squire waited
until "all the household had retired to rest for the night," then
"dipped its hinder parts in tar" and set it free in one of the runs.
This rat ("tarred but not feathered," as Dr Hobson originally and
facetiously remarks) is said to have scoured up and down "every
underground burrow," so that the other rats smelling "an odour of
all others the most offensive to the rat . . . thought it most prudent
to take themselves off." But the remedy was only temporary, for,
while mentioning "this laughable circumstance" to Dr Hobson, the
Squire added that he had repeatedly "scared away" rats by leaving
in their runs a "mixture of tar and finely chopped garlick."

To Dr Hobson, and to Dr Hobson alone, the world is indebted
for the only extant account of a passage in Mr Waterton's adventurous and original career, which must have occurred in the early
1820s. Dr Hobson, writing about 1865, dates this piece of "experimental ingenuity" at "more than forty years ago"—which fixes
it within a few years. Whether it was the result of identifying himself with "the feathered tribe" he so much delighted in watching or
from some more Watertonian cause we are not told; but the fact is
that, as Dr Hobson apologetically puts it, the Squire "conceived
some crude and ill-digested idea that the act of flying was within
his grasp."

Admirable as Dr Hobson was, the admission must be made that he did not always recollect all the important circumstances connected with what he was telling and, for all his amazing verbosity, was not always successful in making perfectly clear what he did recollect. Mr Waterton, he tells us, "invented and manufactured duplicates of a peculiar character of mechanism." They were "substitutes for wings," and were "fixed on each arm . . . and united by their then surrounding the thoracic and dorsal portions of the trunk." This is unhappily vague. The Squire's legs, as we shall have occasion to note again, were remarkably developed owing to the enormous exercise they got through wanderings and saunterings, barefoot and otherwise, and climbings of innumerable trees. Unluckily he did not tell Dr Hobson how they were to be dealt with for flying purposes, except to complain that "a man's legs, however symmetrically formed, were inconveniently long and heavy for an atmospheric trip." The only time in his life when he found his legs in the way was, he added, "when he attempted to fly."

Something in addition to wings was invented, but vexatiously enough, Dr Hobson speaks only of "the remaining mechanism he conceived necessary to be attached to the other parts of the body." Equipped with his wings and other "mechanism" (whatever it may have been), the Squire with his invariable intrepidity mounted to the roof of a lofty outhouse at "an elevation of several yards," from which he proposed to launch himself into the air and to fly. "Several yards" suggests anything from fifteen to thirty feet—an awkward height to tumble. But at the last moment "an intimate friend accidentally walked into the farm-yard." Who was he? Dr Hobson, who loved a Latin tag as much as the Squire, simply says rather enigmatically that he was one "alicui toto pectore deditus." Whoever he was, he must have had extraordinary influence over the Squire, for he actually persuaded him to choose a lower perch, so that when he did attempt to fly and "woefully" came "in contact with mother earth," no great damage was done beyond what in Walton dialect was called "a foul shak." The experience was not wholly wasted, for even out of defeat and bruised bones the Squire could gather wisdom:

"Since that egregious and unpardonable blunder of mine," he confided to Dr Hobson, "I have realised the rebuke given by Apelles, 'Let not the cobbler go beyond his last—Ne Sutor ultra crepidam.'"

With the failure of the attempt to "Navigate the Atmosphere," discouragement from "mounting the hobby-horse," and the merely intermittent growth of the great wall, time must have hung heavy on the Squire's hands. War with the rats may have been some consolation, but when they had fled—temporarily—from the horrors of tar and garlic, there was little in the way of "knowledge and exercise" to occupy his energy. Yet though he asserts that the autumn departure of the bird migrants "scarcely caused me to turn my face to the south," he was not yet ready to settle down into a life of Walton Hall pottering. His pique with the "illiberality" of the Treasury, which for a time put a stop to the growth of his museum, could not last for ever. Nor had he by any means abandoned ornithology, as the building of the wall proves.

Discovery of a famous book on birds sent him off on his travels again. This was Alexander Wilson's *American Ornithology,* the first volume of which appeared in 1808. Six more volumes had appeared when Wilson died in 1813, and the eighth and ninth were issued posthumously by Wilson's Philadelphian friend and biographer, George Ord, who was to become a life-long friend and correspondent of the Squire and to inoculate him with his own dislike for Audubon, the rival of Wilson. It may seem odd that so enthusiastic a lover of birds as Waterton should have remained in ignorance of so important a pioneer book until ten years after the author's death—but we have to remember how greatly international exchange of knowledge and culture was interrupted by the wars with France and the United States. At all events, once the Squire had his enthusiasm roused by *American Ornithology,* he instantly decided that he must go to the United States. As he puts it, "the almost expiring flame" of ornithology in him was "fanned up" by Wilson's "animated description of the birds."

A priori, one would suppose that few persons were less likely to enjoy America than the Squire. He was proud of his old family, in politics a most uncompromising Tory, and in religion more Catholic than the Pope; whereas the people he was about to visit were, or professed to be, egalitarian democrats, republican Whigs and dissenters. But, then, extremes sometimes meet, and both could at any rate join in detestation of the moderate episcopal and aristocratic government and society of England. Moreover, Waterton went with a very different point of view from the arrogant, self-satisfied, provincial attitude unfortunately too common among the English of that time. He did not arrive in New York with the tacit assumption that he was conferring an immense benefit upon the New World by bringing it the refined civilisation of his person. On the contrary, he gave himself the salutary warning that "a man generally travels into foreign countries for his own ends," and therefore "it rather becomes him to court than expect to be courted," and "with this in view he will always render himself pleasant to the natives." With such an attitude he was not likely to be repelled by people so naturally friendly as the Americans.

With his hazy chronology and flighty habit of hopping inconsequently from subject to subject and back again, the Squire has made it difficult to reconstruct his North American trip accurately. How long, for instance, did he stay in New York before starting for the Erie Canal and Niagara? He does not say. Nor does he say when "the beautiful packet *John Wells*" left England or when it reached America. He does say the passage was "long and cold," and that he left New York for Buffalo and Niagara in July (1824). It seems reasonable to suppose, then, that although he delayed his description and impressions of New York until the end of his stay, he must have started his American experiences by at least a few weeks there.

In 1824 New York was still a small town compared with London and Paris, and did not extend much beyond the region now occupied by the Wall Street sky-scrapers; but the Squire had the wit to see that it was destined to become "the commercial capital of the New World." The houses on Broadway, he thought, had a "stately appearance," and he would stand there for hours on end "to observe the passing multitude." He was charmed by the fact that he saw "very few dogs, still fewer cats, and but a very small proportion of fat women." "The ladies of New York," and indeed of every place he visited in America, aroused his respectful enthusiasm. Under their influence and at the age of forty he suddenly discovered a critical admiration of the sex and a dogmatic assertiveness on the topic of women's dress which would be stupefying in a man less accustomed to go his own way and to know his own mind.

"Nothing," he says, "can surpass the appearance of the American ladies when they take their morning walk from twelve to three in Broadway." They rejected, it appears, all the "extravagant superfluities" of Paris fashions, keeping only what was "becoming to the female form." The Squire then launches out on an enthusiastic but critical description of how the American ladies wear "the Leghorn hat," and gives it as his opinion that their dexterity may be "fatal to the passing swain." He agrees with them whole-heartedly on their "abhorrence of caps," and asserts that "a rosebud or two, a woodbine, or a sprig of eglantine look well in the braided hair; and if there be raven locks, a lily or a snowdrop may be interwoven with effect!" Anticipating the future, he urges the "head milliners" of London to go to New York instead of to Paris.

What was the cause of this extraordinary metamorphosis? What suddenly changed into a critic of women's clothes and elegance this Yorkshire hermit whose main occupation was building a Chinese wall between himself and the world, this barefoot wanderer who even piqued himself on dressing like a tramp, this *censor morum* who at other times could not sufficiently despise "the caustic gossip of the tea-table" and "the dissipations of nocturnal gadding"?

The answer must be "the fair Albanese." But before recording the too scanty notices he has left of this fascinating and "highly polished female," we must be allowed to approach her by way of a Watertonian digression. When the Squire took his place on the steamboat which was to carry him up the Hudson from New York to Albany, he was ill-furnished with letters of introduction. He was one of those, he tells us, "who depend much upon an accidental acquaintance," on meeting someone whose "mild eye and sweet and placid features seem to beckon." Such a person the Squire picked out from among the "great number of well-dressed ladies and gentlemen" on the steamboat. Thus American "stranger gentleman" did the honours of the Palisades, and at Albany took the Squire to the best inn, and put him in the way of making other and agreeable acquaintances.

From Albany, the Squire made his way to Lake Erie, and then, finding it was "the season of roving and joy and merriment for the gentry of this happy country," he joined the "thousands" who were on their way to "the springs and lakes and the Falls of Niagara." Unfortunately, getting out of the stage-coach near Buffalo the Squire, in his unhandy way, stumbled on a rut, and sprained his foot severely. This was a sad interruption to a pleasant life of travel and sociability with well-dressed ladies and gentlemen. Instead of sending for a surgeon, the Squire determined, as usual, to be his own doctor. He recollected that a "very violently sprained ankle" had been treated many years before by holding it under the pump two or three times a day. He decided that the cure for his sprained foot would be to hold it under the falls of Niagara, which he fancifully asserts discharge "670,255 tons of water a minute."

This whim he actually carried out, "hobbling down the winding staircase" and holding his leg under the spray. Now this was the kind of thing which would please the American sense of humour, and a certain popularity would instantly attach itself to the crazy Britisher who treated a sprained ankle by holding it under Niagara Falls. For a day or two he would naturally be quite a character among the holiday visitors. Just at this juncture the Squire was invited to a dance, where he had to sit immobile with his leg up, and suffer the humiliation of being asked if he had gout—he who had never drunk port in his life! At this most unpropitious moment there entered a young American girl from Albany "with such a becoming air and grace that it was impossible not to be struck with her appearance."

Clearly the Squire was very much struck indeed, and the more he looked upon "the fair Albanese" the more he was convinced that "in the United States of America may be found grace and beauty and symmetry equal to anything in the Old World." He yearned to dance with this delightful and highly polished female, but there he was, nailed to his chair, and compelled to watch her dancing with others. This was intolerable; so that, both to clear himself of the imputation of gout and to recommend himself to the lady, he made the following entry in the hotel album:

"C. Waterton, of Walton Hall, in the county of York, England, arrived at the Falls of Niagara in July 1824, and begs leave to pen down the following dreadful accident:

> He sprained his foot, and hurt his toe,
> On the rough road near Buffalo.
> It quite distresses him to stagger a-
> Long the sharp rocks of famed Niagara.
> So thus he's doomed to drink the measure
> Of pain, in lieu of that of pleasure.
> On Hope's delusive pinions borne
> He came for wool, and goes back shorn."

Feeling, however, that his awkwardness in expressing his real meaning through the difficulties of rhyme and attempted metre had betrayed him into impoliteness, he added this:

> N.B.—Here he alludes to nothing but
> Th' adventure of his toe and foot;
> Save this—he sees all that which can
> Delight and charm the soul of man,
> But feels it not,—because his toe
> And foot together plague him so.

Dissatisfied with the inn album as a circulating medium for this composition, the Squire gratified the eager curiosity of the world by including it in the published editions of his *Wanderings*.

But what of the "fair Albanese"? She disappears from the narrative as abruptly as she enters it; for the Squire was too much of a gentleman to publish a line which might cause a lady's blush. We do not know if he ever saw her again, or if she joined him in travelling with that "family from the Bowling Green, in New York," who were so "highly accomplished" and whose "young ladies sang delightfully." Perhaps nothing more came of this radiant vision. Perhaps he offered—and she most unaccountably refused—to share with her the rat-infested museum and bird sanctuary at Walton. But it must have been her influence which made the American journey so delightful to the Squire and inspired him with so much enthusiasm for country and people. Did she appear also at Saratoga, whose visitors receive from the Squire this emphatic compliment?

"There is a pleasing frankness and ease and becoming dignity in the American ladies; and the good humour and absence of all haughtiness and puppyism in the gentlemen must, no doubt, impress the traveller with elevated notions of the company who visit this famous spa."

Not but that America could also make its contribution to the more serious side of life. When in the Squire's company we reach Philadelphia, it is at once possible to abandon the realm of conjecture into which we are forced by his reticences about the fair Albanese, and to re-enter the world of solid fact. Here the Squire made the acquaintance of Mr Charles Wilson Peale, one of those early American painters whose reputation was based on the fact that he had been permitted to paint a portrait of Washington, and who added to a precarious income by selling copies of his picture. The Peale Museum in Philadelphia contained specimens of his work as a painter and also the skeleton of a mammoth, which enchanted the Squire. "It is," he asserted vehemently, "the most magnificent skeleton in the world." Mr Peale had four gifted sons, whom he had named Rembrandt, Raphaelle, Titian and Rubens. Rembrandt and Raphaelle inherited their father's artistic gifts, but Titian and Rubens were on the side of the mammoth bones, though Titian is still favourably remembered for his drawings of animals.

This was a family after the Squire's own heart, and whenever he mentions them it is with respect and affection. He developed such an admiration and liking for Charles Peale that he—who could never afterwards be induced to sit for his portrait—docilely permitted Mr Peale to paint that picture of him, with a stuffed bird and a decapitated cat, which passed from the Peale Museum to the possession of Mr George Ord of Philadelphia, from him as a gift to Walton Hall, and is now in the National Portrait Gallery of London. It was through the Peales that Waterton met the then celebrated American naturalist, George Ord, who became a life-long friend and correspondent, and stayed at Walton Hall whenever he visited Europe. Their common admiration for the genius of Alexander Wilson was a bond between them. Another bond was their inability to appreciate J. J. Audubon, whose work as ornithologist and artist they united in disparaging.

The chronology of this tour has the usual Watertonian vagueness; and though the itinerary is more than usually clear, I am not certain whether he was twice or thrice in New York. After leaving Niagara, he says he went down from Ontario to Montreal and Quebec. He must have spent several days in Montreal, as he had time to become acquainted with the professors of the College; and several more days in Quebec, since he and his American friends saw "all that was worth seeing" there. They returned to Montreal "for a day or two" before going to Saratoga, visiting Ticonderoga and Lake George on the way. He speaks of a "stay" at Saratoga, and when he left, "bade farewell to the charming family" with whom he had passed "so many happy days." He still had to go back to Albany and New York and to visit Philadelphia—and his Philadelphia stay included "an excursion down the Delaware to the neighbourhood of Salem" with Mr Titian Peale, when he went to look for birds and found live mice in his bed.

The Squire says he left the United States when "the sun was within a week or two of passing into the southern hemisphere"—a somewhat Dantesque way of indicating the first half of September. But considering that he travelled either by steamboat, canal or stage-coach, and that he made several stops, including whatever length of time was needed for the Niagara Falls cure of his sprained foot, he seems to have done an enormous amount in ten weeks or less. Moreover, in the *Essays* he elaborates a little on the bare statement in the *Wanderings* that, owing to the autumn cold in New York, he "contracted a bad and obstinate cough." The "severe cold" he there tells us was the result of "having incautiously taken a hot bath in the City of New York."

The adverb "incautiously" gives the impression that taking hot baths was not one of the Squire's common indulgences; though, when we come to the interesting affair of the civetta owls, we shall find the record of another disastrous hot bath. But did the Squire catch cold in New York before he went to Philadelphia or afterwards? And then, as we have only ten weeks at most for his wanderings in America, what are we to make of his statement that "I was bled eight times, and I lived for six weeks on little more than bread and tea"? Did he diet in this way while he travelled and on board ship for the West Indies, for which he departed "at the urgent entreaty of Doctor Hossack," all of whose skill could otherwise not "have saved me from consumption"?

However the chronology is arranged, it is certain that he sailed for the Caribbean, and that the ship was "thirty days" in making Antigua—a delay which the Squire records in gratitude, since they thus missed a destructive hurricane in which their vessel would probably have perished if they had made the voyage in the usual time. From Antigua they proceeded to Barbados, stopping at Guadaloupe, Dominica, Martinique and St Lucia. The Squire recorded that "the difference between the French and British islands is very striking—the first appeared happy and contented; the second were filled with murmurs and complaints."

He had intended to go on to Trinidad; but, as inevitably must happen, the communications between these various islands were—and to some extent still are—difficult; and he could not find a vessel carrying passengers from Barbados to Trinidad. So, for the second time, he abandoned an attempt to strike out a new line of wandering, and took ship for the familiar Guiana. He did not stay in Georgetown, but "proceeded without loss of time to the forests in the interior." Why did he make this excursion? And how does it happen that he did so little after this long journey? Apart from confirming his observations on the sloth, attempting but again failing to get his "claret tapped" by a vampire bat, and picking up one or two birds for his collection, he seems to have done nothing and to have nothing to report.

Several explanations of this disappointing inactivity have been put forward. The Squire was still suffering from his "incautious" hot bath; he was low-spirited, regretting his American friends; he pined for the "fair Albanese"; he was not going to exert himself to capture rare birds and animals in order to pay "mail" to the caterans of the Customs. Probably there is something in all these conjectures, but there seems to be yet another possible line of explanation for this brief and eventless raid into the jungle.

Two or three years of sulking in his tent must have convinced even the obstinacy of this ornithological Achilles that he was going the wrong way about it to punish the Treasury. Even he could scarcely imagine that when My Lords Commissioners met they greeted each other in tones of subdued grief, saying: "Good God! my lord, but for our folly in taxing Mr Waterton's specimens we should now be in full enjoyment of his incomparable method of stuffing birds." The indifference of these stony-hearted villains to their punishment must have been apparent even to the Squire, and he must surely have realised that all he had done was to deprive himself of the fame of his discovery. Some other punishment had to be devised.

Moreover—and this is also conjectural—we must remember that in Philadelphia the Squire had found unexpectedly congenial company. Mr George Ord and two of the Peales with the pictorial Christian names were enthusiastic and competent naturalists. It is reasonable to suppose—especially in view of the triumphs of taxidermy included in the elder Mr Peale's portrait—that the Squire would have communicated to them the manuscript of his immortal essay, *On Preserving Birds for Cabinets of Natural History*, and possibly even the script of the first three "Wanderings." These energetic Americans would naturally pooh-pooh the nonsense of boycotting the Treasury, and also any old-fashioned scruples the Squire may have had about its being ungenteel for the twenty-seventh lord of Walton to enter into competition with low author fellows. Mr Ord especially, scenting a useful and certainly fearless ally for his battle of Wilson versus Audubon, would urge publication.

An author seldom needs much persuasion against depriving the world any longer of the fruits of his genius.

And then at some time or other—perhaps in that incautious hot bath, perhaps not until he reached Barbados—the Watertonian thought came to him. He would print the *Wanderings*, yes; and yes, he would include the immortal pamphlet on Preserving Birds. But he would also at one Watertonian sweep demonstrate his unique skill in taxidermy and lampoon the Treasury. . . .

His fourth wandering to Guiana was undertaken, I submit, solely for the purpose of obtaining a specimen of that hitherto unknown animal, the Nondescript.

IX

AMONG the many traits which endear the Squire to his readers must certainly be numbered his impetuosity. It was part of that generosity of spirit which made him a defender of unpopular causes and an over-zealous denouncer of all he thought infamous. Equally characteristic were his compassion and his irascibility. He was not one of those sluggish calculating men who take no risks, always pause to consider, put themselves craftily on the winning side with seeming disinterestedness, and walk off with the world's praise and pelf. He could be patient and tenacious of purpose, as in the building of his great wall, and working out his discoveries in taxidermy, and even in his feuds with Swainson and Audubon and the rest. But let him once "take a notion" to do something or other, he was all on fire until he could carry it out, however whimsical it might be, and however much a colder man would have foreseen dangers.

So it was with this affair of the Nondescript—no sooner had the revelation come to him than he rushed instantly into action. In this connection, the Squire's biographers seem not to have stressed sufficiently the extreme brevity of his fourth wandering in Guiana. No doubt the vagueness of his chronology accounts for this, but even from his whimsical way of counting time we can see that his total stay in Guiana cannot have exceeded six weeks, and was probably much less. On his Dantesque reckoning, he left the United States about the middle of September; he was "thirty days" in reaching Antigua, which brings us to the middle of October; he went ashore there, and at four other islands on the way to Barbados, where he must have stopped some days at least looking for a ship. It is several hundred miles from Bridgetown to Georgetown, so that, all told, another thirty days—bringing us to mid-November—seems a moderate estimate for a sailing vessel. The Squire left Guiana for the last time "towards the close of December, 1824," characteristically infecting his hand with "a chegoe" so that during the voyage he might observe its *modus operandi* at leisure. His whole stay that time in "the wilds" cannot have been a month. In other words, as soon as he had obtained the Nondescript, he sailed for England by the first available ship, in spite of the fact that he had supposedly been sent to a warm climate for lung trouble, while a moderately rapid voyage would inevitably bring him to England long before the northern winter was over. And, in fact, he himself reports that he reached the Channel in "dismally bleak and cold weather" which favoured his "old foe, an affection of the lungs." For a period of no less than six months "the late lamented Doctor Gilby of Wakefield grappled" with this "old foe."

Such a trifle as a six-months' battle with tuberculosis naturally did not impede the Squire's plans in the least. The great wall marched on whenever the deal drawer had enough solid tin to pay for it. And he arranged with the London firm of Mawman (sinister name for a publisher) to issue the *Wanderings in South America* with a frontispiece of the Nondescript, drawn by his "young friend, Mr J. H. Foljambe, eldest son of Thomas Foljambe, Esq., of Wakefield."

What was "the Nondescript"? Although for his own purposes —and detriment—the Squire made a mystery of it, there is no reason why we should. The Nondescript was the skin of a Red Howler monkey from Guiana, manipulated with such skill that it appeared to be a stuffed specimen of a hirsute late Georgian gentleman. There was more than one exquisite Waterton reason for perpetrating this dangerous freak—although he himself clearly hints at its origin by describing the Nondescript immediately after his account of the Red Howler monkey.

"The features of this animal are quite of the Grecian cast," says the Squire, whose assertion may be checked by reference to the engraving of the Nondescript. He brought back "only the head and shoulders," because he was "pressed for daylight" and also found him too heavy to carry. In his heavy style of joking, he suggests that somebody else should go out and secure another specimen. But then he lets the taxidermical cat out of the bag, and allows us to see that the primary reason for creating the Nondescript was to produce such a specimen of the art of taxidermy as would, from the Watertonian point of view, strike every observer with admiration and delight.

"If," he says, "this head in question has had all its original features destroyed, by what means has this hitherto unheard-of change been effected?" Well, of course the Squire knew, and he naïvely expected people to ask him to demonstrate his wonderful new method, and then to praise him as he deserved. But, of course, they did nothing of the kind. Some took it literally as yet another "curio" from the "wilds"; some maliciously pretended to believe that the Squire had slain and stuffed some "native Indian" in order to make an arrogant display of his "stuffing powers," and inveighed against "Mr Waterton's wanton cruelty"; and one malicious (or perhaps merely obtuse) specimen of the race of Yorkshire baronets, re-marked: "Dear me, what a very extraordinary-looking man Mr Waterton must be." Only Sydney Smith, the most distinguished and the most favourable of the first reviewers of the *Wanderings,* was not deceived:

"In this exhibition," he says of the Nondescript, "the author is surely abusing his stuffing talents, and laughing at the public. It is clearly the head of a Master in Chancery—whom we have often seen basking in the House of Commons after he has delivered his message."

It seems quite obvious that, in addition to a startling advertise-ment of his "stuffing talents," the Nondescript was intended as a caricature of the Squire's enemy, the secretary to the Treasury, Mr J. R. Lushington. I know of course that Waterton denied in his *Autobiography* (1837) that he had ever wished "to pass off this extraordinary thing either for the head and shoulders of a man . . . or those of an ape." Many years later, Dr Hobson, repelling "sus-picions of the gravest and most diabolical character . . . vile insinua-tions and widely disseminated under-currents . . . severe and abso-lutely uncompromising remarks and not a few nauseating aspersions . . . malicious gnashing of teeth currently whispered" emphatically asserted—the Squire's authority supporting him—that there was never "the slightest intention that this unique work of art should represent, by physiognomical similarity, any particular individual whatever."

But long before this the Squire, even, had become aware of what a mistake he had made in perpetrating this grotesque combination of revenge and self-advertising. Not only had most non-specialists failed to see his point, but the few specialists had bitterly attacked him, while doubtless more than one possible victim had silently fitted on this simian cap—to adopt Hobsonian phraseology. Doubt-less Waterton felt he had as good a right to deny that the Non-descript was meant as a caricature of a Treasury official as Sir Walter Scott believed he had to deny the authorship of the Waverley novels. But the way the denial is made in the 1837 edition of the First Series of Essays is such as to suggest the very thing the writer pretends to deny. As a footnote, immediately under the denial, is

printed Mr Lushington's offensively official letter, although the
course of the Squire's narrative might more reasonably have led to
the quotation of this letter two or three pages earlier. Taking everything into consideration, I am convinced that, among other things,
the Nondescript was intended as a caricature of Mr Lushington and
a Watertonian retort to his "illiberality" in 1821.

If the *Wanderings* were attacked by closet naturalists, who were
as infuriated by the story of riding the cayman as they were by the
Nondescript, they had a considerable public success. Sydney Smith's
favourable review contained more than one of his parson-about-
town jokes, which were certain to be endlessly repeated at dinner
tables by persons who could furnish no conversation of their own;
and thus unwittingly advertised the book. It is an error to take *au
pied de la lettre* the Squire's preliminary remarks about the book
having "little merit" and his offering it "with a hesitating hand."
The acrimony with which he answered its detractors, as well as the
tone in which he writes of it later, shows that he thought very highly
of it. To speak gravely of the Squire as "modest" is to show a mis-
understanding of his character. He had virtues and endearing qualities, but he was far from modest. His own writings show that he
was not only exceptionally obstinate, but had an exceedingly high
opinion of Mr Waterton of Walton Hall, which he did not hesitate
to maintain to the point of downright rudeness:

"The Squire," says his intimate friend, Dr Hobson, ". . . would
not at all hesitate to support his own side of the argument by very
energetic language, and, occasionally, by a tartness and an asperity
of expression somewhat ungracious, and, unfortunately, also by a
very decided insuavity of manner." That coming from someone
who really was devoted to the Squire's memory is clear enough. He
goes on to say that Mr Waterton was "impatient with anyone
hazarding an opinion at variance with his own," adding in his
intolerably pompous and prolix manner, ". . . if merely the most
trifling difference of opinion was ventured to be expressed in the
mildest and most gentle manner possible . . . no one was exempt
from the reception of a testy or a somewhat irascible punition, nor
did anyone possess the slightest immunity from this infliction in
consequence of age, friendship or sex." Such was the Squire's
"modesty," particularly about matters of natural history and taxidermy, not to mention Hanoverian rats, his numerous enemies, and
"the Church by law established"!

Waterton's *Wanderings* have been so often quoted and referred to in this narrative that, even if he has not read them, the reader must have a fair notion of their merits and demerits. The book has with difficulty obtained a precarious hold on the memory of posterity, and then rather as a piece of genial eccentricity, a literary *lusus naturae*, than as a serious contribution either to science or belles-lettres. The absence of construction, of ordonnance, so characteristic of the literary work of amateurs, is in the *Wanderings* so flagrant as almost to suggest doubts of the Squire's sanity. I do not know any book which has survived oblivion so badly put together as the *Wanderings*, except—strange coincidence—Dr Hobson's stupefying *Charles Waterton* which, to be sure, we only read because of what it has to tell us about its eccentric subject. Dr Hobson we can all mentally reconstruct from his book—garrulous, consequential, prolix, pompous and flighty. The *Wanderings* are a more complex problem. There is a similarity in the flightiness of mind which can seldom dwell on any topic for long, which is incapable of arranging topics in any sensible order, and baffles the reader by irrelevant returns to some subjects which have already been treated. They even share the same mania for otiose Latin quotations and unprosperous jests.

How then did it happen that the *Wanderings* were a contemporary success and are still readable and read? Well, the Squire not only possessed the unique and amusing character we are investigating, but, in spite of his affectations, his slap-dash carelessness and mannerisms, he really had in him the makings of a writer, both scientific and literary. He had, in the first place, the literary common sense (which is not too common) to choose subjects which entirely interested him, and not those which happened to be fashionable or which he imagined might curry favour with the public. He had genuine gifts of observation in natural history, as is demonstrated, for example, by the information contained in his remarks on the sloth and on the Indian methods of compounding curare. On the literary side his descriptions of the tropical forests as seen from the river, of his battles with boas and the cayman, and—in a very different manner—of his experiences in American society, all have merit. That the reader is continuously reminded of the Squire's odd prejudices and quaint mannerisms is no bar to enjoyment, but rather increases it.

Upon the whole the Squire seems to have treated with sensible contempt the yelpings of the closet naturalists who fell upon his accounts of the cayman-riding and of the Nondescript. There was, however, one exception, and that was the remark of William Swainson, already quoted, about the Squire's "constant propensity to dress up truth in the garb of fiction." Waterton was infuriated by this and never forgave or forgot it, or missed an opportunity of trying to retaliate on Swainson. Now, in matters of natural history the Squire was a careful observer, and nobody who gets to know him can doubt that he was a strictly honourable and truthful man. But then his vagueness introduces difficulties in his chronology (as we have seen), and when he relies wholly on memory, he is apt sometimes to contradict himself. It was perhaps his consciousness of these, in general trifling, mis-statements, which made him resent so deeply Swainson's remark.

But the Squire's conscience may perhaps have caused him to misinterpret his critic's statement; for while it is certainly a severe rebuke to the Squire's errors of fact and complacent little exaggerations, it is just and true when applied to his manner. I have quoted his description of the sloth with its imitation of Tristram Shandy, whose style Waterton so constantly copies. But, in addition to this, references to Don Quixote and the Metamorphoses of Ovid and other Latin poems might very justly be described as showing a "propensity to dress up truth in the garb of fiction." Take, for instance, the following sentences from his mystification (in itself a totally unscientific and "fictional" piece of writing) about the Nondescript:

"Some gentlemen of great skill and talent, on inspecting his head, were convinced that the whole series of his features had been changed. Others again have hesitated, and betrayed doubts, not being able to make up their minds whether it be possible that the brute features of the monkey can be changed into the noble countenance of man: 'Scinditur vulgus.' . . .

"Let us suppose for an instant that it is a new species. Well; 'Una golondrina no hace verano': One Swallow does not make summer, as Sancho Panza says. . . . Perhaps, gentle reader, you would wish me to go in quest of another. I would beg leave respectfully to answer that the way is dubious, long and dreary; and though, unfortunately, I cannot allege the excuse of 'me pia conjex detinet,' still I would fain crave a little repose. I have already been a long while errant:

> Longa mihi exilia, et vastum maris aequor aravi,
> Ne mandate mihi, nam ego sum defessus agendo."

And so on and so forth in the same style. Here the style is perhaps rather that of Burton's *Anatomy of Melancholy* than of fiction, but it is certainly not scientific—and then, after all, the whole thing was in itself a "spoof"! Small wonder that the naturalists of the day looked down their noses at the *Wanderings*. Even in more recent times it may be observed that naturalists are not too anxious to claim Waterton's *Wanderings* for their particular part of the world of intellect. Notice, for instance, how Mr Edmund Selous eludes responsibility:

"To me, indeed, the *Wanderings* seems, not so much a work of natural history, as a literary work with that theme, amongst others, for a background, lightly and discontinuously touched upon. It is a pomp and pageant of the tropical forest, into the lively procession of which all enters that happens to pass—birds, monkeys, snakes, peccaries, 'tigers,' and tapirs, ants and ant-bears, falling in and then out again, with the trees and the rivers, the savannahs, hills, vistas, Indians, and wourali poison—the account of which last, in the hands of its producers and users, is excessively interesting."

That is felicitous criticism, but the reader will observe how careful Mr Selous was to stress the literary side rather than the scientific. In America an equally generous critic and competent naturalist, the late General Theodore Roosevelt, has this to say:

". . . a century ago Waterton's *Wanderings* marked the beginning of the literature wherein field naturalists who are also men of letters have described for us the magic and interest, the terror and beauty of the far-off wilds where Nature gives peace to bold souls and inspires terror in the mind. Gilbert White and Waterton added in new ways to the sum of achievement of men of letters. Each made a contribution to literature. . . ."

Such are some of the qualities which recommend Waterton's *Wanderings* to readers of more recent times, though it will be noted that the two naturalists are, as I have pointed out, far more willing to praise the Squire on literary than on scientific grounds. In his own time most of the scientific writers and reviewers were against him simply because he was too little of a disciple of scientific method and manner. They resented his refusal to use Latin scientific names ("jaw-breaking words" he called them, like any uneducated person) while peppering his pages with quotations from the classics puritanically re-written by the Jesuits. But the Uncle Toby and Don Quixote *pastiches* would appeal to the more literary audience, and a sprinkling of well-worn Latin tags was still evidence of gentility in his class, though any approach to a more exact knowledge was voted "mean" and "parson-like." Moreover, the Squire's humour, which now is most successful when least intentional, was then in its broadest and flattest moods best suited to an audience of country gentlemen. Whether the Squire was quite such a pioneer as General Roosevelt generously implies may admit a query. It is true that Cook and Dampier, Anson and Jack Byron were mariners, and Bruce, Clarke and Burckhardt had many other interests before natural history. The great predecessor was undoubtedly Alexander von Humboldt, whose account of his "wanderings" in South America began to appear in an English translation as early as 1814. But Waterton is certainly the pioneer among travelling English naturalists, preceding Darwin, Wallace, Huxley, Bates, Belt, and how many others down to the admirable Mr Ivar Sanderson.

Thus, although accurate appreciation of any book even a little out of the ordinary seems doomed to wait until after the author's death, Waterton in his own lifetime could console himself for the stupidities and malevolences of contemporary comment by the most satisfactory of salves—his book was all along being steadily bought and read.

The next year, 1826, saw the completion of the three-mile wall round Walton Hall park, which converted it into the first sanctuary for wild birds. The wild-life sanctuary has proved to be the only method of saving many species of mammals and birds from extermination in the United States and Africa; and even in Australia, where protection is supposed to be national and effective, the sanctuary has great value. All these are a development of the Squire's "eccentric" defence of his park against poachers, gamekeepers, foxes and other destroyers of wild life. Furthermore, Waterton was a pioneer in pleading for a mitigation if not a total abolition of the "sportsman's" and gamekeeper's and farmer's war on wild birds. He did this by showing that the destruction of crops, eggs, young chicks by wild birds was either exaggerated or untrue; and by demonstrating the interest to be found by any intelligent person in making friends with the birds and carefully observing their lives. Did anyone before Waterton realise the immense advantages of watching wild creatures through binoculars or a telescope from a place of concealment? America is full of Audubon Societies for the protection of wild life, though, in spite of his great book of coloured engravings, Audubon did nothing towards the establishment of wild life protection and sanctuaries. Waterton gave much of his income and much of his life to further these aims, and yet remains without acknowledgment in his own country and abroad, while even his name is omitted from books of reference.

The Squire's efforts to defend the "feathered tribe" from its enemies were not always marked by the tact and conciliatory manner which are advisable when trying to protect the weak who are supposed to be noxious from the strong who undoubtedly are so. "In the good old sensible times," says the Squire, the "rook was styled *frugilegus*. It is now pronounced to be *prædatorius*." So far so good; the point, as they say, is well taken. But then he goes on to say: "Who knows but that our Great Ones in Ornithology may ultimately determine to call it up to the house of hawks?" It was tempting, but was it altogether good tactics and in the best interests of the birds, to indispose the whole class of closet ornithologists, and then to take an unhandy swipe at the House of Lords, whose agreement was necessary for any legislation in defence of wild birds, and which was crammed with fox-hunters and pheasant-killers?

Gamekeepers were of course less likely to read essays on birds— they were practical men whose contribution to civilisation was to cover barn and stable doors with desiccating and decaying corpses of birds and small mammals. For this they were salaried, and received guinea tips from the visiting sportsman. But even gamekeepers and sportsmen might hear rumours of this sort of thing:

"The kite, the buzzard and the raven have been exterminated long ago by our merciless gamekeepers. Ignorant of the real habits of birds, and even bent on slaughter, these men exercise their baneful calling with a severity almost past belief. No sooner have they received from Government their shooting licences, than out they go with the gun, and under one pretext or other, they kill almost every bird which comes in their way. Our game laws are at the bottom of all this mischief.

'—*Illis, non saevior ulla
Pestis, et ira Deum, Stygiis sese extulit undis.*'"

And so he goes on, deploring that he has seen none of these birds (1813), adding with appropriate tact and relevance: ". . . like the family of poor Charley Stuart (God rest his soul!), they no longer appear on their own native land."

These examples could be greatly multiplied, as anyone familiar with the Squire's writings knows. But it is time to take a look at

Walton Hall and the newly enclosed park, as well as at a few of the Squire's doings and dodges therein. The full details and description must be looked for in the Squire's own scattered but numerous notices, the eccentrically methodless reportings of Dr Hobson, and the narratives of such eye-witnesses as Wood and Moore. It must be remembered that their descriptions relate to the house and park and "dodges" as they were in the Squire's last years, and that there are no means of discovering the dates of all the different "improvements" and "dodges." Nor is that of much importance, the important thing being that the Squire had made for himself an endless occasion of occupation, interest and observation, while to the end of his long life he was always planning and carrying out some new "dodge" or improvement—the welfare of the wild birds being really the main consideration after the Squire's own entertainment.

Agricultural land was included within the wall along with the lake and kitchen gardens and other appurtenances of the Hall (including the grotto), and these were still farmed in his obstinately unproductive way. The house itself stood on a small island in the lake, connected with the park only by an iron bridge, fancifully described by Dr Hobson as "an ornamental object in the scenery." The house was a plain brick structure dating only from the second half of the eighteenth century. In the Middle Ages the island site must have formed a useful defence to the small castle which had been built there for the lords of Walton. This seems to have been destroyed, or perhaps only re-modelled in early Tudor times. At all events this house had possessed an oak-panelled hall ninety feet long, but at the time of re-building in the reign of George III, the panelling was either burned or used to build a pigeon-house. It is useless to regret the destruction of the old house, though why people who were so obstinately conservative in so many obstructive ways should have chosen not to be conservative in the one respect where that would have earned the gratitude of posterity is a question. But if a motive is looked for, it might surely be found in the multitudes of rats, which continued to swarm in the new house as in the old, in spite of all the measures taken by the official rat-catcher of Stonyhurst.

All that remained of the old buildings was the fortified water-gate which, as we have already seen, was believed to show signs of "the besieging influence of that daring Puritan," Oliver Cromwell. This stood on the island to the left of the iron bridge as you approached the house, and this was one of the many nesting places the Squire prepared. As early as 1813 he induced barn owls to nest there by building on it "a place with stone and mortar, about 4 ft. square," and a "thick oaken stick" as a perch. (In 1831 he had "four broods," and was hopeful of nine the next year.) He had noticed that the starlings regularly left Walton in spring, and conjectured it was for lack of nesting-places. When he prepared twenty-four nesting "crannies" for them in the old tower, he had the satisfaction of seeing every one of them occupied by starlings. A few years later he could boast that "this year, seven pairs of jackdaws, twenty-four pairs of starlings, the barn owl, the blackbird, the robin, the redstart, the house-sparrow, the chaffinch, have had their nests in the old ivy tower."

He was equally successful in attracting other birds, and towards the end of his life gave Dr Hobson a list (which the doctor prints) of 122 species of birds which had "sojourned or been seen" within the park limits since its enclosure. It was in 1833 that the Squire wrote in great glee to Mr George Ord in Philadelphia to inform him that at last the herons had "bred here for the first time." Incidentally, the Squire's massive sense of humour came into play even in the protection of wild birds, for he reports exultantly to Mr Ord that "I have made jackdaws hatch magpies, and magpies jackdaws." The eggs of carrion crows had been successfully hatched and the young reared by rooks; and rooks had performed the same service to young carrion crows. "It is quite laughable to see a brood of young jackdaws following an old magpie, and vice versa." By "vice versa" we may take it that the Squire did not mean "old magpies following a young jackdaw," but "young magpies following an old jackdaw."

Encouraged by his success in getting starlings to build in the "ivy tower" the Squire—at some unspecified date—built beside it "two towers . . . for these birds." The base was so constructed that cats and rats could not possibly climb to the nestlings. The entrance to each nesting-place was "closed by a cube of stone, having one of the corners squared away." The space left was sufficient for the mother bird to reach her nest, but the whole stone could easily be removed either for observation or cleaning. Wood reports that in the sixties the starlings nesting in these towers had become "so tame that they have no objection to being watched, and even after the stone is removed the bird sits calmly serene on her eggs, following the intruder with a fearless gaze." The Squire was equally successful with water birds, which came in large numbers to feed in his lake and to nest beside it when they discovered that they were entirely safe there.

At the other end of the "ornamental" iron bridge were the stables, masked from sight by one of the yew hedges in which the Squire so much delighted, since they gave him shelter from the cold winds which were such an affliction to his "chilly frame." Where the stream left the lake the Squire eventually built a "substantial hovel" as a bird-observation post for himself or a shelter for the gamekeeper in rough weather. Later, having given permission to poor persons to fish the lake for their food, his kindness went further, and supplied the "exhausted and half-starved" fishermen with "an easy and refreshing arm-chair" which was "permanently fixed" in the said hovel. This stream ran past the garden beyond the stables and, after being crossed by two or three "naturally formed stone bridges," flowed through what Dr Hobson enthusiastically described as "one of the loveliest grottos, probably, in England."

Both Norman Moore and Dr Hobson refer to this "grotto" as "a paradise," though Dr Hobson says it was "earthly" and Sir Norman "sylvan." It was a sunken garden which included a small cave, a stone table with benches, a "small temple, having an obtusely formed conical roof" and, on the higher land above the cave, "a large and circular temple . . . supported by eight stone pillars." Here, in what Moore calls "a small square house of one room," the Squire would build a fire in winter time, but leave the door wide open so that, as he put it, "he could talk to cock robin and the magpies." On the "brink of the precipice" above the small temple the Squire put up a cross which he asserted was "the first . . . erected and exposed to public view in England after the Reformation." Not far from this was "a border of the spruce-fir grove," and there the Squire, "ever anxious to gratify all" and "more especially the juveniles," put up a swing, wherein, as Dr Hobson complacently notes, "many a buxom country girl has joyously received the swinging attentions of her devoted swain."

These were some of the more conspicuous features in the newly enclosed sanctuary. Oddly enough, the greatest difficulty had not been the seemingly enormous task of building a wall long enough to rival the town walls of Lucca, but the opposition to the Squire's closing a right of way which ran through the park. Once his legal right to that was established, the wall was a question of frugality and saving. The Squire was accustomed to say facetiously that he had "built the wall with the wine he didn't drink." And there was a good deal in the boast. Suppose he had been a three-bottle man like his ancestors, drinking claret of a medium country-gentleman sort at five shillings a bottle. If he had lived to keep it up for forty years, he would have drunk about ten thousand pounds' worth of wine.

If he had been a three-bottle man, we may well doubt whether he would have preserved so long his astounding agility in climbing trees. Except on occasions when he encumbered himself with a ladder, tree-climbing seems to have been one of the only two occupations in which the Squire never had an accident. On some unspecified occasion when helping masons move large blocks of stones, he contrived to get his thumb squashed to a pulp, and even his coolness in putting the fragments together resulted in a deformed thumb and a long abstinence from writing. The other outdoor occupation in which, strange to say, the Squire never had an accident was boating. According to Dr Hobson, the Squire delighted his friends both by "his graceful handling of the oars" and "scientific management of the sailing boat"; and the doctor boasts that he never had a mishap. Perhaps not, but the friends seem to have had their fears, since he adds that Mr Waterton constantly called their attention "to objects of interest" in order "to free them from the fear of a watery upset," which the Squire's reputation and "mishaps" in so many other forms of activity must have rendered extremely probable to the apprehensive guests.

It was to a great extent this love of tree-climbing which gave the Squire his love of trees. Even as a boy, it is said, he planted young trees which he lived to see and to climb when they were fully grown. Once the wall was completed and the trees comparatively free from the poachers shooting at real or dummy pheasants in the dark, the Squire was able to take care of them with the skill which has been since developed by modern "tree-surgeons." By skilful roofing and plastering to keep out the rain, he saved many a decayed tree or even stump, and then adapted it to suit some bird's nesting habits. The Squire's making of dummy pheasants to deceive poachers and growing yew hedges to protect himself from cold winds have been mentioned; but the final and triumphant stage of his method of pheasant preserving shows a most ingenious use of his knowledge of trees, pheasants and poachers. Near the house the Squire planted a thick shrubbery of yews, and surrounded them with an impenetrable wall of hollies entered only by a locked and spiked wicket. Having decorated the trees in the coverts with dummy pheasants, he lured the birds each evening to the yews by a train of beans and a sack or two scattered under the yews. He put down beans in preference to other grain, because the small birds could not eat them, and under the thick yews they were hidden from the rooks. The pheasants followed the train of beans, gorged themselves on those under the yews, and then flew up to roost in the branches above them. If awakened in the night by the popping of unauthorised guns in the coverts, the Squire could chuckle and go to sleep again —the poachers were welcome to as many dummies as they could shoot, and dummies were all they were likely to get. The wall itself was not a better protection.

The Squire was so accustomed to climb trees on every fine day either to read or to watch birds or both that it never occurred to him how strange his naïve references to it must sound to those who had long been incapable of such feats, if they had ever practised them even when boys or girls. Ordinary men and women, as well as sedentary closet naturalists, were naturally surprised—and if of a suspicious nature incredulous—when they read such statements as the following from a country gentleman who had decades ago reached years of discretion without, however, acquiring much of that quality. Writing, for instance, of the carrion crow, he says enthusiastically:

". . . many an hour of delight do I experience, when, having mounted to the top of a favourite aged oak which grows on the border of a swamp, I see him chasing the heron and the windhover through the liquid void. . . ."

And, again coming to carrion crows, though nominally discussing rooks:

"Last spring I paid a visit, once a day, to a carrion crow's nest on the top of a fir tree."

And, still more characteristically mingling his hobbies:

"When the delicious season of spring sets in, I often get up into the topmost branches of a wide-spreading oak; and there, taking the *Metamorphoses* out of my pocket, I read the sorrow of poor Halcyone. A brook runs close by the tree, and on its bank I have fixed a stump for a resting-place to the kingfisher."

Some people, on reading such passages, docketed the Squire as boastful and untruthful. Now, he certainly had the highest opinion of himself as a field naturalist, a taxidermist and a repository of ultimate and indisputable theological truth, and, as Dr Hobson has told us, would resent the slightest questioning of his supremacy with "insuavity." Of course, the Squire may have the crow over us on the Day of Judgment, but then he may not. For his pretensions in natural history he certainly had some justification; while the inaccuracies and contradictions in his publications are mostly only the result of carelessness and lapse of memory. Most people, even in his own day, recognised that he was too honourable a person to dream of intentional deceit except in what he considered such lawful jokes as the Nondescript. But as all these oddities of behaviour, adventure, opinion and habit strengthened upon him and became known, from his writings and from gossip, was it surprising that even his admirers admitted he was "eccentric," although this word "eccentric" infuriated the Squire when applied to himself as much as Swainson's remark about "dressing truth in the garb of fiction," and probably for the same reason? He could not help secretly feeling, though he would never have admitted it to anyone, that there was a foundation of truth in both.

And now he was on the verge of yet another wild adventure which the world naturally dubbed "eccentric." At the age of forty-eight, with all his whims and odd habits and prejudices strong upon him, he suddenly took it into his head "to commit matrimony," and with a convent-bred girl of seventeen who, as the Squire certainly knew, would profoundly alter his ancient stock by bringing to it genes inherited from her "Arowak" Indian grandmother.

X

THE girl who had been chosen by Squire Waterton as a bride —for in the peculiar circumstances it seems highly improbable that she could have chosen him—was Anne Edmonstone, younger daughter of his old friend Charles Edmonstone of Mibiri Creek. Just as the Squire was descended from kings and saints, so, strange to relate, Anne Edmonstone was descended from Robert II and Robert III of Scotland, and from Lady Godiva. On the other side, even the gratuitous "princess" conferred by the family on her maternal grandmother, Minda, cannot make her anything but a "poor wild sister" from the Guiana forests. In the eighteenth century a Scottish gentleman from Banffshire, by name William Reid, married Minda "daughter of an Arowak chief." This Reid was a close friend of Charles Edmonstone, and, by the influence he had acquired among the Indians through his marriage, was useful to Edmonstone in his battles with gangs of escaped slaves. Charles Edmonstone married Helen, daughter of Reid and "princess" Minda, the "Arowak," and she was the mother of Anne.

There is a tradition that in 1812, when Anne was a new-born baby, the Squire held her at the font in Demerara and announced that when she grew up he would marry her. On the face of it this has all the appearance of a typical Watertonian freak, but apart from the fact that anyone would feel there is something repulsive in the idea of a man of thirty-one affiancing himself to a new-born baby, the Edmonstones would not have permitted a remark in such doubtful taste, whether made jokingly or in earnest.

In the absence of any information as to how this marriage came about, perhaps a little conjecture may be allowed, with the warning that it is conjecture and not biography. We do not know exactly how long Mr and Mrs Charles Edmonstone survived their residence in Scotland, but it cannot have been long; he was elderly and suffering from wounds received in fights with the slaves; and for her, a native of tropical Guiana, the climate of Scotland would be as fatal as that of Guiana too often was to Scots. I have noted the interesting fact that in 1820 the Squire sailed from the Clyde, and not from Liverpool as on all his other wanderings in America. Why, on that occasion, did he go as far north as Scotland? There must have been a reason, and it could only have been something involving the Edmonstones. What is more likely than that Mr Edmonstone, finding his health failing and knowing that his wife was a stranger to European ways, should have commended his children to the care of the Squire, knowing him to be a kind-hearted and honourable man? Judging from the Squire's numerous references, there was no man he admired and liked more than Edmonstone, who of course was fully aware of it. The 1820 journey to Scotland may have been either to take leave of a dying Edmonstone or to make arrangements for the orphaned girls, supposing Edmonstone was then dead. The choice of the English Convent at Bruges for their education sounds very like the Squire.

The Edmonstone girls were provided for in the matter of money, but what they needed was a protector and a home; and these of course were for a time provided by the convent and the nuns. But the girls could not stay in a convent indefinitely, and propriety would have been shocked if three girls of marriageable age but in no way related to the Squire should take up their abode permanently at Walton Hall. This problem must have given the Squire anxious moments of Watertonian thought as he pondered it at the top of a favourite tree or as he stuffed a bird, for while he might not have cared about his own reputation, theirs was another matter. The Watertonian if not the obvious solution was to marry one of the girls, which made the others his sisters-in-law and thus regularised everything. Whether he discussed this with them directly or through the Mother Superior, whether he proposed for Anne or for any of them who would sacrifice herself for the others, whether they tossed up or Anne volunteered, are matters that can never be known. The sole known fact is that the arrangement was made for him to marry Anne.

Before starting out to wed his bride in Belgium, the Squire came to a characteristic resolve—once more he would extirpate the Hanoverian rats which still continued to infest Walton Hall. There would be no more half-measures such as tame tiger-cats, or frightening the Hanoverians with tar and garlic, but radical measures of permanent efficacy, founded on a lifelong study of the vermin. All rat holes were closed "with stone and mortar"; the outer doors were bound with hoop iron, and the pavement outside the house "relaid with particular care." Useless sewers were filled up, and those necessary repaved and closed at each end with movable iron grates. "The cat and the owl" were encouraged to take care of those which might "still linger in the environs." As a matter of fact, the rats were not driven from the stables and other outhouses until the Squire rebuilt them in 1839. And even in the sixties Dr Hobson noticed outside the Hall an ingenious stone rat-trap, containing "an enticing and fatal powder" compounded of "brown sugar, oatmeals and arsenic . . . well triturated in a mortar."

Having made this ample preparation for the reception of the young bride, the Squire, well-satisfied, set out for Bruges, where he was married to Anne in the convent church at the Watertonian hour of 4 a.m. on the 11th May, 1829, the bride having spent the previous night in the school dormitory.

Now, four o'clock in the morning is an awkward hour for any girl to be married, even if the bridegroom is a beautiful young man with flashing eyes, a black moustache and a white satin cravat. Anne Edmonstone's bridegroom was hardly that. It was only a very few years later that he boasted of himself as "still quite free from rheumatic pains" and so supple he could climb trees "with the utmost facility"; an accomplishment always looked for in a husband by romantic young women. His height was five feet eleven and a half inches; his face, he confesses, "anything but comely," " furrowed" by the suns and rains of the tropics, and of "a tint which neither Rowland's Kalydor, nor all the cosmetics on Belinda's toilette, would ever be able to remove." His hair was cut very short and had been dark, but then had "the appearance as though it had passed the night exposed to a November hoarfrost." His legs had "great muscular power," and were so disproportionate to the rest of him, that he compares himself to "Tithonus placed on the lower part of Ajax." If he were exhibited at a fair, the Squire surmised that some "learned jockey" might exclaim, "He is half Rosinante, half Bucephalus." Yet he was certainly well-preserved, as Dr Hobson so quaintly bears witness in the already quoted statement that at the age of seventy-seven the Squire gratified his friends by "scratching the back part of his head with the big toe of his right foot"—another romantic accomplishment which must have been most gratifying to the young bride. To this may be added the fact that at home his clothes and his hat in particular were often so shabby that he was mistaken for one of the labourers on his own estate. It is true, however, that he sported real gold buttons when he went to Wakefield, but the police had to beg him to desist because they had so much trouble to protect him from being robbed.

Mr. Waterton Mounted on the Cayman when Living

The Distant Mansion, the Ruin, the Little Island and the Lombardy Poplar

It is said (and the statement if untrue is so *ben' trovato* that it ought to be true) that by way of entertainment on her honeymoon, and to celebrate her first glimpse of the great world after being shut up in a convent for years, the seventeen-year-old bride was taken to see the collections of stuffed animals at Antwerp, Ghent and Paris. Delicious hours of emancipation and tasting the worldly and fashionable pleasures appropriate to the wife of an English gentleman of family and fortune! Then came the return to Wakefield and Walton Hall, where doubtless the heretical church bells were set ringing for the Squire's bride, and the assembled tenantry cheered and were "regaled" on roasted ox and strong ale, which, tradition asserts, were at that time actually obtainable in England. The carriage would drive up to the ornamental iron bridge, and the bride would enter her new home.

It is perhaps of some interest to consider what she found there. As they came towards the bridge the Squire would explain to Anne an object on the southern side of the house called Boulby's Sun-dial, a piece of stone cut into twenty equilateral triangles forming ten sundials, which, on the rare occasions when the sun shone, recorded the time in ten different towns—a freak which so much delighted the Squire that he presented the ingenious Boulby with twenty guineas. From the bridge the sight of the four sycamores beside the Hall would remind him to tell her the laughable fact that "the dismal screams" of the owls borne on "the midnight wintry blast" had often frightened out of her wits the aged housekeeper, who was waiting at the big folding doors of the main entrance to welcome her new mistress. Of course, he could not let her pass the doors without calling her attention to the facetious knockers, the joint invention of the Squire and the talented Captain Jones of climbing fame. If you tried to knock with the grinning one, you found it was so secured that it could not be moved, and the grinning face seemed to mock you "with intense delight." The scowling knocker, which did work, seemed "as if suffering intense agony from the blows you had just given it."

Fortunately, it was not until 1861 that the Squire acquired and placed "at the foot of the grand staircase" that *lusus naturae* he purchased from "Mr Roberts, the taxidermist at Scarbro'," so much to the delight of Dr Hobson—namely "the head of a sheep, having a horn growing from one of its ears." But there must have been much to startle the young bride and to haunt her in this fantastic museum which she had so rashly made her home. Before ever she reached the foot of the grand staircase, she had to encounter a joint product of the Jones-and-Waterton genius, the "singularly conceived and inimitably modelled representation of the nightmare," enough in itself to murder sleep:

"This horrid incubus has a human face, grinning and displaying the frightfully formidable tusks of the wild boar—the hands of a man—satanic horns—elephant's ears—bat's wings—one cloven foot, the other that of an eagle widely expanding his terrific-looking talons, and the tail of a serpent. . . ."

. . . With the motto, obligingly translated by Dr Hobson into English for the benefit of ladies: "Sitting on the region of the heart I take away sleep."

It is to be hoped that Anne had strong nerves, for this horrific spectre was a mere greeting on the vestibule, and more taxidermic terror lurked for her as she was ceremoniously conducted to the matrimonial chamber. The "enchanting staircase," as Dr Hobson called it, displayed in cases mysteriously secured to the banisters stuffed specimens of brilliantly plumaged birds (the Squire despised plain birds, however rare or interesting) from the native Guiana she had left at too early an age to remember. If these were a little reassuring, their influence was immediately dissipated by a large painting (due also to the genius of the Squire's Jones, who certainly deserved the epithet of "gigantic" far more than Ruskin's Ned Jones) hung on the wall side of the staircase, depicting the Squire and his native companions on the banks of the Essequibo, as they haul and he rides the cayman. At the top of the stairs—poor Anne!—she had to face the grinning jaws and "fearful frame" of "the veritable cayman" itself, together with "the actual line and hook" with which the "poor wild brother" had nabbed the elusive reptile.

And this was only the beginning. At the top of the "enchanting staircase," behind the cayman, was a very large room called the "organ gallery"—it had perhaps been old Mrs Waterton's music room—and this was a combination of a natural history museum and a chamber of zoological horrors. It still lacked the "young chimpanzee, sitting with a negligently easy air on a cocoa-nut," but there were plenty of other objects attractive to a young lady, including a "vast number of crabs, lobsters and insects." There the "great coulacanara snake" lay "coiled in dreadful folds, his eyes dully gleaming under their brows, and his head idly reposing on the pillow of his own body." In cases close at hand were "venomous serpents lurking amid foliage"; one asleep (what a relief in this zoological melodrama!); one with "angry head" and "forked tongue quivering and threatening fangs erect"; and still another "bearing off a fluttering victim in its jaws."

There was "a huge ant-bear" with "his bushy tail curled over his back," and "enveloping him in a cloud of hair." And there was a sloth, "stretching out its neck," and "wearing a peculiarly pitiful, wistful look."

The Nondescript, to which no doubt Anne would be introduced at the earliest possible moment, may already at that time have been banished to "the extension staircase"; but the "organ gallery" and other parts of the house were already becoming crowded with the Squire's taxidermical freaks, particularly those "distasteful and nauseous" representations of famous Protestants which Dr Hobson found so repulsive to good manners, being contortions "of the most disgusting creatures that his flight of fancy could conceive, from the animal, nay, from the painfully loathsome reptile creation." In addition to these exhibitions of Christian charity were such freaks as the Noctifer, "made of the gorget and legs of a bittern, and the head and legs of an eagle-owl, skilfully blended." A political lesson was enforced by a preserved tortoise with the head of "an exceedingly stout but exceedingly worried man," who was supporting the national debt of eight hundred millions sterling, plagued by the *Diabolus bellicosus*, "a sort of grinning lizard all over abnormal spikes and horns"; the *Diabolus ambitiosus* "with outspread wings"; *Diabolus illudens*, and *Diabolus cæruleus* "with open mouth and sharp teeth."

If, shrinking from all this conglomeration of skill in taxidermy, satire, facetiousness and charity, the bride fled to the drawing-room miscalled hers, she would have found that its chief if not sole use was to act as a bird-observation room, with a large telescope ever poised at the window.

And it would have been most ill-received by the Squire if she had ventured to use the prerogative of a bride and to suggest the relegation of these creatures embalmed in corrosive sublimate to the attics and the stable lofts. Only her doubting the one true faith would have caused more consternation and rage, as is attested by Dr Hobson's much-quoted story of the Bahia toad. Calling one day, Dr Hobson noticed that the Squire's temper was "ruffled," and asked if he felt "poorly." To which he "excitedly replied":

"Yes, I am grieved to the backbone, Mr ——, whom you would

just now have met in the carriage-road, and who professes to be enchanted and in raptures with the works of God's creation, has just left the house; and, what do you think? he coolly turned up his nose at my Bahia toad, calling it 'an ugly brute.' "

This, the Squire added, was enough "to put me out" for a week; so he politely left his guest on the staircase "to his own cogitations."

Anne's worst trial was probably not even the feverish night-mares haunted by diabolical Protestants in the form of distorted toads and lizards, but the visits of the female "county." By this time the Squire had become a notorious character and the source of endless gossip about his eccentricities. Match-making Mammas had of course long ago given him up as a hopeless old bachelor, undesirable for even a portionless niece of advancing years; so the news that Squire Waterton was married, and married to a child of seventeen straight out of a convent, and to a child whose mother was a half-caste, was sensational. No doubt the Squire had long before this rid himself of the friendship of the many; but with a spectacle like this to be enjoyed and a guileless bride to be quizzed, old feuds would certainly be brushed aside at least for the duration of one unwanted call. "Dear Mr Waterton—I always liked him, in spite of his odd ways and brusque manners—and that poor young thing must be so lonely—we should forget and forgive and be neigh-bourly—we must call, dear, as soon as the horses are re-shod." And doubtless Anne had to endure the lorgnettes and sweet gibes of every hag and harpy from Wakefield to Scarborough.

And now conjecture, so unavoidable in the case of this strange match completely hidden in discretion, may be abandoned for the facts of biography. Early in the April following her marriage, Mrs Waterton gave birth to a son, who was named Edmund; and about three weeks later, on the 27th April, 1830, she died, aged only eighteen.

XI

ANNE'S unexpected and pathetic death was the greatest moral shock the Squire ever experienced. Of course, he had the usual religious "Morton's fork" line of argument which meets any situation. If he prayed and things went well, then it was evidence of divine benevolence and interference on his behalf. If he prayed and things went wrong, then it was a trial of faith sent from heaven. The tragical event of Anne's death, so cruel and wasteful and needless in a world ruled by Divine Providence, did not of course shake the Squire's faith:

". . . It pleased Heaven to convince me that all felicity here below is no more than a mere illusive transitory dream; and I bow submissive to its adorable decrees. I am left with one fine little boy. . . ."

Such is the Squire's only public comment on this intimate disaster, written some six or seven years after the event, and its pious resignation was undoubtedly sincere. But if we recollect his peculiar character, it is easy to see how this blow shattered him. As we have been watching the Squire's life, we have seen him to be egotistic, opinionated, aggressive, intolerant, but naïve, warm-hearted and charitable to the poor. Above all things he loved to plan out his actions in his own eccentric, freakish way, and he had planned this Watertonian marriage with special care and complacence. He must have felt that a marriage involving such benevolent motives was peculiarly to be blessed. In any event, being the person he was, the Squire would never have undertaken this odd wedding of hoary forty-eight with ignorant seventeen if he had not felt perfectly confident that he was carrying out the unspoken commands of Divine Providence. And this was what Providence responded with—slaying the innocent girl in child-bed, and leaving the pious Squire at nearly fifty with a motherless baby.

That particular problem was dealt with by calling in, first his sister Mrs Carr, and then Anne's sisters Elizabeth and Helen, who became permanent members of the Walton Hall household. But the Watertonian solution to his own agonising problem as a widower after less than a year of marriage was far harder to solve. Some have hinted that he was smitten by remorse at the thought that by marrying a girl so young he might have been guilty of her death in child-bed. This I do not believe. In the first place, she was not so young especially for that epoch and for one of her mixed race; and then the fact that he had only entered on this marriage with the full sanction of the Church would be quite sufficient discharge to his conscience. It was not remorse: it was the hope and faith of meeting her again in heaven which dedicated him to her memory, and made him symbolise his separation from all other women by never again entering a bed. Henceforth, keeping faith with his dead wife, he slept on the floor.

It is true that in his curious little essay *On Fresh Air* the Squire has hinted at a very different origin to a habit which had become (in 1844) so notorious that even he felt some public explanation was needed. There was every reason for not giving the true cause, especially for a man who was so genteelly reticent about his wife that he never mentions her in any of the extant letters written during their married life and only once or twice and very briefly after her death. In the essay *On Fresh Air* he indulges in a naïve and transparent equivocation. He does not say that he himself has adopted this habit of sleeping on the floor and for these reasons, but "a person, on whose veracity I could depend." Very naturally, knowing his habits, the Squire's readers assumed that he was the person who determined never to sleep in a bed because, when travelling, "the bed might have been occupied by a rough-skinned, pimpled victim to turtle soup and Curaçao." In 1844 this person had "not passed a single hour in bed for fourteen years," which takes us back precisely to 1830, the year of Anne's death. "My apprenticeship to the hard floor only cost me a fortnight and after that all went right." In other words, this "person of veracity" has had the Squire's experience of sleeping on the floor, but conceals his true reason for adopting a habit so extraordinary in a civilised man. It had nothing to do with dislike for "pimply aldermen," and was not a habit brought back from Guiana, for the simple reason that it did not begin until 1830.

None of the persons who have left records of their acquaintance with the Squire knew him before 1830. Dr Hobson knew him longest and most intimately, "for nearly thirty years," he says, which dates the beginning of their friendship to a little after 1835 —about five years after this strange resolution of sleeping on the

floor was taken. All agree in essentials as to the ascetic life lived by
the Squire when they knew him, though the medical adviser tells
us that when "the Pope's padlock was taken off his grinders" (i.e.
after Lent or other obligatory fasts) "he was incautious and by no
means ordinarily discreet as regards the consumption of solids."
After fasting "he would gratify his palate (until very late in life)
with a hearty relish of rich soup and also solids in the way of animal
food," with the inevitable result of dreadful pains from the shrunken
stomach, and a hasty call for the doctor. It is a curious fact that
people who are most rigid in abstaining from strong drink of any
kind are apt to be gluttonous in eating. The Squire was no exception.

In most other respects the Squire's routine of living after Anne's
death was ascetic. Besides water he never drank anything but "excessively weak" tea with much sugar but no cream. He went to bed
about nine o'clock, and invariably lay on the floor. His only covering was a "far-worn cloak" and "a napless blanket," while "his
pillow was a slightly hollowed-out beech-wood block." There was
one occasion when the wooden pillow was not used. For some Watertonian reason, when he was aboard ship he always slept on deck and
then used his "velvet cushion," which consisted of "the outward
soles of his strong shoes, which were furnished with a profusion of
strong nails." When at home, so Dr Hobson tells us, the Squire was
invariably up by half-past three, when he lit a fire, and worked at
"some natural history pursuit" until eight. At this point Dr Hobson
characteristically breaks off and forgets to give us the rest of the
Squire's day, being somehow diverted into a discussion of *The
Testimony by Milton, and also by Ovid, to the beneficial effects of
Sleep,* and thence to other topics. Luckily, Norman Moore has left
us a less flighty account of the Squire's daily habits, but this belongs
to a later period of his life.

It is Moore also who has preserved for us a significant piece of
traditional gossip about the Squire's reaction to Anne's death:

"Grief overpowered her husband, and for a week he spoke to no
one. Religion gradually brought comfort to his mind, but he never
sufficiently forgot his sorrow to be able to talk of her. He put up
over the mantelpiece of the usual sitting-room a picture of Saint
Catherine of Alexandria, which had some resemblance to her; and
when he sat with his eyes fixed upon it, or was lost in reverie, those
who were nearest to him knew what was in his thoughts."

Incidentally, it may be noted that his private chapel was dedicated
to Saint Catherine. But where did he get this picture of the Saint

which resembled his wife? Strange to relate, the first item of news
we learn about the Squire after this desolating episode of Anne's
death is the extraordinary announcement that on his return from
a trip to Germany he bought a collection of one hundred and forty-
eight pictures at Wurzburg.

Why did he do that? The story is partially told by the Squire
himself in a pamphlet (published in 1855), entitled *Catalogue of
Pictures at Walton Hall near Wakefield*. The Squire had been stay-
ing at Huttenheim on a visit to a Mr Forster, secretary to the Prince
of Hohenlohe, who was sponsoring a miraculously cured nun. It
was possibly from him that the Squire heard of an old Bavarian
gentleman, named Berwind, who owned a collection of pictures.
Herr Berwind courteously permitted the Squire to see them, and
informed him that they were for sale as a collection, but not in
separate items. After looking at them in the morning, the Squire
returned for another inspection at four o'clock, and "ere the sun
had set, I became the purchaser of his collection."

Now, this is certainly far from being the maddest of the Squire's
freaks, but as related is surely one of the most unaccountable. If he
had been an æsthete, a connoisseur, an ardent collector of Old
Masters, there might have been some consolation to a broken-
hearted widower in acquiring a hundred and forty-eight pictures.
But until this moment his interest in painting had been severely
limited, hardly extending beyond the portrait of himself by Mr
Peale of Philadelphia, to the battle of the cayman, and the portrait
of the Nondescript by the ever-memorable Jones. It may be that
the Squire found in this collection the Saint Catherine picture re-
sembling his wife, of which Moore speaks, and that rather than
lose it he bought the whole collection? That would have been a
truly Watertonian gesture, and otherwise there seems not even a
Watertonian reason for this sudden purchase of a hundred and
forty-eight dubious Old Masters. True, the catalogue contains no
separate St Catherine, but number 91 appears as: "The Holy
Family and St Catherine by Otto van Veen," but Moore speaks
only of "a saint's head."

There are some Watertonian attributions in this collection, for
among others it contained pictures by Paolo Veronese, Rubens,
Vandyke, Wouvermans, A. van Ostade, Cranach, J. B. Tiepolo,
Agostino Caracci, Holbein and Michelangelo. Quite a bargain!
And the impact of this on the small but choice collection already
hung at Walton Hall makes curious reading in the catalogue:

Before the Squire and his new art gallery had reached home, he contrived to involve himself in another of those nearly fatal accidents which he had either avoided since his return from Guiana in 1825 or (more likely) has omitted to record as too commonplace and repetitious. This was nothing much, a mere brush with death in the somewhat unexpected form of a battle in the streets of Bruges. After the French revolution of July 1830, the Belgians—then part of the kingdom of the Netherlands—revolted against the authority of the Dutch king. On his way home the Squire stopped at Bruges to visit the convent in which the Edmonstone girls had been brought up. Hearing musketry fire, he could not resist going into "the large square" to see what was going on, and with his usual tact placed himself between the opposing forces. "I thought," he says cheerfully, "that I might as well live to see the row another day," and accordingly tried to take refuge in an open doorway, only to have the door slammed in his face by a fat old woman. "Thank you, old lady," he says he said; "Felix quam faciunt aliena pericula cautam." How he got away he forgets to tell us, being obviously in a great hurry to finish off this section of his *Autobiography*. For some reason he forgets the years 1830–37, and in their place inserts a defence of his veracity in the *Wanderings*, followed by an earnest plea to Protestants to join the one true faith:

> *I pray for those who now have got*
> *A creed infected with the rot,*
> *And wickedly have set at nought*
> *That which our ancestors had taught.*
>
> *I pray for those who, having thrust*
> *Our holy altars in the dust,*
> *Defiled the places where they stood*
> *With crazy tables formed of wood.*
>
> *I pray for those who, having slain*
> *Our flocks that grazed the peaceful plain,*
> *Did force their pastoral defenders*
> *Into Jack Ketch's hemp suspenders.*

I also pray for those who made
A tyrant king the Church's head;
And let him waste our sacred treasures
'Mid rogues and knaves, in filthy pleasures. . . .

And so forth. Just how charitable the Squire really felt when praying for his enemies may be judged from his dealings with Audubon, Macgillivray, Swainson, Rennie and everyone else who either questioned his omniscience as a naturalist and his pre-eminence as a taxidermist, or published results at variance with his own views. This is illustrated by the very first use he made of an invitation from R. C. Loudon to contribute to the *Magazine of Natural History,* which he received just before he set out on the "saunter" to see the miraculous nun, and this ended in his buying a picture-gallery. His earliest contribution to that periodical—or at any rate the first of the reprints included in the *Essays*—is an attack on Professor Rennie. What had the Professor done to arouse the Watertonian wrath? Well, in bringing out a new edition of an *Ornithological Dictionary* he had quoted some of the Squire's remarks on the humming bird, and had acknowledged them as coming from "the eccentric Waterton."

As I write I have before me more than one early edition of the First Series of Waterton's *Essays,* and every one of them on page iv gives those fatal words the prominence of a footnote all to themselves. *"The eccentric Waterton"*—just that, and nothing more. For my part, while acknowledging the heinousness of the offence, I have always felt that the professor meant no harm. He was, I imagine, a mild, overworked man with a large family and myopia, and in discharging his underpaid editorial duties, thoughtlessly used the academically accepted cliché: "The eccentric Waterton." Now, it is no use for us to beat about the bush and to try to pretend that the Squire was not eccentric. Of course he was eccentric; we should not love him if he had not been eccentric. That "eccentric" was unintentionally a compliment. What says William Blake? "Listen to the fool's reproach! it is a kingly title!"

Very likely these professionals, who had to work for their living, had got into the habit of using "eccentric" as a sneer to soothe a little their envy as they reflected that the Squire had an ample un-earned income which permitted him to go anywhere he wanted when he wanted, and to publish any nonsense he liked with im-punity, or not to publish at all if he chose. However that may be,

Professor Rennie's "eccentric" galled the Squire exceedingly. It gave him, he said, "no other sensation than that which a man experiences when he receives a pinch which he knows he does not deserve." And, by way of revenge, the Squire writes a review of the Professor's book in which he rudely disables the Professor's judgment in that delicate matter of the incubation of water-fowl. Would he have taken the trouble to do this if he had not wanted to be revenged for that "eccentric"? He resented it and Swainson's remark about "dressing truth in the garb of fiction" far more than Macgillivray's sneer that the Squire was "a carrion crow." But then Waterton had a fondness for carrion crows, and frequently served them to his friends as rook pie—even to "two convalescents"—exulting secretly as they placidly ate the food they would have rejected with horror if they had known what it was.

This offer from Loudon's *Magazine* to print the Squire's contributions was a godsend. It was not only that the work provided a real distraction from his grief or even that it gave him opportunities for carrying on the quarrels with other naturalists which occupied so much of his attention. The *Wanderings,* in spite of the critics and their own shortcomings, had in them so much that was lively, quaint and amusing that their success with the public had been durable; and any author who has once successfully "tasted ink" is easily persuaded to return to the bottle. Waterton was eager to do so, and needed only a pretext. The writing of the first series of *Essays* and of the section of the *Autobiography* which accompanies them must have amused his leisure during the seven years preceding their publication in book form. How successful these *Essays* were as they first appeared is pleasantly illustrated by a remark of the Rev J. G. Wood. When he was living in Oxford, he says, the Ashmolean Society regularly received the *Magazine of Natural History,* and "I used to watch impatiently for each successive number, in the hope that it might contain an article from Waterton's pen."

The subjects of the Squire's controversies in Loudon's *Magazine* and in American periodicals are not without interest, yet hardly likely to be very entertaining to modern readers. In too many cases they were animated more by vindictiveness and wish for personal victory than by disinterested love of scientific truth, though the Squire had this merit—he appealed to his own first-hand experience out-of-doors while his opponents often could only appeal to the authority of books. As he said of Rennie, that evil perpetrator of the insulting "eccentric," the professor was better educated in books than in bogs—and in a discussion of the habits of marsh birds knowledge of bogs was the more important. The strong personal feelings evoked in the Squire by these polemics frequently produced an acrimony which fringes the absurd, when you consider that the fiery arguments raged about such important topics as whether the Squire was or was not an "amateur," whether vultures find their prey by sight or by scent, whether Audubon's rattlesnake in the Mocking Birds plate was or was not correct in its delineation of the snake's right fang, whether a Salempenta should or should not be scientifically called *Teius teguexin,* and so forth. The heat radiated by the combatants was excessive. But then, like most exacting critics, the Squire was sensitively restive as soon as his critical methods were applied to himself. As Dr Hobson has already told us and repeats more than once, the Squire was noticeable for his "excessive degree of sensitiveness and susceptibility" and "his unfortunate tendency to too readily 'champ the bit.'"

A better use of Loudon's *Magazine* was shown by the essays putting forth the Squire's views on the protection of wild birds. In essay after essay he published arguments now almost universally accepted in English-speaking countries, but then so far ahead of the time that they were ranked among "Waterton's eccentricities." He pleaded for an end to the brutal indiscriminate slaughter of wild birds, saying that some supposedly noxious birds were in fact either harmless or positively beneficial to mankind, and that others, which admittedly did harm for a few weeks of the year, made up for it by their services during the remainder. The pleasure of having birds close at hand, living fearlessly close up to the house (he argued), more than made up for their depredations; and if they carried off his spring chickens and ducklings or thinned his early peas and cherries, well, he "grudged them not." Even as early as 1833 he appears to have made one very distinguished convert. In that year Alfred Tennyson wrote:

> O blackbird! sing me something well:
>   While all the neighbours shoot thee round,
>   I keep smooth plats of fruitful ground,
> Where thou mayst warble, eat and dwell.
>
> The espaliers and the standards all
>   Are thine; the range of lawn and park:
>   The unnetted black-hearts ripen dark,
> All thine, against the garden wall.

It must not be supposed that after Anne's death the Squire subsided wholly into an unadventurous life of sedentary and literary occupations. He was constantly at work on his land, on such jobs as "helping a man to stub some large willows" or (as in 1828) building refuges for wild ducks and other water birds to nest in. During the year 1834 he began to rebuild his semi-ruinous outhouses, "an immense pile, composing an oblong square of forty-five yards in length, and thirty-six in breadth," not counting the "dog kennel, fowl-house, sheds and potato-vaults," all of them swarming with rats and mice, in spite of the much-boasted extirpation of the Hanoverians from Walton Hall. It was about this time, too, that he discovered with much pleasure a new way to combine ornithology with the risk of a broken neck by having himself lowered over Flamborough Head for the eggs of guillemots and razorbills, and down the Raincliffe (July 1834) for the eggs of cormorants. His experiences are graphically described in essays which have already been quoted here for their diatribe against the slaughter of birds. With the passage of time the Squire lost none of his old whimsical mannerisms in writing. Indeed, they rather grew upon him, as may be judged from his peroration to an essay on the cormorant:

"Stay here, poor wandering mariner, as long as it pleases thee to do so. The sight of thee puts me in mind of the happy hours I spent in reading the *Metamorphoses* at the Jesuit College. Well do I remember how beautifully the poet tells thy affecting story, before thou wert reduced to the necessity of diving for a livelihood. I do not care if thou takest all the eels in the lake. Thou art welcome to them. I am well aware that thy stomach requires a frequent and a large supply. So, pr'ythee, help thyself."

Even with these diversions and the stimulus of an occasional "saunter" through Belgium and Holland, the Squire was not content with his life. He "sighed for the comforts of a warmer sun," and would indeed have started out in 1839 on a long trip through the south of Europe but for the fact that his distinguished American friend, George Ord, "the accomplished biographer of Wilson" (and enemy of Audubon), announced that he was coming on his promised visit to Walton Hall. The trip abroad was postponed, and under the stimulus of this good news the Squire found energy to finish the long-protracted work on his outbuildings. Having accomplished this task to his satisfaction, he penned the following odd boast:

"When I am gone to dust, if my ghost should hover o'er the mansion, it will rejoice to hear the remark, that Charles Waterton, in the year of Grace 1839, effectually cleared the premises at Walton Hall of every Hanoverian rat, young and old."

As this was the third time that he had "permanently" got rid of his Hanoverians, it is natural to wonder whether after all further campaigns may not have been needed against these tough and ugly customers. The use of arsenic against the rats seems to have brought up the old topic of curare poison and its possible use as an antidote for hydrophobia. The suggestion that curare might be an antidote for hydrophobia was not a mere whimsy of the Squire, as modern writers assume, but a serious suggestion from the head of the London Veterinary College. Mr Sewell was wrong, of course, but not absurd. In those pre-Pasteur days hydrophobia was incurable; Sewell, like others, had seen that the disease is accompanied by dreadful paroxysms, while the Squire's experiments had shown that curare has "sedative and narcotic qualities." Therefore, argued Sewell and the Squire after him, curare might prove to be a remedy, while "if the worst come to the worst," it would at any rate "render death calm and composed, and free from pain."

It will be remembered that after the curare experiments on the donkey in London in 1814, the resuscitated animal was named Wouralia and taken to Walton Hall. There she died in February 1839. Almost at the same moment a Nottingham police-officer, making his night rounds, heard the yelping of a dog trapped in a hole underground. Very unwisely this tail-wagger's friend did not wait for daylight, but went at once to the aid of the frenzied dog, which promptly bit him in the nose. Six or seven weeks later the unfortunate policeman developed hydrophobia, and the entire medical faculty of Nottingham had to admit defeat. At the last moment, when it was already too late, even if curare had been an effective remedy, the doctors called on the Squire, who promptly rushed intrepidly to the rescue; but when he came tearing up with his wax-coated ball of "wourali," all was over for the policeman.

Soon after this the Squire was persuaded to repeat at Nottingham his donkey-poisoning experiment of 1814, in the presence of the Nottingham doctors and with "my worthy friend, Mr Sibson" presiding over the fatiguing but indispensable bellows. Two asses were stabbed, and the first one proved to be a very strenuous business indeed for worthy Mr Sibson, who had a solid seven hours at the pumps before the donkey recovered—and even that was illusory, for it died three days later. "The second case," says the Squire, "occupied a much shorter space of time, and was quite successful."

Inevitably this repetition of the grotesque curare experiments on donkeys suggests the majestic influence of Dr Hobson. Writing just after the Squire's death, Dr Hobson says they had been friends for "close on thirty years," and from the Squire's own description of how he called in Dr Hobson to cure his dysentery on his return from Italy in 1842, it is certain that by then they were already close friends. Their first acquaintance could not have been later than 1839 or much before 1836, and must have been somewhere between those dates. Of course the Squire may have met Dr Hobson along with the "Nottingham faculty" over the 1839 experiments, but it seems far more likely that it was Dr Hobson who staged the whole thing. He practised in Leeds, and it was certainly he who in later years staged the famous demonstration of rattlesnakes. Knowing how much the Squire's vanity was delighted by a little innocent showing off, Dr Hobson was happy to arrange for meetings of "professional men" who could henceforth testify that the Squire's tales about curare and snakes were true. And this was an important service, if you consider how much the Squire's accuracy and veracity had been questioned.

With all deference to Sir Joseph Banks, Sir Norman Moore, the Rev J. G. Wood, the Jesuit Fathers and Daddy Quashi, the most remarkable of the Squire's friends and the most congenial to his spirit was certainly Dr Hobson. Since the days of Robert Burton, few writers have been so lavish of Latin tags as these two Yorkshire cronies, and Dr Hobson's *Charles Waterton, His Home, Habits and Handiwork* is by a miracle of literary good fortune the perfect complement to that golden document, the *Autobiography*. It is true that these excellent men, especially the physician, rudely dispel any lingering illusions that a classical education produces correct writers. Long ago the disputes of philologists proved that a profound knowledge of the classics often fails to make men more humane, more tolerant and more serene. But there was still a belief that drilling in the classics saved even amateur writers from some of the worst and commonest faults, such as slovenly and inconsequent construction, obscure and incoherent expression, prolixity, mixed metaphors. Alas, they are all horribly present in Dr Hobson's writing, as they are to a less extent in the Squire's. Dr Hobson offers his reminiscences of the Squire without any order, in a series of disconnected "bits" thrown together at random. He is monstrously prolix, and mishandles the language in grievous fashion. Consider, for example, this stupefying sentence:

"I quarrel not with any opposing party-spirit, from whatever cause it may emanate, nor even with a jaundiced or malevolent eye, if such should prevail, nor with any diversity of opinion that may be entertained; indeed, it would be unreasonable in me to calculate upon casting my net with such exquisite skill as to secure every variety of fish by a single draught."

Even that fades into insignificance, and becomes almost lucid and elegant, when compared with the peroration in which the doctor terminates his biographical labours:

"All our grief, however, will not restore to us the loss of that for which we vainly mourn. Submission to the fates decreed is, or, at all events, ought to be, on all occasions, our sheet anchor, and although 'lowering our flag' is seldom an agreeable act, yet it may be a politic and just one. Humanly speaking, we find it difficult to train our unwilling minds to kiss the rod that inflicts the scourge of heart-ache, and, even under wholesome correction, to bravely but patiently meet and endure the worst, yet, after all, the only legitimate, and, I may truly add, praiseworthy remedy we possess is 'to stoop to conquer.' "

Yet, in spite of such gongorisms, Dr Hobson had the seeing eye, and has noted many interesting traits and "habits" of the Squire which others suppressed or failed to note. For instance, it is to Dr Hobson that we owe—among other valuable information—the description of how the Squire used to pretend to be a dog, and rush out growling to bite his friends' legs. It was Dr Hobson, and Dr Hobson alone, who illustrated the Squire's "remarkable suppleness of limb, and elasticity of muscle" by the now famous anecdote of his scratching the back of his head with his big toe. Then, it was Dr Hobson who watched with intense interest as the almost octogenarian Squire "bounded in one of his jocose moods" over "a stout wire fence," which, when scientifically measured by the doctor, turned out to be exactly three feet six inches high. And it was Dr Hobson who can still awake in us his own breathless suspense as he watched his venerable friend

". . . hop on one leg along the brink of a rock forming the highest terrace in the grotto, whilst the other leg was dangling over the chasm below; and, when thus hopping, at a rapid rate, he would whirl himself entirely round in the air, and, dropping on

The Grotto in the Grounds of Walton Park

Funeral Boats on Walton Hall Lake

Reproduced from the issue of the Illustrated London News, dated June 17th, 1865.

the other foot, would return again by hopping back on the contrary leg."

Not to multiply instances, let us be satisfied with one more Hobsonian masterpiece—his account of how the non-eccentric greeted his medical friend when he drove over from Leeds for dinner and a "confab":

"In order to manifest his warmth of heart and a welcome reception to his friend, the Squire would, on my arrival, even in the most boisterous weather, or in the depth of winter, nay in a snowstorm, come out to meet me at the bridge, without hat or any other covering on the head, although his hair was always cropped as short as the most dexterous expert in the hair-dressing line was able to cut it. He would frequently come out to welcome me, even in his slippers, and prove his pleasure to receive me by actually dancing down the whole length of the broad flagged walk, occasionally throwing one of his loose slippers from his foot high up in the air above his head, and expertly catching it in its descent. The wetness of the flags underfoot, or a shower overhead, never constituted any impediment to an exploit of this character with Mr Waterton, when he was even approaching his eightieth year."

XII

MR. GEORGE ORD had returned to Philadelphia, and Dr Hobson was busy among his patients; no more experiments in poisoning donkeys with curare were for the moment called for; all available trees and precipices had been repeatedly climbed and descended; so there was really nothing of importance to hinder the Squire from accompanying his heir on the grand tour. A captious or Swainsonian critic might perhaps ask whether a child of ten, as Edmund was in 1840, could be expected to make the best use of an experience reserved by all other fathers for their sons after they had completed their University years. Doubtless the Squire had his Watertonian reasons for this reversal of the accepted rule—besides, he was extremely anxious to make the trip himself.

It must have been well worth while to see this expedition start off from the Hall. The time was the spring of 1840, and probably the ponderous travelling carriage with the Waterton arms on the panels was still obligatory. There, by the stables on the other side of the iron bridge, they must have assembled as the last bags and parcels were stowed away; the Squire as usual gave his last solemn charge to the gamekeeper ("to protect all hawks, crows, herons, jays and magpies as he valued his place"); the Miss Edmonstones were handed ceremoniously to their seats; two servants scrambled into the dickey; the coachman called to William to "run 'em out"—and they were off on the long road that led to Rome.

This was the longest and most ambitious of the Squire's saunterings in Europe, and we may guess how much he enjoyed it from the fact that his account of the journey occupies a disproportionately large section of his *Autobiography*. There have been many more or less "mad" Englishmen who have made this tour. By an odd coincidence in this very year 1840, the greatest of English æsthetic travellers, John Ruskin, set out for Rome with his parents, having obtained a year's respite from Oxford. A comparison of Ruskin's tour with Waterton's cannot fail to display the happy diversity of human character. Unfortunately, they did not meet, but one cannot help speculating whether the unpublished jottings of other travellers may unconsciously have recorded some aspect of the Squire's party as they jogged gravely across Europe, from one collection of stuffed animals to another, from holy church to miraculous relic. Among all the mad English travellers, Waterton is unique in the fact that for him the grand tour was almost wholly confined to birds and bigotry.

They started off by way of Hull to Rotterdam, and there, through the offices of "an honest tar," the Squire found in a "house for poor decayed sea-captains" the skipper who had taken him to Spain nearly forty years before. The Squire always concealed his charities, but we may be sure he did not start for Holland until he had done what he could to make this old friend comfortable. Holland reminded the Squire of Demerara and of how "British mis-government" had driven the industrious Hollanders from that former Dutch territory into Surinam. Turning to more serious topics, the Squire proceeds: "The Stork is carefully protected in Holland." He discovered a bird-merchant who had some good specimens of wild fowl, but the museum of zoology at Leyden was "wretched in the extreme"; "the Japan monsters" at The Hague were so "clumsy" the Squire was convinced he "could do better work" with his left hand. Moreover, the wicked change of religion (he does not tell us who was "the royal goat" of Holland) had left the Dutch churches in a state of "nudity and gloom."

He was glad, then, to move on to Belgium, which had kept its churches more or less intact, and the Squire noted with glee that whereas there were no Protestant English in Holland, they swarmed in Belgium—to look at the churches, according to him. In proof of this he cites one cultured Englishman who boasted that he had "knocked off thirteen churches that morning." The Waterton party had stopped at Amsterdam to look at pictures, but Antwerp was made far more memorable by the presence of the renowned Mon-sieur Kats, who "had succeeded admirably in breeding and rearing the summer duck of Carolina," and in addition owned a priceless "baboon from the coast of Africa." Naturally, Bruges could not be passed without a visit of the whole family to the convent so bound up with memories of Anne. And here the Squire fell into the sin of covetousness, for he admits frankly that he longed for two pictures, one "of a boy laughing at his own performance on the fiddle and . . . a representation of a dead bittern suspended by one leg in the Academy of Arts."

At Ghent the Squire brooded mournfully over legends of the "half an ox" he believed had been boiled daily by the monks for the poor in a "huge cauldron called St Peter's pot"—a custom discontinued, in spite of the fact that Belgium had not been corrupted by wicked Protestants. He praises the Béguines, and naturally they remind him of Corporal Trim, while he cannot see Dendermond without tender thoughts of my Uncle Toby and Lieutenant Lefevre, "the most feeling and pathetic story ever told by the tongue of man." The party then sauntered on to Aix-la-Chapelle (afterwards a favourite resort of the Squire, second only to Scarbro' in his affections), and this spa provided him with material for moral scoldings on the topics of gambling and high living, compounding, like the rest of us, for sins he was inclined to by damning those he had no mind to. Perverse indeed must the visitors to Aix have been to indulge in these vices when "kind Providence has afforded" the town "an inexhaustible flow of salubrious water." From the disgusting spectacles of gastronomy and gambling the Squire turned to the more "salubrious" company of two ravens and a willow-wren he found in the suburbs.

Thus they loitered away the summer, but eventually "old Boreas" drove them south, along the Rhine to Strasbourg and "Freyburg," where they found a talented German waiter who had written a poem in English on the cathedral—a precious relic which the Squire unhappily lost in his shipwreck. The Alps he crossed on foot, in the hope of seeing some of "our rarer European birds," but, as was to be expected at that time of year, he saw no birds whatever. On entering Italy Miss Helen Edmonstone remarked "with a considerable archness of countenance" that she was "sure we are in Italy now," and, looking up, the Squire saw "a matronly looking woman with her fingers in full chase among the long black hair of a young damsel." In a similarly arch but prolix manner the Squire concurred, and in that modest tone which has endeared the British tourist to the whole world. There were no vermin in the slums of Wakefield.

Naturally the Squire bitterly laments the filth of Italian hill towns, but does admit in a manly way that "at a distance, the appearance of the Italian towns and villages, surrounded by olive groves and cypress trees, is perfectly enchanting." On the other hand, "there was nothing in any of the museums" to show that they had reached the taxidermical standards of Walton Hall. A slight consolation was that in Bologna he saw "two male turkeys with a very thick and long tuft of feathers on their heads." Florence was a sad failure. All it had to offer was a bird and a mouse, a piece of heart and liver, supposed to be "petrified," but in the Squire's view "probably hardened by corrosive sublimate." He "left the room with disappointment" in his looks.

And now we approach one of the most notorious of the Squire's many misadventures. I do not refer to the interesting fact that on the road from Florence to Rome he saw very few birds, nothing but some coots and crows, "a heron or two," and "a noisy blackbird." No, I am thinking of his entrance into Rome. "Having been accustomed to go without shoes month after month in the rugged forests of Guiana, I took it for granted that I could do the same on the pavement of his Holiness Pope Gregory the Sixteenth." Rising at the usual Watertonian hour of three in the morning, the Squire roused his friend, Mr Fletcher, and together they started to walk the last twenty miles of the way from Baccano to Rome—of course in the dark, the Squire of course barefoot, with his shoes and socks in the pockets of his greatcoat. Gossips later asserted that this barefoot pilgrimage was an expression of the Squire's ultra-Catholic piety, but this he strenuously if not truthfully denied, claiming that he did it only for "easy walking and self-enjoyment"—a rather flimsy plea since, on his own showing, he had not walked barefoot since he left Guiana fifteen years before.

It was a frosty night, the pavement was hard and rough, and all went well for several miles, but when ". . . we halted to admire more particularly the transcendent splendour of the morning planet, I saw blood on the pavement; my right foot was bleeding apace, and on turning the sole uppermost I perceived a piece of jagged flesh hanging by a string." Now is the moment to brace the nerves, for "seeing that there was no chance of replacing the damaged part with success," the Squire "twisted it off." Naturally, Mr Fletcher was "horror-struck" and very sensibly suggested that they sit down and wait for the carriage. But the Squire had no intention of enduring that humiliation. Asserting that "the pain would be excessive as soon as the lacerated parts would become stiff by inaction," he crammed his feet into shoes, and—will it be credited?—the rest of the way to Rome was "a very uncomfortable walk," as well it might be considering that even "the sound foot . . . had two unbroken blisters." Only two months of lying on a sofa—the Squire's one concession to physical disability since his mute pledge to Anne kept him out of all beds—were needed to restore him to walking health.

Nearly a quarter of a century had passed since the celebrated

Jones and Waterton duo had delighted the Roman populace and
annoyed the Holy Father by their unauthorised climbing of St
Peter's and the Castello. There was a moment, probably soon after
his recovery from this dramatic entrance into the City, when the
Squire was sorely tempted to renew this climbing of Roman build-
ings. It happened thus. The family lodged in the Via de' Due
Macelli, which runs from the foot of the Spanish Steps towards the
Piazza of the Holy Apostles. Not far beyond that, and close to the
Palazzo Venezia, is the Church of the Gesù, where Waterton heard
Mass every morning at the crack of dawn. Passing the Church of
the Apostoli one morning he saw a Solitary or Rock Thrush (the
Passer solitarius of the Psalmist) fly from the Palazzo Odescalchi to
the belfry. Later on he saw it nesting "only a few yards from my
window," in the upper part of the Collegio di Propaganda Fide.
The Squire "longed to get it," but, instructed by former experience, he sadly refrained, as he reflected that "the Romans would not
understand my scaling the walls." Not to end this story unhappily,
let it be added that he found the bird nesting abundantly "in the
stupendous ruins of the Baths of Caracalla" and in the Colosseum.
"It lays five eggs of a very pale blue. They much resemble those of
our starling."

In Rome Waterton spent his time between the bird market and
the churches, particularly in the Gesù, and disdained to renew acquaintance with the "galleries and palaces" whose transient attrac-
tions he had exhausted in the winter of 1817–18. Under date
December 1840, he wrote to Mr Ord of Philadelphia: "I go to the
bird-market at the Rotunda every day, and when I fall in with a
rare bird in good order, I buy it and take it home in order to prepare
it." After another page or more of the usual truculent sneers at
Audubon, Swainson, Jameson and Macgillivray, and a jeer at the
bird collection of the Prince of Canino (Charles Bonaparte), the
Squire concludes: "The whole of my time has been taken up, from
light till dark, in preserving birds, and in modelling the head of a
porcupine."

In those days Rome was a very good place for finding wild birds,
and to some extent still is. Unluckily for the wild birds, their æons-
old line of migration is along the west coast of Italy, where in spring
enormous numbers of many species of birds are trapped, snared,
netted and shot with ruthless avarice. Even in winter a century ago
the abandoned Campagna abounded in game and wild birds. A
footnote to the Squire's essay on The Roller lists the game and wild

birds he found in the Roman bird market during a single season. It is a good deal longer than Dr Hobson's list of all the species of birds recorded by the Squire during a lifetime of observation at the Walton Hall bird sanctuary. Collecting these birds from the "bird-men"—"at first they were shy with me, but as we got better acquainted, nothing could surpass their civility"—pleased the Squire far more than "ferreting out antiquities and visiting modern schools of sculpture and of painting."

Except for his 4 a.m. Mass in the Gesù, the Squire seems to have given his attention rather to the bird market and bird-preserving than to the many church festivals which occur in Rome. Yet there was one annual celebration which the Squire certainly would not have missed even for the sake of securing a new bird. Between January 17th and 23rd (in those days, at all events) the animals were brought to be blessed at the Church of Sant' Antonio Abbate. This saint was the celebrated hermit of whose legendary temptations in the Thebaid so much has been written, and not—as might be supposed—the Portuguese Sant' Antonio di Padova who preached to the fishes. Why the much-tempted Antony became the patron saint of animals is variously accounted for, but the ceremony of the annual benediction must have been curious and picturesque—certainly enough of an oddity to delight the Squire. The ceremony began with the peasants' animals and continued throughout the week, ending up with the blessing of horses belonging to the Pope and Roman nobles. Naturally enough, during the ceremony the Squire got into an acrimonious argument with an English Protestant who denounced this blessing of the animals as "superstitious folly," while the Squire furiously maintained that it was "an act replete with Christian prudence."

During the summer the whole family made an excursion to Naples, and on his way there the Squire was happy to see "more birds . . . than I had observed in the whole of the journey from England." This put him into such good humour that at one moment when they were "resting the horses at a little inn by the side of the road" he felt impelled to enrich the world with yet another Watertonian jest. Near at hand he saw "a very large herd of Italian buffaloes," wild-looking animals, and was warned by some Italians not to go near them, as "they would gore me to death." Here was a challenge not to be refused. Having marked a couple of trees to which he could retire if necessary, the Squire started towards the animals, and "they all ceased eating and stared at me" in a threatening way which would have been infinitely alarming to the average urban person. But not to the Squire, who was fully equal to the situation:

"I immediately threw my body, arms and legs into all kinds of antic movements, grumbling loudly at the same time; and the whole herd, bulls, cows and calves, took off as fast as ever they could pelt, leaving me to return sound and whole to the inn, with a hearty laugh against the Italians."

The reason for making the journey to Naples in the hot months when everyone else avoided it was not so much to see the wild birds as to be present at the annual miracle of the liquefaction of St Gennaro's blood, which is scheduled to take place on the 19th September. It was a show dear to the Neapolitan populace, who could be excited into rebellion by a judicious withholding of the miracle, and who showed their edification when it happened by noisy demonstrations of happiness, including bottles of gunpowder, which at the joyous moment were "religiously popped."

No unlettered peasant could have been more impressed than the Squire, who first kissed the case containing the phial, and then the phial itself once every hour for five hours after the blood had liquefied, which miracle occurred "precisely at a quarter before two in the afternoon." After calling upon the testimony of Sir William Hamilton to the efficacy of St Gennaro in arresting eruptions of Vesuvius—the honest Squire evidently mistook the old *philosophe's* irony—he winds up his description of this exciting day with a passionate declaration:

"Nothing in the whole course of my life has struck me so forcibly as this occurrence. Everything else in the shape of adventures now appears to me to be trivial and of no account. I here state, in the most unqualified manner, my firm conviction that the liquefaction of the Blood of St Januarius is miraculous beyond the shadow of a doubt. Were I to conceal this my conviction from the public eyes, I should question the soundness of both my head and heart, and charge my pen with arrant cowardice."

So that settles it. Yet who, more than the Squire, better illustrates Napoleon's dictum that from the sublime to the ridiculous is but a step? His next recorded adventure, told at tedious length, was a futile squabble on a stercoraceous theme, involving the false but obstinately pressed charge of a Neapolitan sentry that the Waterton horses had sullied the precincts of St Elmo's castle and therefore must pay a fine, while the Squire as vehemently persisted that the culprit was not his horses but "a moderately sized jackass." Finally, they sent for the officer commanding the guard, and he "with a look full of good-humour to the ladies," accepted their explanation and bade them continue their drive.

Their next excursion was a trip to Sicily, which in those days could be uncomfortable, not only from bad food and crude lodgings, but from the bandits still surviving from the epoch of the Napoleonic wars. It was not the bandits, however, but the officials of the passport office who picked the Squire's pocket and roused in him his customary rage against the petty sharking official. Taking advantage of a flaw in his passport—probably put there intentionally to afford a pretext for insulting and robbing a foreigner—the Sicilian bureaucrats amused themselves by sending him from one office to another, making him wait in the heat of burning sun, and mulcting him of various fees. Little else was recorded of Sicily. Like the rest of his countrymen, the Squire was duly shocked by the exhibition of mummified human bodies in tattered finery. Indeed, most Europeans would have shared his feelings of horror and amazement that a Christian people could endure to parade the corpses of near relatives in such a manner, but only he could have enforced the lesson in taxidermy implied:

"These shrunk and withered remnants of former bloom and beauty brought to my mind the exhibitions of stuffed monkeys which we see in our own museums. . . ."

Soon after this experience the family returned to Rome, and a period of eight or nine months "went smoothly on" with little or nothing of Watertonian interest. Little Edmund was much noticed, and every effort was made (as it turned out, with complete success) to impress indelibly on his mind the seal of the one true faith. The Squire busied himself with preserving "a fine gobbo, or white-headed duck," together with "a very handsome red-crested duck" and "a Roman lizard, very difficult and tedious at the tail." Altogether during his Roman sojourn the Squire "preserved eighty birds, a porcupine, a badger, some shell-fish, and a dozen land tortoises," all of which were fortunately sent overland to Livorno when the time came for them to leave.

And here, just as the Squire leaves the City, we come upon a problem—did he or did he not have an interview with the Holy Father? Among his many non-eccentric points the Squire had determined never to occupy any of the decorative official posts in England, because he disapproved of the national religion. Thus, there was no official uniform he was entitled to wear. Another wise decision was his irrevocable refusal ever to wear evening dress. And so, in 1817–18, he had been compelled to abandon his hopes of a papal audience, for Vatican etiquette was as rigid as the Squire's prejudices, and insisted on either evening dress or something which might pass as an official uniform.

Now, once again, he was leaving Rome, after a residence of nearly eighteen months. Was it fair that so zealous, perhaps over-zealous, a son of the Church, one who had refused everything "genteel and confidential" for conscience' sake should go away without the consolation of an interview which was granted sometimes even to wealthy heretics? According to modern writers, the Squire never had his interview; but they have overlooked a passage in Wood's memoir which seems to imply that he did eventually see the Pope, through a stratagem which must have been devised by wiser heads than the impetuous Squire's. According to Wood, someone among the Squire's friends recollected the Demerara commission of 1808, when, as history gratefully records, "he carried Lord Collingwood's despatches up the Orinoco." Had not even the Demerara militia a uniform? They had, but unluckily the Squire had not brought his with him. Whereupon, some of the Squire's friends in the Royal Navy, said to include Captain Marryat, improvised a Demerara militia uniform from the Squire's usual blue coat with gold buttons, enhanced by naval epaulettes, and the sword and cocked hat of a Captain in the Royal Navy. Some joker urged the Squire to complete this remarkable costume with a pair of spurs, but this he rejected, ever anxious to shun the ridiculous, and reflecting perhaps that he must kneel to kiss the Pope's foot and that at such a memorable moment an entanglement with spurs was to be avoided.

Pope Pius VII (Chiaramonti), the pontiff who had been so much scandalised in the winter of 1817–18 by the climbing of St Peter's, was no more. It seems possible that the Holy Father's just displeasure over this freak may have accounted for Waterton's not being presented to him, and not so much the difficulty over a suitable costume. The Pope who received Waterton, if Wood's evidence is accepted, was his third successor, Gregory XVI (Capellari). Though such interviews with exalted personages must necessarily be brief and formal, the pontiff must have heard tales of the Squire, and he was always so wholly himself that perhaps they got at once beyond the banal and conventional. If they conversed in Latin, as they assuredly would, did His Holiness understand the Stonyhurst pronunciation? What did that urbane and lettered prelate think of this weird member of his vast flock? What did they talk about? Would the Pope have understood the Nondescript, the Nightmare, Mrs Bennett the rumpless fowl, the other strange actors in the Waterton saga? We shall never know. But that some such interview did take place seems definitely implied by Wood's phrases, slightly ambiguous as they are.

The Waterton party started on their return journey to England from Rome in the middle of June 1841. They had decided to make the journey from Cività Vecchia to Livorno by ship, and went on board the *Pollux*, a "steamer of two hundred horse-power" at 4 p.m. on June 17th. (The Squire, it will be noted, for once is most punctiliously accurate about dates and times.) The weather was "charmingly serene," but the Squire "remarked" (or rather afterwards said he remarked) "a want of nautical discipline" on the ship. Luckily for them, they all slept on deck, the Squire having in his pocket "Mr Macintosh's life-preserver," while his cheek rested on "the velvet pillow" of nail-studded shoe soles.

"Suddenly our sleep was broken by a most tremendous crash." They had collided with another small steamer, the *Monjibello*, bound from Livorno to Cività Vecchia. The *Monjibello's* bow smashed into the Watertons' after cabin, and would probably have killed all those who might have been sleeping there. Its bowsprit hit the *Pollux's* funnel, and knocked it overboard. In a second all was panic and confusion. The Squire, having coolly collected his family, inflated and put on his life-preserver (he says nothing of theirs) and "entreated them to be cool and temperate." Instantly they "obeyed me most implicitly," for Edmund fell on his knees and prayed fervently to the Blessed Virgin, while Miss Edmonstone "kept crying out in a tone of deep anxiety, 'Oh, save the poor boy, and never mind me!' "

They were saved, in point of fact, by the Napoleonic action of Prince Canino, who happened to be on board the *Monjibello*. As soon as the collision occurred, he rushed aft, knocked down the steersman, took the helm and prevented the two ships from drifting apart. This action undoubtedly saved the lives of the *Pollux* passengers, for their ship was sinking fast, and their only hope was a swift transference to the less-injured *Monjibello*. The Squire, "confiding in the valuable life-preserver," remained on the *Pollux* almost to the last, though he very nearly perished in the desperate clasp of a "fine young German woman" crazy with terror, who threw her arms round him and refused to let go. In the end all were saved but one man. Now came the question of what was to be done with the injured and overcrowded *Monjibello*? The accident had occurred just off the coast of Elba, and Prince Canino, relying on his prestige as a Bonaparte, directed that the ship should make for Portolongoni, never doubting that permission would be at once granted to land the distressed *Pollux* passengers, all of whom were suffering more or less from shock, while some had on nothing but their night clothes. The Prince had reckoned without the bureaucrats. The *Monjibello*'s ship's papers named its ports as Livorno and Cività Vecchia, and the port lunatics insisted on sticking to the letter of the documents and forced the leaky, overcrowded ship to return to Livorno. When they at last reached that port, only the wrath and insistence of Prince Canino saved them all from twenty days of close imprisonment in quarantine!

According to the Squire, the whole blame for this accident lay with the captain and first officer of the *Pollux*, who were sleeping below when it happened. The captain rushed on deck in such a panic that he did not even wait to put on his trousers, but saved himself in nothing but his nightshirt. The Squire had instantly made himself medically useful on the *Monjibello* by setting the dislocated shoulder of a priest, and was then called to prescribe for the *Pollux* captain, whom he found "sighing, sobbing, and heaving like a broken-winded horse." The Squire was asked to bleed him, but so great was his wrath with this "dastardly *sans-culotte*" (as he pleasantly nicknamed the trouserless captain) that he denied himself even that exquisite pleasure, and merely recommended that the captain should be "taken on deck and drenched well with sea water." Nor did this (if it was carried out) serve to appease the Squire's wrath, for on the way north he took a Watertonian revenge by writing the following poem in an inn album:

> *The* Pollux, *once so fine,*
>   *No longer cleaves the wave,*
> *For now she lies supine,*
>   *Deep in the wat'ry grave.*
>
> *When she received her blow,*
>   *The captain and the mate*
> *Were both asleep below*
>   *Snoring in breechless state.*

If I the power possess'd
I'd hang them by the neck,
As warning to the rest,
How they desert the deck.

Our treasures, and our clothes,
With all we had, were lost.
The shock that caused our woes
Took place on Elba's coast.

The losses were serious enough, coming as they did close upon a bank failure which cost the Squire and his sisters-in-law eight hundred pounds. The eighty birds, stuffed porcupine, lizard and all the rest were safe, but the party lost their letter of credit, cash, English passport, diaries, books, a holy relic from the catacombs, an ivory crucifix, various "objects of art," and the "costly wardrobes" of the ladies.

Nor was this the end of their vexations. At Basle, on their melancholy way home, in spite of warm letters of recommendation from Prince Canino and Prince Torlonia, the churlish Swiss banker refused to advance the Squire any money; and he was only released from this unpleasant position by a loan from—of all people!—the brother of that pestiferous Whig, Lord Chancellor Brougham. And then, just as the Squire was quitting Italy, his philanthropic instincts urged him to enrich his native land with the gift of a dozen live civetta owls. This bird had long delighted him by its interesting behaviour; for "standing bolt upright, it curtsies incessantly, with its head somewhat inclined forwards, while it keeps its eyes fixed on the approaching object." How natural then the conclusion that "the civetta would be peculiarly useful to the British horticulturist." But tragedy lurked for these gifted owls:

"All went well after this, until we reached Aix-la-Chapelle. Here, an act of rashness on my part caused a serious diminution in the family. A long journey and wet weather had tended to soil the plumage of the little owls; and I deemed it necessary that they, as well as their master, should have the benefit of a warm bath. Five of them died of cold the same night. A sixth got its thigh broke, I don't know how; and a seventh breathed its last, without any previous symptoms of indisposition, about a fortnight after we had arrived at Walton Hall."

The Squire was ever unlucky with hot baths. That 1824 bath in

New York had resulted in a temporary condition of tuberculosis. This one resulted, not only in the unhappy fatalities to the owls, but greatly aggravated a dysentery which the incautious saunterer had picked up in Italy. Unfortunately, arrival in England did not put an end to this distressing state of health, and the Squire's mind naturally turned Hobsonwards. But duty had first to be done and Edmund placed as a boarder at Stonyhurst, with written exhortations from his father which the Squire somewhat incautiously printed among his essays. Only when that obligation was discharged and the Squire had tottered home from Stonyhurst did he feel justified in calling for medical aid "upon my invaluable friend, the justly celebrated Doctor Hobson of Leeds." Then began a mighty contest. As befitted so good a friend and so conscientious a physician, Dr Hobson instantly drove to Walton Hall, yet "such was the invincible composure of his countenance" that none of those present could guess whether he thought the Squire was seriously ill or the reverse. With reinforcements from "our worthy family surgeon, Mr Bennett," the doctor seemed to have compelled the dysentery to yield to "the masterly arrangements of this renowned" practitioner. It was but a temporary victory, lost through the Squire's imprudence:

"On one cold and frosty morning I had occasion to cut away the shoots from certain stumps of trees on the bank of the brook. My foot betrayed me, and I slipped in the water up to the middle. As this accident had placed me in a more commodious position to trim the brambles on the sides of the brook I remained in the water for upwards of an hour. The dysentery appeared again, and again Doctor Hobson triumphed."

Once again the triumph was short-lived. The dysentery returned, and now for the third time it yielded to Hobson and yielded for ever. If we may judge from what the physician has himself recorded, the Squire was very ill during at least one of these attacks, since "for a lengthened and intensely anxious period he lay in an utterly helpless, hopeless, and totally unconscious condition, and for many, many hours, appeared to be hovering between life and death."

XIII

IT was "on the 10th of May, in the year of our Lord, 1842, there being abundance of snails, slugs and beetles on the ground," that the Squire released the five surviving civetta owls from their cage, and turned them loose on his bird sanctuary. He was now within less than a month of his sixtieth birthday. Inevitably the circle of life began to narrow for him once more as it had narrowed in 1830 with the birth of his child and death of his wife. Wanderings had now long been abandoned, and henceforth even saunterings were greatly reduced, almost limited to Scarborough and Aix-la-Chapelle, except when some attractive miracle demanded a longer pilgrimage, such as that 1844 journey to the Tyrol, which he prolonged to Venice, Rimini and Rome. There were still adventures, quarrels and accidents ahead of him, but more and more his life tended to centre on Walton Hall and its park, which in these latter years reach their full rich development as manifestations of their owner's personality.

It is the tendency of biographies to end in "a cloud of anecdotage." This may be deplorable, but is unavoidable if you consider that most lives are prolonged beyond their period of maximum activity to an epoch of reminiscence and anecdote. A great life suddenly cut short, like Byron's at Missolonghi, permits the biographer to avoid this unravelling of the threads of action and personality into little stories. But when a man lives to be over eighty, even one so original, so physically strong and active and so vitally interested in his pursuits as the Squire, there cannot help but be a fading away into routine and small talk. Moreover, it is especially during these last years that any man of mark makes his third-generation friendships, and it is from their admiration—so much more disinterested than the blame or praise of his contemporaries—that we learn something of the personal traits and doings which bring a lost character back to a shadowy life in the imagination. But the Squire did not meet even Hobson until he was well over fifty, while Moore and Wood—more discreet though less racy—did not come on the scene until years later. Thus, their detailed memories refer only to the Squire in his old age—they knew nothing of the young man who struggled with *vomitò negro* in Malaga or triumphantly rode the cayman in Guiana. And yet, though the Squire went through all the seven ages of man, he mentally remained all his life a schoolboy "with shining morning face." He had been a pickle at Tudhoe and Stonyhurst, and a pickle he remained until the end.

In most respects he hardly evolved much beyond the mental age of fourteen to sixteen. Consider, for instance, his attitude towards religion, natural history and literature, which were the chief interests of his life. How like a schoolboy he adopts and maintains the views and prejudices of his instructors. He shows his independence only by opposing their opponents. His attitude towards those who do not share his black-and-white prejudices irresistibly evokes the truculent schoolboy. "What's this? Protestants? Fellows not on our side? Let's jolly well lamm them one, and serve 'em right if it hurts." And again: "Swainson? Audubon? Closet naturalists who didn't agree with our side? Well, let's jolly well lamm them too." Instead of filling the margins and blank pages of grammars and histories with caricatures of old Queen Bess and Dutch William and old Lushington, the Squire worked with immense pains and skill to produce his taxidermical horrors from toads and lizards and monkeys. He made life an apple-pie bed for the infidel, and at eighty was still playing the practical jokes of eight. As an old man he may be found still quoting the Latin tags of his boyhood, and even then quoting them from the expurgated texts of his schooldays.

Even his sound belief that natural history is better studied out-of-doors than in the library and museum was due less to the scientific principles involved than to the simple fact that a schoolboy prefers to bunk about the fields and to climb trees rather than work in class. He had a telescope to watch wild birds, and deserves commendation for it, but he had no microscope to study details of structure. In many county families the hobbies of the boys included the catching and stuffing of fish, foxes, birds and insects. Where Waterton surpassed them was in doing it so well, with so original a technique, and, above all, by his evolution from a mere catcher and stuffer to the builder of his bird sanctuary. Yet even as an observer he had failures as well as notable triumphs. He was right about the sloth and the ant-eater and some of the English birds, but he was wrong about the skunk, the vulture and the Gibraltar baboons. Unfortunately, he was unable to learn from a rival, and was as violently assertive in defence of his blunders as of his discoveries.

A recent writer blames this on Stonyhurst, adding: "What does he know of any of those great landmarks like Homer or Dante or Goethe? He had been fed on orthodox pap, on Virgil, Dryden and other *safe* writers. . . ." The prejudice and absurdity of this are obvious. No public school in the 18th century gave instruction in Dante, and Goethe was then a contemporary author who had scarcely been heard of. As to Homer—I have before me the list of authors expounded by pupils at the Stonyhurst "public exhibition" of 1807 (the earliest extant), and they include Xenophon, Homer, Pindar, Sophocles and Demosthenes. The Squire knew no Homer because he did not take Greek. And it is curious criticism to complain that eighteenth-century Jesuits did not aim at turning out twentieth-century atheists.

The schoolboy quality of the Squire's humour and practical jokes is only too obvious. In his later years, that series of uncouth taxidermical jokes, "The English Reformation Zoologically Illustrated," became well-known and was visited by many people. According to Joseph Hatton, these included the Archbishop of Canterbury, but this is a little hard to believe. The series was constantly being developed:

"If there was an uglier monkey than usual in the menagerie-offerings which were made to him, he stuffed it to represent Old Nick, or labelled it 'John Knox.' Titus Oates, Cranmer, and Bishop Burnett were illustrated from reptiles of the lowest order. 'Mother Law, Church, and her Dissenting Fry' were made up chiefly of toads, and 'Queen Bess at Lunch' was an appalling combination of lizards and newts and other unhallowed things, such as might have strengthened the hellish mixture of the witches' cauldron in *Macbeth*. Beetles and flies, as emblems of the devil, bore their part in this strange medley of polemics."

This primitive humour extended from the Hall to the park. Inside the house was the human headed tortoise with an enormous weight on its back, labelled "John Bull and the National Debt." In the park, a filbert tree, sprung no doubt from a nut dropped by some rodent, grew up in the centre hole of an abandoned mill-stone, which the tree eventually raised several inches from the ground. It was of course also nicknamed "John Bull and the National Debt." Twelve trees were named after the Apostles, and a deformed one which groaned in high winds was of course "Judas Iscariot." Near the grotto was "another union at variance with the laws of nature," and this consisted of a spruce and an elm which had been made to grow twisted round each other. As the inevitable result was "a miserably stunted growth of both trees," the Squire exultantly named them "The Union of Church and State"—a polity he only approved in the Papal States.

As he got older the Squire's interest in Natural History tended to be concentrated more and more on what Dr Hobson calls "unique abnormities." This was not necessarily unscientific, for in biology study of the abnormal and the pathological has often yielded important knowledge on other lines. But the Squire disdained such study, and his interest was little more than a schoolboy's natural delight in freaks. His eagerness to show off any new acquisition of this sort was intense. He would send off at once for his "dear Dr Hobson," who would find the Squire "eagerly looking out . . . always on the tip-toe of expectation":

". . . The moment my foot overstepped the threshold of the entrance-hall door, his anxiety was manifested to introduce the subject of the previously noticed novelty—probably some unique abnormity in the animal kingdom or the feathered tribe might be prepared and conspicuously placed so as to create intense surprise or 'love at first sight.' . . ."

Dr Hobson's testimony is supported by other evidence of this love for "abnormities." On July 5th, 1842, the Squire wrote to Mr Ord: "I got, the other day, a milk-white hedgehog. It is a perfect albino with pink eyes." In his essay on the rook, the Squire diverges into a description of a crowing hen which he had "received with abundant thanks" from an old woman. These sex reversals in fowls are far from uncommon, but in the Middle Ages were looked upon with superstitious horror—the unfortunate bird was indicted for heresy and burned alive. The Squire had outgrown that phase of Merry Europe and highly prized such "abnormities." But though he describes them with quite scientific accuracy, he does not hazard an explanation.

Less amusing from the point of view of the victims to these pleasantries was the Squire's habit of naming his living bird freaks after his friends and medical advisers. Thus the name of "Mrs Bennett" given to the Squire's cherished freak, the rumpless fowl, came from his surgeon, Mr Bennett. This bird, so strangely truncated by harsh fate, was not "unique," and the Squire has pointed out, perfectly justly, that it is only a variety of the common barnyard fowl. "Mrs Bennett" was particularly dear to him, not only on account of her "abnormity," but because she proved a point which had been debated with much acrimony. According to the Squire's opponents, the oil-gland in birds supplied them with oil which they spread over their feathers with their beaks. The Squire had denied this. Now, Mrs Bennett had no oil gland, and yet her feathers appeared as sleek and oily as those of other birds. Her fate was that of many favourites. She was slain out of jealousy by a large Malay fowl, and the mourning Squire could do nothing but preserve her in his inimitable style. For years she had inhabited that "decayed edifice," the water-gate, which, in Dr Hobson's words, "afforded, for many years, a safe and unmolested retreat, and comfortable roosting-berths, for a beautiful rumpless fowl and his jet-black mate."

Another even more famous character in the Waterton saga is the duck, "Dr Hobson," which a recent writer has involved in much needless confusion. "Dr Hobson" was not hatched at Walton Hall, it was not a female bird, nor was "Dr Hobson" the duckling which was "hatched with its head reversed, having its bill, as regards its horizontal position, appearing and indeed actually situated immediately above its tail," so that when food was placed on the ground, behind its tail, this duck always had to seize it by turning a somersault.

"Dr Hobson," it is true, was one of this strange brood which were hatched in 1857 near the home of "the late Mr Ainley, Surgeon, of Bingley," a man "intrinsically shrewd and well skilled in ornithology." He mentioned the fact to Dr Hobson, who instantly urged that the ducklings should be bought for the Squire. When Mr Ainley went to buy them he found, to his disappointment, that he was "only just in time to secure a solitary male, the remaining number having been destroyed from a vulgar and superstitious idea . . . that, if anything assuming an unnatural or a monster-like form should be allowed to live, some bad luck would attach to the owner." This "solitary male bird" was "Dr Hobson," and had nothing abnormal about it except that it was "devoid of a particle of web between the toes." The duck lived at Walton Hall for over two years, and when it was somehow killed and found at the top of the weir, the Squire preserved it as a valuable gift for its human namesake.

Among other mis-statements about the Squire and his works is Norman Douglas's assertion that "the park contained an agglomeration of weird contrivances for catching this, and killing that." It is true that on one occasion—but only one—a gun-trap was set for a fox which had managed to scale the wall. And it is true that there were permanent traps for rats and mice. But otherwise all the "weird contrivances" were designed, not for "catching and killing," but for the fostering and preservation of wild life or the comfort of domestic animals. When the Squire rebuilt his outhouses, he added several devices and features which prove his warm if eccentric love of animals. The stables were re-designed in such a way that no horse was kept in solitary confinement in a separate stall, but so that "the horses could converse with each other after their work was over." The Squire was convinced that the pig is naturally a clean animal, and lives in squalor only because of human ignorance and laziness; and therefore arrangements were made to keep the new pigsties very clean. He believed that dogs are unhappy when deprived of a wide view, so he re-sited his kennels in such a way that "the hounds should be able to see everything that was going on." In consequence, it is said, Walton Hall was henceforth spared those dismal yappings and howlings which make dogs a public nuisance.

The Starling Tower was designed in such a way that neither cats nor rats could enter it to destroy the nesting birds. After much thought he worked out and had built a lofty dove-cote which kept the birds safe from rats and also from the more cunning human thieves, who stole them to sell to the promoters of pigeon-shooting matches. So successfully was this done that the Squire could report with pride how this single cote in one season provided him with 875 young pigeons. Again, it was contrary to his principles to prevent his cows from conversing with each other over gates, but as he found they would lean against them and break them down, he devised a protection by hanging a strong chain along the weaker side of the gates. As we have noted, the water birds were protected during the breeding season and after by a rigorous closing of the lake to fishermen and all boats. The Squire's jacket pockets were always kept filled with scraps of bread "for distribution to all living creatures" that asked for them, and he was "delighted" by the confidence of the wild birds which mobbed him as they begged for scraps and crumbs.

He cared little about his dogs. "I never knew him pay the least attention to them," says Dr Hobson. But he was devoted to cats. There was one cat nicknamed "Whitty," a "very beautiful and enormously large" cat which eventually weighed fully sixteen pounds. This cat was a great favourite, and was allowed an unlimited licence to poach. In a letter dated 1846 the Squire mentions another favourite cat, "Tommy Pussy," which, he says, had just brought him in "a half-grown rabbit." The Squire knew that well-fed cats make the best mousers, and the daily feeding of the cats was an event which is differently described by different authors. According to the Rev J. G. Wood, they were fed on fish caught in the lake, especially pike, which were chopped up on a wooden block near the stables. Although not a cat might be visible when the chopping started, half a dozen blows brought them swarming round like "alley cats round a cat's-meat man." According to Dr Hobson, who may be writing of what happened in Lent, the Squire would carefully collect in an old newspaper "scraps of fish and their bones" and take them to the saddle room. There he would pound the bones with a hammer, calling out, "My pretty, my pretty!" With this call alone he could at any time assemble "the whole feline retinue."

The Squire's benevolence was not limited to animals. His creed prescribed good works and alms-giving, and he was as scrupulous in carrying out these injunctions as in keeping Lent, hearing Mass and visiting holy relics. Because he kept literally to the Gospel injunction: "Take heed that ye do not your alms before men, to be seen of them," we hear only occasionally and by accident of one or two of his life-long charities. As a schoolboy he had given a beggar-woman all he had to give—a precious darning-needle which was invaluable to him for blowing birds' eggs. Even in his noble charity and material kindness there was still something of the schoolboy, as Dr Hobson unwittingly reveals when he boasts:

"Almost invariably, on my leaving the hall, when about to return home in the evening, I was sure to find my great-coat pockets well stuffed with apples, pears, filberts or some other fruit which might be then in season, whilst my carriage box was as repeatedly most liberally stored with cherries, eggs, and other edibles."

Only once or twice do we hear directly from the Squire of his benefactions. He tells us that the Second Series of his *Essays* was published as "an unsolicited donation to the widow of my poor departed friend, Mr Loudon." But there was an obvious reason for mentioning what he calls "this trifling present." It was made to advertise the widow's need, not the Squire's generosity. Sir Norman Moore says of him:

"His widespread charity was unostentatious. He never put his name to a subscription list, though he often gave, and he silently allowed himself to be abused for not contributing to a fund to which he was one of the largest donors. . . ."

The Protestant clergyman, J. G. Wood, pays him even more enthusiastic compliments which perhaps are a little gushing. This often-quoted passage is the basis for the panegyrics of Waterton as a "saint" and a "great gentleman." Here it is:

"It was perhaps eccentric to have a strong religious faith, and act up to it. It was eccentric as Thackeray said, 'To dine on a crust, live as chastely as a hermit, and give his all to the poor.' It was eccentric to come into a large estate as a young man and to have lived to extreme old age without having wasted an hour or a shilling. It was eccentric to give bountifully and never allow his name to appear in a subscription-list. It was eccentric to be saturated with the love of nature. It might be eccentric never to give dinner parties, preferring to keep an ever-open house for his friends; but it was a very agreeable kind of eccentricity. It was eccentric to be ever childlike but never childish."

Now, three or four of these statements are perfectly true, but the remainder, particularly Thackeray's, are either exaggerated or false. If we want something more than these vague laudatory generalities, we must apply to Dr Hobson's circumlocution office, which, however wordy and tedious, gives us facts—and facts which were all endorsed by the Squire himself in his eightieth year. Dr Hobson bears emphatic witness to his charity:

". . . Liberality to the neighbouring poor, of every political shade, and of every religious creed, was a marked trait in the character of this good and kind-hearted man."

When anyone in the district was too poor to pay for a doctor, the Squire paid Dr Hobson to go, and in addition supplied medicines and food. If "the patient could walk," he or she was fed in the servants' hall; if not, food was sent to the cottage. The sick were given bread, meat, milk and eggs; and "the needy" who were in health received "broken meats." "New shoes to the naked feet were seldom refused."

But, Dr Hobson laments, "Mr Waterton had an inordinate, and, I am sorry to acknowledge, in my opinion, an injudicious amount of credulity in his composition." Too often his generous kindness was abused by swindlers. Even in giving shoes to "naked feet" he had to devise a Watertonian scheme he hopefully believed would protect him from rogues. He ceased to give money to such applicants, but instead handed over a worthless old pocket-knife. When this was given to the local cobbler, it was a symbol which instantly procured the stranger a pair of shoes, for which naturally the Squire paid. Dr Hobson, who had heard of this odd proceeding, ventured to ask if the story were true, and instantly received this hearty answer:

"Yes, you have got the right sow by the ear. It is as true as that Pope Pius the Ninth is a holy man."

He then went on to explain why he had resorted to this device.

"Many years ago," the Squire related, "a miserable, half-starved-looking wretch, and apparently terribly footsore, met me near the village of Walton, and entreated charity in such a piteous tone, and in such apparently genuine humility, that my flinty (scientifically termed, siliceous) heart was softened—and having nothing less than half a crown in my pocket, I was speedily minus that amount. In the latter part of the day, on passing through Sandal, on my way to Wakefield, I accidentally came in contact with the scoundrel who had done me out of half a crown in the morning. Although very drunk, he recognised me by a most familiar 'How do you do, old boy? I owe you one; come into the public-house, and I will treat you with a pint of heavy wet, out of your own half-crown, as I have fifteen pence in button park yet.'"

Far from being touched by this rollicking mendicant's wish to share his good fortune with a benefactor, the teetotal Squire was much offended.

"This drunken exhibition so annoyed and so thoroughly disgusted me," he said, "that I set my wits to work to discover a better method of affording relief to the poor than by giving them money."

Hence the "dodge" of the pocket-knife, which the Squire seems to have thought was rogue-proof, without reflecting that a well-made pair of new boots could easily be exchanged by an unscrupulous thief for a good deal of beer. Even the astute and worldly Squire, backed by the subtle device of the knife, realised on one occasion that he had been nearly cheated—indeed, would have been but for his gamekeeper. One day, an "object of distress in the form of a man," had told his tale and begged for new boots so persuasively that the Squire was already fumbling for the knife, when his gamekeeper hurried up and whispered to his master that he had seen "the vagabond" take off and hide his own boots. At that very moment, the gamekeeper added, he had them in the game pocket of his shooting-jacket. Instantly the Squire replied aloud:

"Jack, do you think my shoes would fit this poor fellow?"

"No, sir," the gamekeeper answered, "yours won't fit him, but I have a pair in my pocket that seem to be about his size." Then, turning to the beggar, "Try them on these poor feet of yours."

Of course the beggar instantly recognised the old boots and "his countenance fell to below zero." The gamekeeper, with all that excessive zeal of reprobation felt by subordinates in authority for the unfortunate, wanted "to inflict summary punishment" with his dog whip. But the Squire, "begged the scoundrel off, substituting a threat to imprison him, if he should ever appear in the district of Walton again."

We owe our knowledge of another benefaction of the Squire to his inability to withhold from the world a typical example of his schoolboy humour. The Superioress of the Convent of the Good Shepherd at Dalbeth had written to ask, in right Scriptural terms, for "some of the crumbs which fell" from the Squire's table. Now this was touching a sore point, for the Squire was not rich as rich men went, and those confiscations by the "royal goat" always rankled. Naturally, you could not threaten the Superioress of a convent with a dog whip or imprisonment, so he replied in Watertonian terms as follows:

". . . All the crumbs which fall from my table are mortgaged to a huge Cochin-China fowl, which receives them in payment for awaking me by his crowing every morning at three o'clock. But as he does not feed on my cheese, I find that I can spare a mite from it. Pray accept it; and if you enter the trifling donation in your book, please put it down as coming from a friend. I always make this stipulation on similar occasions."

As the Squire hardened more and more into a "character" of something more than local celebrity, anecdotes clustered about him, and people came from afar to admire or to quiz him. It is hard to accept Wood's statement that the Squire was "utterly unconscious" of his eccentricities, that "he thought himself the most commonplace of human beings," and that "he had no idea that he was doing anything out of the general course of things if he asked a visitor to accompany him to the top of a lofty tree to look at a hawk's nest." This sounds more like hagiography than biography. A rather different impression comes from the Doctors, Moore and Hobson, and from the Squire's own writings and recorded sayings. If Wood had been literally exact and the Squire really was "utterly unconscious" of his own "abnormities," how is it that he penned this curious defiance and declaration to all "students of external anatomy"?

". . . I respectfully beg leave to inform them that I have been gifted by Nature with vast powers of leg and toe: I can spread all my five toes; and, when I am barefoot in the forest, I can make use of them in picking up sundry small articles from the ground. Having an uncommon liking for high situations, I often mount to the top of a lofty tree, there to enjoy the surrounding scenery; nor can I be persuaded that I risk 'life and limb' in gaining the elevated situation. *These, no doubt, are qualities and propensities aberrant from the true human type. . . .*" (My italics.)

Of course, the Squire was being sarcastic, but I detect a certain self-gratulation in that "aberrant." Obviously the Squire was admirably free from all forms of silly self-consciousness, but he would have been one of his own "jackasses" if he had not been conscious of his peculiarities and enjoyed the notoriety they brought him. He loved to tell anecdotes about the amusing situations arising out of his habit of wearing shabby clothes and shabbier hats. He was charmed when a new footman in the service of a neighbouring family showed him into the servants' hall and announced to the lady of the house that "an old man wished to see her." The Squire had another favourite story about a farmer who happened to meet him in Walton and, mistaking him for a labourer, said:

"Good morning, my man; can you direct me the road to the Hall belonging to Squire Waterton? I want to try to buy some wood of him, but they tell me he is a queer old chap if he happens to be the wrong side out; do you happen to know aught of him?"

This was an opportunity not to be missed, so the Squire (ever ready, at least in retrospect) instantly replied:

"Yes, I know him well. Indeed, no one in all the neighbourhood knows him so well, or is so much in his company as I am. He is as queer as Dick's hatband; you will have to get up early in the morning if you mean to get to the blind side of the old Squire."

"Well, this is a lucky hit," the Squire said the farmer went on, "you are the very man for me; come into 'the public' close by, and I will stand a pint of beer, and bread and cheese also, if you will make it worth my while."

The old vow to Father Clifford and his own consequence made the Squire decline to enter a public-house, but he advised the farmer to go to the Walton Hall woodman, and took care to meet the pair "accidentally" after the bargain had been completed. Of course the woodman respectfully saluted his master, and of course the "countryman" was filled with a laughable confusion when he "realised the mess he had got into."

If we may judge from the portrait of the Squire published in the *Illustrated London News* in 1844, he still wore in London his blue coat and gold buttons, with a black stock and decent top hat. Presumably he was thus dressed when he had the "most amusing adventure" in a railway carriage with "a very fine and portly-looking gentleman" and his "elegant daughter." The Squire was so much pleased with this tribute to his fame that he sat down instantly and wrote a full account of the meeting to Mr Ord in distant Philadelphia. The portly man, it appears, told the Squire (not knowing him from Adam) that "Waterton lived not far from Wakefield," in "a very curious house replete with most exotic curiosities, and with a moat round it full of most extraordinary reptiles." Waterton, he said, had been dead for four years, but had a son then travelling in South America.

"Ah," said the Squire, enraptured by all this garbling of fact, "Waterton must have been a blade. He has left us some tough stories in his *Wanderings,* too tough to swallow."

The portly one rose nobly to the bait.

"No," he said earnestly, "although I never knew Waterton, I am sure he was an honest man. I read his character in his works."

Of course the story ends with the Squire revealing his identity to the stupefaction of the portly one and daughter, who "stared like stuck pigs," and the intense satisfaction of the flattered Squire. But not all these stories of mistaken identity turned out so flattering to his self-esteem. There is for instance the story of the officers—a story too long-winded to re-tell in detail—who came to look at the Squire's pictures and began "actually quizzing him and indulging in rude and personal remarks." He thereupon sent them to the house of a neighbour to look at his pictures, and disguised himself to meet them in "a faded red wig—an old green shade over one eye —an eye-glass over the other—a thread-bare coat so stuffed as to give to his figure the appearance of a hunch-back—drab-coloured smalls, with white stockings—and a crutch used to *apparently* relieve a crippled limb." Thus disguised the Squire showed the officers round the pictures in his friend's house, making them admire bad pictures and censure good ones, while they kept on abusing "that old devil Waterton." When he "thought he had sufficiently gulled the would-be proficients," he revealed himself with a bow, saying, "Your humble servant, Charles Waterton."

"Their apologies," says Dr Hobson exultantly, "to their credit, were abject, and the verbal castigation they received from the Squire was as severe as it was merited, inducing those brave warriors to hand out the white flag, and humbly sue for peace."

What these "verbal castigations" could be when the Squire's vanity was really touched, as it was by the least criticism of his skill as a taxidermist, is shown by the story of "the man-milliner," a "self-opinionated and conceited young coxcomb" who had the impudence to doubt that the Squire was the greatest and most perfect taxidermist in the world, and even ventured to criticise his preserved peacock. It is true that the "man-milliner" spoke with an insolence and condescension deserving rebuke, particularly as he spoke to an old man in his own house. But the verbal bombardment he received certainly bears out Dr Hobson's statement that the Squire's rebukes were marked by "very energetic language and, occasionally, by a tartness and asperity of expression somewhat ungracious, and, unfortunately, also by a very decided insuavity of manner."

Here is what the Squire said to the "precocious and inexperienced popinjay" who had dared to criticise the mounting of his peacock:

"Sir, I should degrade myself by holding any cavilling argument with so mere a stripling as you, and, the more especially, as it is palpably evident, from your remarks, that your ignorance far outshines any ordinary qualifications which you may possess in the bewitching science of ornithology. Go home, sir, I beseech you, and carefully pore over some elementary A.B.C. work, relative to the anatomy of the peacock, and endeavour to ascertain *where* the tail of the peacock is situated, as, at present, your ignorance may constitute *self-bliss,* but it must give much pain to your friends if they happen to possess any knowledge whatever of natural history."

In controversy with other naturalists the Squire habitually indulged in an "insuavity" which can hardly deserve Thackeray's "saintly," and of a domineering assertiveness and rudeness which may be natural to "a great gentleman, one of a long race of untitled nobles," but are unacceptable to scientists, especially when he attacked men of reputation for supposed errors while making worse ones himself. A few quotations from his letters to Ord will show the feelings and language he indulged in:

"My former letter to him" (i.e. Swainson) "galled him tremendously, and pointed out to the public pretty clearly his lamentable ignorance of real ornithology. I was informed by our consul in Palermo that Swainson is about to settle in Australia, having offered

his museum for sale. He seems to be an utterly disappointed man."
(December 1st, 1840.)

"... Swainson, and Jameson, and Macgillivray, and all his other
supporters shall have their ignorance brought home to them. I will
prove their consummate ignorance. ..." (December 1st, 1840.)

"Cuvier, though a great philosopher, and a most honest gentleman, knew no more about the real habits of most birds than I did
about his grandmother" (January 30th, 1846.)

"And now let me request you must earnestly to write a critique
on Audubon's work. That ornithological impostor ought to be
exposed." (July 3rd, 1835.)

"So much for Audubon's drawing and Swainson's critique.
These two men ought to be whipped!" (July 3rd, 1835.)

"Your comments on Audubon's raven are admirable. He is indeed an arrogant fool! Only think of heaven imposing on such a
fellow the task of writing the history of your birds!" (July 3rd,
1835.)

"As for Audubon, of course, he will catch it to his heart's content; neither shall I let Sawney (i.e. Professor Jameson), with his
forty-three titles, escape till I have flayed him alive." (July 3rd,
1835.)

"Fearing that you might have a dozen of naturalists on your
back for daring to call in question the authority of Jenner, I have
already taken up the club on your side. ... The whipping which I
gave to Parson Morris in the magazine of this month ought to have
appeared in the one of last month. ..." (March 4th, 1836.)

Unluckily, the Squire was apt on occasions to behave as if
natural history in general and ornithology in particular belonged to
himself and his rather obscure friends, while nobody—even the
friends—could be anything but his inferior and pupil in taxidermy.
Perhaps this was true, but how unwise to proclaim it in language
so heated! The fact that he himself had suffered from the ignorant
disparagement of other writers when he published his *Wanderings*
should have made him more restrained and courteous when he criticised with such boisterous contempt the work of famous naturalists,
such as Audubon and du Chaillu. The Squire's attempt to criticise
Audubon's rattlesnake (in the *Birds of America*) is either dishonest
or very stupid, as anyone can see by comparing the criticism with
the plate. One is glad to note that the Squire was right when he
criticised the "Washington Eagle," but how much better if he had
remembered to say that he was informed of Audubon's mistake

by George Ord and did not discover it for himself. He could not possibly have known as much about the birds of America as Audubon, who gave up his life to the study, while the Squire at most spent a few weeks of sight-seeing in the United States. He was even more incompetent to criticise du Chaillu's account of the gorillas he was the first to find in Africa in their own haunts—the Squire never was in Africa and never saw a gorilla in a wild state. His controversy with Swainson receives this comment from a modern naturalist, Edmund Selous:

"For me, the most entertaining feature of the great Waterton–Swainson controversy is the equally assured and erroneous assertions —especially negative assertions—which each of the frowning champions makes in regard to the habits, powers and possibilities of the animal, or family of animals, around which it raged, and particularly the curious and interesting manner in which some of these *ex cathedra* cocksurednesses can be checked and their falsity exposed."

All this, however unpalatable, must be faithfully set down if we are to obtain a complete and honest picture of the Squire, and not merely another arrangement of freakish and saintly qualities. When Sir Norman Moore says that Waterton "flogged two generations of quacks" and includes among the "quacks" not only Swainson but Audubon, he spoke from the partiality of friendship and perhaps from ignorance. In later life the Squire tolerated no naturalists except those who came to consult him in the pleasing attitude of discipleship, and he was far too unyielding to learn anything from his superiors, such as Darwin, Wallace and Bates. This, of course, indisposed many good men, and in the long run meant that he was denied the just praise due to his unwearied observation, his courage and energy in exploring the jungle, his delicate methods of taxidermy, and his invaluable work as a pioneer in the creation of wildlife sanctuaries.

XIV

THE Squire's last years were comparatively tranquil, but, like their predecessors, were marked by interruptions, accidents and untoward events. One of these was the establishment of a "soap and vitriol works" close to Walton Hall, which brought destruction to its trees, polluted its waters, and came near to making a premature end of the park as a bird sanctuary. The soap-boiler appears to be that unpopular character referred to by one of Ruskin's correspondents in *Fors Clavigera*. He was an energetic man, who rose from humble circumstances to the ownership of a factory, and a typical example of the nineteenth-century industrialist pushing his own fortunes in complete disregard for public welfare and his neighbours. No capitalist was so ruthless as the enriched workman, and in the 1840s there were insufficient laws for the control of noisome and dangerous industries, so that this factory was permitted to pour out blighting fumes and poisonous waste products over land belonging to the Squire and others, with no redress but cumbersome and expensive and above all slow methods of legal action for committing a public nuisance. The Squire's trees died by scores, his cattle refused to drink from the poisoned stream, herons and other birds were diminishing, and even Miss Edmonstone developed, or thought she had developed, lung troubles.

This was an unlooked-for and unhappy threat to the work of a lifetime, with the first bird sanctuary in England threatened with partial or complete destruction. What made it the more exasperating to the justly incensed Squire was that the factory had been built on a paltry three roods of land, which at one time had belonged to the Waterton family and which the Squire for twenty years had been vainly endeavouring to buy back. It was unlike him to haggle over money when he really wanted something, so that the refusal to sell to him and then selling to an upstart may have been dictated by personal dislike and jealousy of the old gentry.

With so many motives for annoyance and impetuous action the Squire did not behave with his usual irascibility and haste. Perhaps he was sobering with age or perhaps he was influenced by the cooler judgment of his neighbour and fellow sufferer, Sir William Pilkington, with whom he was associated as joint plaintiff. Still, even Sir William could not prevent the Squire from privately calling their opponent "a fellow" and "this vitriol vagabond." According to Dr Hobson, the Squire had tried persuasion before going to law, perhaps on those lines.

The chief account of this law-suit is contained in a long letter to Ord, dated November 19th, 1848, when the law proceedings had still to go to appeal. Thus, if Mr Philip Gosse is right in putting the beginning of the nuisance as early as 1843, it lasted an intolerably long time. Naturally enough, in his account of the affair to his Philadelphian friend, the Squire is heartily and indignantly on his own side; but from the figures he gives it is impossible to agree that the arbitrator was such a scoundrel or his award so unfair to the Squire. From the Squire's own account this "unjust" arbitrator "doomed our adversaries" to pay £6,000, including "the *whole* of the expenses in the first suit." Waterton had claimed £2,200 damages, and was awarded exactly half that sum. But (says the Squire indignantly) the arbitrator "neutralised all this" by ordering Pilkington and Waterton together to pay one-eighth of the arbitration costs. These totalled £528, so that the Squire had to pay all of £33, leaving him a net award of £1,067. This was doubtless not so much as the Squire honestly believed he ought to receive, but it hardly justifies his saying of his £1,100: "I shall touch little, perhaps none of it, by his saddling me with a certain portion of the expenses," or that "arbitration law, nine times out of ten, is certain death to the breeches pocket," or that "surely grandson Jonathan can manage his lawyers better than his old, stupid, perverse and profligate grandfather Bull does." At this distance, and going only on the Squire's own account, one would say that the arbitrator acted very fairly, considering that on the other side (which the Squire never thinks of) were involved a man's whole capital, a necessary if noisome industry, and the living of his employees.

Whether driven out by the factory fumes or, as he says, by his own restlessness, the Squire and the Edmonstone girls set off in the autumn of 1844 on a "saunter" which took them to Rome by way of the Tyrol, Venice, Loretto and Rimini. Edmund is not mentioned, so presumably was left at Stonyhurst, being then about fourteen. In his *Autobiography* the Squire has not much to say about the Italian section of this journey, which for much of the way covered familiar ground. Between Pesaro and Ancona they had one of the familiar accidents to carriages, common enough at the time.

but fortunately nobody was hurt. One of their horses fell when they were "going at full gallop," and "in an instant, both itself and the off leader were on their backs." By good luck they just escaped "a total smash," and the Squire notes with satisfaction that the "two sisters behaved nobly . . . not a shriek, not a sigh."

There are a few zoological notes. They saw a civetta owl and a "young hero, who was wrestling most manfully with a jet-black half-grown pig," and noted the interesting fact that "cats were plentiful." But the Squire's travel interests were centred more and more on religion and miracles. It seemed to go along with his passion for "abnormities," such as the malformed duck and the sheep's head with a horn growing out of its ear.

By far the greater portion of the Squire's story of this saunter is taken up by an interesting account of his visit to a celebrated Tyrolese nun, called "the Ecstatica." His description shows how vividly he could write when he avoided petulance and Latin tags and Shandyean humour and other crotchets. True, the solemnly related episode of the Ecstatica handing out "holy prints" to the Squire and his sisters and the servants inevitably recalls Panurge consulting his oracles, but the account is written so accurately that it might almost be quoted as a clinical description of the case.

The journey to Rome is passed over in silence, except for the complaint that he saw practically no birds "from Calais to Rome." Nor does he tell us when the party returned to Walton Hall, but instead breaks out into a poem on Protestants:

> *Villains, bent on holy plunder,*
> *Strove to drive from Albion's shore,*
> *What had been her pride and wonder,*
> *For nine hundred years and more.*

During the course of this pious composition the Ghost of Queen Elizabeth is made to address the Anglican bishops in these terms:

> *Whilst you Bishops here are boasting*
> *Of the reformation-tricks,*
> *My poor soul is damned and roasting*
> *On the other side of Styx.*

It was in 1845 that Miss Edmonstone began to suffer from lung trouble and was ordered to Madeira by whatever doctor it was (probably Dr Hobson), who guessed that she wanted an excuse to get away from the factory fumes. The lungs cannot have been very seriously damaged, since the patient recovered before she even reached Madeira. There the sisters spent the winter, but the Squire did not remain in this "terrestrial paradise" for the excellent reason that there was "not sufficient in the bird line to give me an occupation for half a year."

With the passing of the years the Squire did not acquire the caution which might have spared him the accidents which had dogged him throughout life. Dr Hobson tells us of two accidents, one of which is confirmed by a letter from the Squire, unfortunately not dated in the printed version. Both accidents arose out of operations in the park. According to Dr Hobson, the Squire found a "specially favourite amusement" in "trimming his beautiful fences with a light hedging bill." (By "fences" the doctor must surely have meant "hedges.") On one such occasion, as was no doubt inevitable with him, the Squire "accidentally cut his foot very severely with this sharp hook." The surgeon began lecturing his patient on the "inexpediency and danger" of this rustic occupation, and then enjoined "absolute rest . . . and an elevated and horizontal position" together with continuous applications of cold water. When the surgeon made his call next day, he and the whole household suddenly discovered that the Squire had disappeared. He was at last found standing ankle deep in cold muddy water wielding his hedging bill. In answer to the surgeon's "respectful and really serious remonstrances," the Squire "gravely insisted" that he was only carrying out the medical orders given—he had cut a hole in his shoe to allow the cold water to reach the wound freely, and as "he was not walking, he contended that the limb was at rest."

This accident is evidently the one referred to by the Squire in his undated letter which goes on to say that as he had not been feeling up to the mark he had just "let out about five-and-twenty ounces of blood." The event was witnessed by one of the Jesuit Fathers, and "Warrener, my servant, was my cup-bearer, and in a pet I called him a noodles, and he said, 'He might well be one, as he had not never seen nobody bled before.'" Just a week earlier, the Squire adds casually, he had fallen off a ladder "in full twelve feet of descent soss upon the earth." Luckily this occurred in Lent, when the Squire was scrupulously fasting and hence "meagrely supplied within" so that he "literally bounced upon" his feet in "an instant, and then continued my occupation."

There is no recorded instance of the Squire suffering any tree

accident when climbing without a ladder, but in the winter of 1850
a second ladder accident was very nearly fatal to him. He had invented some sort of a "machine" (Wood, who tells the story, is
vague about this) which he used when pruning the higher branches
of fruit trees. "He had been repeatedly warned that the machine,
not having side stays, must fall if the weight were thrown on one
side." He was up twenty feet from the earth, and Edmund, after
repeated remonstrances, went away "saying he would not be res-
ponsible for an accident which he foresaw but could not prevent."
Our obstinate schoolboy of sixty-eight would not listen, but with
his usual obstinacy and self-confidence persisted in doing what he
wanted to do—with the inevitable result foreseen by everyone but
himself. Down he came—"soss"!—and this time with such a
crash that he was "partially stunned," while "the heavy ladder and
machine" fell on his arm and smashed the elbow-joint.

It is instructive to turn from Wood's to the Squire's own account
of this disaster. He was, he says, "correcting an over-grown luxuri-
ance in a tree" when "suddenly the ladder swerved in a lateral direction. I adhered to it manfully, myself and the ladder coming
simultaneously to the ground with astonishing velocity. In our fall
I had just time to move my head in a direction that it did not come
in contact with the ground—still, as it afterwards turned out, there
was a partial concussion of the brain; and, add to this, my whole
side from foot to shoulder, felt as though it had been pounded in
a mill."

The usual self-inflicted remedies were instantly resorted to, and
a blood-letting of thirty ounces was followed by "a strong aperient."
The Squire firmly believed that this would have put all to rights,
in spite of the badly smashed arm, but for another accident which
occurred almost immediately afterwards. To suit his crippled state
the Squire (for some exquisite reason) had dressed himself in a
Scottish plaid, and thus attired sat down to dinner. During the meal
the plaid "went wrong on the shoulders," so the Squire stood up
to put it right. The servant waiting on him thought he meant to
leave the table and silently pulled away his chair. Whereupon the
Squire, without looking round, fell into his own booby-trap and
"came backwards to the ground with an awful shock."

The result of these twin mishaps was truly dreadful. "Symptoms
of slowly approaching dissolution now became visible," the Squire
sent for his lawyer and his confessor and prepared himself for death
"with Christian resignation,"

And here I must interrupt this narrative to point out in connection with these two almost fatal accidents that neither the Rev J. G. Wood nor Sir Norman Moore mentions the fact that it was Dr Hobson's devoted care which saved the Squire's life. When Moore reproduced the greater part of the Squire's narrative, he cut out all mention of his professional rival. Thus, from the Squire's own account of these proceedings, Moore omits these sentences:

"My affectionate sisters, ever on the watch, had telegraphed Dr Hobson of Leeds, their sole remaining hope; whilst my son had taken his departure for a dear friend. The doctor, on his arrival, exerted his giant powers with wonderful precision, ordering the immediate application of leeches and blisters to the head. This masterly practice made death surrender his devoted prey; for although . . ."

After silently omitting that tribute to Hobson, Moore continues as in the Squire's version: "But although I lay insensible with hiccups and subsultus tendinum for fifteen long hours . . ." breaking one of the Squire's sentences in half to avoid giving Hobson any credit. From Moore's version the reader would think the Squire "arose" without any medical aid at all.

The surgeon whose job it was to deal with the broken elbow was less successful. The Squire lived in constant pain and began to suffer from bad nightmares. "I was eternally fighting with wild beasts, with a club in one hand, the other being bound up at my breast. Nine bull-dogs one night attacked me on the high-road, some of them having the head of a crocodile." Ever an advocate of extreme medical measures, the Squire now seriously thought "of having the arm amputated." He had actually decided on this drastic remedy when luckily he listened to the words of wisdom of his gamekeeper:

"Master, I'm sure you're going to the grave," he began gaily. "You'll die to a certainty. Let me go for our old bone-setter. He cured me, long ago—and perhaps he can cure you."

Anything out of the ordinary routine was sure to attract the Squire, and instead of dying or having his arm off he agreed to an interview with the bone-setter, and fixed it auspiciously for Lady Day. The diagnosis, if accurate, reflected no credit on the Wakefield surgeon, for said the bone-setter: "Your wrist is sorely injured: a callous having formed between the hand and the arm. The elbow is out of joint, and the shoulder somewhat driven forewards."

The Squire's stoical courage in enduring the tortures inflicted

upon him by "Chiron the Centaur" (as he instantly nicknamed the
bone-setter) would have befitted a Red Indian or some more than
usually defiant victim of the Spanish Inquisition. During fourteen
days the Squire cheerfully suffered the "potent embrocations,
stretching, pulling, twisting and jerking" held necessary to force
"the shoulder and the wrist to obey" the bone-setter. The elbow
then called for three weeks of "greater exertions and greater attentions." And at the end of these five weeks of torture, the bone-
setter retired with the ominous threat, "I'll finish you off this
afternoon." And a less robust and determined person might easily
have been "finished off" by the next proceedings of this rustic
Torquemada:

"Laying hold of the crippled arm just above the elbow, with one
hand, and below it with the other, he smashed to atoms by main
force, the callous which had formed in the dislocated joint; the
elbow itself crackling, as though the interior parts of it consisted
of tobacco-pipe shanks."

During this agonising ordeal the Squire neither moved nor
uttered a sound. When at last it was over he cheerfully handed his
friendly tormentor an extra five-pound note, and calmly awaited the
return of health and a quiet mind. "Here I am just now, sound as
an acorn."

These ladder accidents and their sequel have carried us ahead in
time of yet another of these disasters. It was one of those events in
which religious obligations were nicely balanced. If he had not gone
to Bruges to witness the procession of "the holy blood of our
Redeemer," he would never have fallen into the sea; but then if
he had not been wearing the "miraculous medal of the Blessed
Virgin" of whom he had repeatedly "asked the favour that I might
not die a sudden and unprovided death," he would have been
drowned.

The Edmonstone ladies had already gone to Bruges, and the
Squire followed them alone, without even Edmund or a servant to
take care of him. It was a very dark night when he reached Dover,
and asked a porter the way to the Belgian boat. "You have only to
cross the little bridge close by here, sir," said this emissary of the
powers of darkness, "and you will be on board the Belgian steamer
immediately." The Squire thanked him, and, clad in his "Italian
cloak, with an umbrella in one hand and a little portmanteau in the
other," stepped on to what he thought was the temporary gang-
way. "O horrible mistake!—I was in fact on the very confine of

the basin—and at the next step, I sank overhead in the water, after having dropped down some fifteen feet."

A plunge into icy water, in darkness, and in that plight, would surely have daunted any but a hero. Even the Squire, who had somehow contrived to get himself under the paddle-box, was on the point of giving up and sinking "through excessive cold and numbness" when the holy medal went into action. A voice with a Belgian accent called: "Courage, and I will save you!" The Squire was hauled aboard, taken on deck "soaked and shivering," and then conducted by two friendly police officers to the "Dover Castle Inn," then kept by a widow Dyver—which the Squire thought an exquisitely appropriate name at that juncture.

As always, the Squire slept on the bedroom floor, but on waking noted from certain "hints from within" that his ducking might have evil consequences. Instead of postponing his journey and resting, as might have seemed prudent, he instantly made up his mind to continue his journey to Bruges. He could have no doubts about his inner condition when he reached that journey's end, for he arrived suffering from "heats and shiverings alternately accompanied by cough and oppression at the chest." This was on the very eve of the procession, which he was determined not to miss. The Squire, having refreshed himself by letting twenty-five ounces of blood, spent four hours with the procession, returned to his hotel, swallowed twenty grains of jalap and ten grains of calomel—and survived.

Little of interest occurred to mark the many little jaunts to Scarborough and Aix with which the Squire amused his old age. Christmas he always spent at Stonyhurst, since the care of Edmund's education had renewed the Squire's familiarity with his old school. It is said that he always managed to amuse the boys each year by some surprising and original feat, such as walking in on his hands instead of on his feet.

Old age did not in the least impair the Squire's unique powers of engaging the affection of animals and of handling the most dangerous snakes with impunity. During a visit to Scarborough he formed a friendship with a young female chimpanzee, named Jenny, belonging to Wombwell's circus. The Squire made a number of observations on this ape, including the important one that she was dying of tuberculosis. When he said farewell, he and the chimpanzee "exchanged soft kisses," and he then privately begged Mrs Wombwell to send him for his museum the body of his friend as soon as she died. Poor Jenny expired sooner than her mistress had expected, and she was "wrapped up in linen by way of a winding sheet," put in a trunk, and forwarded to Walton Hall. Unluckily, the messenger got very drunk, the delivery of the body was greatly delayed, and . . . but let a veil be drawn over the horrid results.

The story of Jenny is related by the Squire in his curious rather than definitive essay on *The Monkey Family*. In the same work he tells us about his encounter with an orang-outang in the Regent's Park Zoo. In this case he was fortunately able to demonstrate publicly his unique abilities and courage in tackling animals and at once making friends with them. This ape had been dangerously angered by the teasing of "a young stripling of a coxcomb," but, though warned of the danger, the Squire fearlessly entered the cage and began examining the animal's hands and teeth. To the amusement of the onlookers, the orang insisted on making a similar examination of the Squire, to which he cheerfully submitted. What else went on can only be guessed from the Squire's reticent statement: "It were a loss of time in me, were I to pen down an account of the many gambols which took place between us."

It will be recollected that the arrival of a live sloth at the London Zoo had given the Squire something of a triumph, by demonstrating that his account of this strange animal was true. A quite unforeseen visit to Leeds of nearly thirty live rattlesnakes now gave him a chance to show that he did actually possess the art of handling venomous reptiles—which the closet naturalists had for so long affected to doubt.

We have two first-hand accounts of this famous display, one by the Squire and one by Dr Hobson. In the main they agree, though Dr Hobson's is the more detailed and lucid. A travelling American was showing his rattlesnakes to pay for a tour of England, and when he arrived in Leeds an idea struck Dr Hobson. He was always eager to advertise his friend the Squire and his doings, and therefore suggested to his professional colleagues that the Squire should be invited to a séance to study and compare the effects of curare poison and rattlesnake venom.

Accordingly, the Squire, the American and about forty doctors met at Dr Hobson's house, together with the rattlesnakes, the curare poison, and numerous live rabbits, pigeons and guinea-pigs. For some reason, the Squire's version omits to mention that these creatures were to be poisoned, and he merely says that the rattlesnakes had to be moved from one box to another. Dr Hobson's story brings up the Squire's part much more strikingly. Before ever the experiments were begun, they struck the apparently insuperable objection that neither the American nor anyone else dared to hold the snakes for them to bite their victims. It was at this moment of frustration that the Squire, from being a mere spectator, stepped forward and became the chief actor in the show by quietly volunteering to handle the snakes.

"Instantly there was breathless silence, when the Squire, on raising the lid of one of the compartments, in the coolest manner possible, fearlessly but gently introduced *within the case his naked hand,* keeping his eye intently fixed on the snake he intended to secure, and in this unprotected state grasped the venomous monster immediately behind the neck, and deliberately removed him from his neighbours, which were loudly hissing and springing the rattle all around his hand. The lid being again closed, Mr Waterton held the rattlesnake in his hand whilst it bit the pigeon, the rabbit or the guinea-pig, and then, on the lid being gently re-opened, he dexterously replaced the snake among his congeners."

A dramatic moment occurred when one of the snakes suddenly made a dart for liberty, and got half-way out of the box. At this most unwelcome apparition the entire medical faculty was seized with dismay. All but Dr Hobson fled out of the room, while "several not only rushed downstairs but even into the street without their hats." With great judgment Dr Hobson instantly but gently pushed down the lid just as the Squire withdrew his hand, and caught the snake firmly but not too hard at its middle. "Mr Waterton, who was as composed as if nothing particular had happened, promptly laid hold of the enraged reptile," held it round the neck and put it quietly back in the box. Could there have been a more convincing and spectacular demonstration of his skill and courage, or that his stories of his encounters with snakes were true?

It is perhaps an anti-climax to mention that their repeated experiments showed that curare poison acted more quickly than rattlesnake venom.

To Dr Hobson we are also indebted for the record of an interesting and pathetic scene with the Squire which occurred in the grotto "many years" before his death. The two friends were watching birds and "musing on the varied character of life" when abruptly and for no apparent reason the Squire's expression changed to one of "unusual gravity" deepening to "intensity of despair." On being questioned, he explained that he was haunted by fears of what would happen after his death to his "vast and varied handiwork." The collection might be dispersed or destroyed, the bird sanctuary violated, all his experiments in taxidermy wasted. As the Squire talked Dr Hobson saw with amazement that tears were running down his cheeks—a thing which the doctor never saw before or after during all the thirty years of their close friendship. From this the doctor inferred that the Squire's distress "must be roused by some additional suspicion betraying a want of confidence in the future, or by some mortification mixed up and amalgamated with his favourite natural history labours." In other words, the Squire by now had come to recognise that Edmund had no interest in his father's life work, and would care nothing about maintaining the collection in the Hall or protecting the bird sanctuary and all its devices for fostering wild life.

Dr Hobson's account of the Squire's daily routine is most fortunately supplemented by descriptions of his habits in old age recorded by Wood and Moore. Both of them, writing after the Squire's death—and not during his lifetime as was the case with Hobson—naturally tend to tone down his eccentricities and to smooth away or to ignore his undoubted "insuavities." Take, for instance, the Squire's kindly habit in old age of throwing open his park to picnic parties, which even included such unusual guests as the inmates of the Wakefield Lunatic Asylum. For Norman Moore all is *couleur de rose*. The Squire was "singularly unselfish," and the visitors invariably well-behaved—"honour proved a more efficient guard than many policemen"—and to show their gratitude these parties gathered before the house on leaving and sang, "The fine Old English Gentleman." But, Dr Hobson hints, the Squire in old age somewhat affected popularity and, enjoying his reputation, was unable to refuse permission to parties "even of dubious cast" who "vociferously and fulsomely flattered his open-hearted generosity." And so far had this amiable weakness got hold of him that, far from the parties gathering before the house, it was the Squire who invariably contrived to stroll out at the appropriate moment for the band to strike up "The fine Old English Gentleman." As to Sir Norman's statement that no damage was ever done by these parties, the fact is that soon after his father's death Edmund Waterton withdrew the permission because the damage culminated in the destruction of one of the fine yew hedges by fire.

The Squire's daily routine remained virtually unchanged until the end of his life. He always, even when over eighty, slept on the floor or sitting by a table, wrapped in an old cloak and blanket, with the familiar wood block as a pillow—of oak says Moore, of beech says Dr Hobson. He nearly always went to bed at about 8 p.m., rose at midnight for a short prayer in his chapel, and slept until he was roused at 3 a.m. by the crowing of his Cochin-China cockerel—the bird referred to in his letter to the Superioress. He then lighted a fire and lay down again for what he called his "half-hour of luxury." By four he was dressed and shaved, and spent the next hour at devotions in the chapel, which was served by Roman Catholic priests of St Anne's, Leeds. From five until eight he read Latin and Spanish, usually *Don Quixote* and the *Life of St Francis Xavier*; wrote; looked over his bailiff's reports and worked at taxidermy. After a light breakfast he went out until noon, often working on his hedges, and in cold weather whenever possible he lighted a fire near which he worked. Between noon and half-past one when he dined, he usually read. Moore's interesting list of his favourite authors includes Dryden, Sterne, Dyer, Goldsmith, White of Selborne, Cobbett and Washington Irving, but is by no means complete. He went out again after dinner, had tea at six and went to bed at eight. What he did in wet or very cold weather is not recorded.

All this refers to the disposal of his hours in extreme old age. In his earlier years it must have been different, particularly before his marriage and the death of his wife. Moore's careful description of the Squire's combined study, work-room and bedroom includes a map of Guiana and the picture of St Catherine thought by the Squire to resemble Anne. The room was "austere," but contained "some prints and pictures" valued by the Squire more for their associations than their merit, among them the St Catherine picture and the portrait of a lobster. The furniture included a few shelves of his favourite books, a washstand, a shaving mirror, and a work table. Wood's assertion that the Squire's personal expenditure did not exceed that of a day labourer on his estate may have been true of Lent, but hardly of other times. The Wood and Moore vignettes of the serene and frugal saint do not altogether square, for instance, with the fact that after Lent the Squire often made himself ill by over-eating. "Seldom any splendid story is wholly true."

On June 3rd, 1864, the Squire unexpectedly invited his sisters to row with him to the far end of his lake, and there showed them a cross he had erected between two great oaks. He then put his arms round the cross, and told them that at this spot he wished to be buried. Until this moment nobody had known the date of the Squire's birthday, but at these words a sudden thought came to Miss Edmonstone. She spoke in Italian, as a servant was with them, and said: "Squire! to-day is your birthday." "He smiled, and bowed assent."

Nearly a year later, in May 1865, when the Squire was close upon his eighty-third birthday, he was healthy and active, still able to perform most of his acrobatic and climbing feats, and his mind was as alert as ever. On the 5th of the month he wrote to his young friend, Norman Moore: "Two nightingales are singing here most melodiously—one in Stubbed-piece, the other in our plover swamp. Cannot you manage to slip over and listen to them?"

At that time Moore was reading for an examination but packed his books and went to stay at Walton Hall. He worked late, and the Squire asked him always to drop in to the work-and-bedroom at midnight for a short talk. At midnight on May 24th Moore "found the dear old wanderer sitting asleep by the fire, wrapped up in a large Italian cloak. His head rested upon his wooden pillow, which was placed on a table, and his thick silvery hair formed a beautiful contrast with the dark colour of the oak." The Squire then retired to his chapel for a brief prayer, and on his return they talked for about three-quarters of an hour about "the brown owl, the night-jar, and other birds."

Next morning the Squire, Moore and a carpenter went out to the far end of the park to make some repairs to the wooden bridges. While they were returning, the Squire caught his foot in a brier and "fell heavily upon a log." He was "greatly shaken" by his fall, and said that "he thought he was dying." He refused all assistance and walked towards the boat, but had to lie down and rest on the way, and then capitulate and ask to be helped into the boat. When he reached home he changed his clothes and waited for the doctor (not Dr Hobson, who was himself seriously ill at this time), and then insisted on walking upstairs, although "bent double with anguish." In order to save trouble to others, he did not go to his own room at the top of the house, but lay on the sofa in Miss Edmonstone's sitting-room.

Unluckily, though both Moore and Hobson were well-known physicians, particularly Moore, neither has told us what the Squire damaged in his fall on the log which gave him so much pain. A broken rib could hardly have been fatal, even at his age, unless it had caused internal injuries. It may be noted that even at this time the Squire still suffered from "agues." An enlarged and protruding spleen is one of the commonest signs of an old malaria patient, and a reasonable inference is that in tripping on to the log the Squire ruptured his spleen. At all events he had no doubt whatever that he was dying, even though next day, the 26th, his pain had considerably diminished. When the women were out of the room he said to Moore, "This is a bad business, a bad case." He retained all his self-possession, and during the spasms of pain often looked up with "a gentle smile," and made one of his jokes.

"Towards midnight," says Moore, "he grew worse. The priest, the Reverend R. Browne, was summoned, and Waterton got ready to die. He pulled himself upright without help, sat in the middle of the sofa, and gave his blessing in turn to his grandson Charlie, to his granddaughter Mary, to each of his sisters-in-law, to his niece, and to myself, and left a message for his son, who was hastening back from Rome. He then received the last sacraments, repeated all the responses, Saint Bernard's hymn in English, and the first two verses of the *Dies Irae*. The end was now at hand, and he died at twenty-seven minutes past two in the morning of May 27th, 1865. The window was open. The sky was beginning to grow grey, a few rooks had cawed, the swallows were twittering, the land-rail was craking from the ox-close, and a favourite cock, which he used to call his morning gun, leaped out from some hollies, and gave his accustomed crow."

XV

THE funeral was delayed until the return of Edmund from Rome, and took place on June 3rd, 1865, the eighty-third anniversary of the Squire's birth, and one year after the visit with his sisters to his chosen burial-place. The funeral procession went by boat across the lake to the grave dug below the cross between the two oaks. It was headed by a boat containing the Catholic Bishop of Beverley and fourteen priests chanting the office for the dead; followed by a boat bearing the coffin and four boats of mourners, the last of which towed the Squire's own sailing boat, empty and draped in black. As the coffin was being lowered, a bird sang from a bush close at hand, a little episode which in time gave rise to the belief that long flights of the Squire's "feathered friends" had followed his body to the grave.

The cross was inscribed with words written by the Squire:

"*Orate pro anima Caroli Waterton, cujus fessa juxta hance crucem sepeliuntur ossa. Natus 1782. Obiit 1865.*"

(*Pray for the soul of Charles Waterton, whose weary bones are buried beside this cross. Born 1782. Died 1865.*)

The Squire's fears for the future of his handiwork proved to have been only too well-founded. His son turned out a spendthrift, and was eventually forced to sell Walton Hall, and to the family of that very soap-boiler with whom the Squire had fought in law, people who cared nothing for his work in the bird sanctuary. The collection was apparently given by Edmund to Ushaw College, but eventually and rightly came into the possession of Stonyhurst. Walton Hall still stands on its island, and descendants of the Squire's Canada geese are said still to inhabit the lake. When Mr Philip Gosse visited Walton Hall, not long before the Second World War, he found that the Squire's chapel had been turned into a lumber room and that his grave lay ruined and neglected.

THE END

THE WATERTON MATERIAL

(1) CHARLES WATERTON

(a) *Wanderings in South America,* first published in 1825, and since frequently reprinted. Best edition that edited by Wood in 1880.

(b) *Essays.* First Series, 1838; Second Series, 1841; Third Series, 1858. Contain many scattered personal and biographical notes and anecdotes.

(c) *Autobiography.* Published in three sections as introductions to the three series of Essays, covering the Squire's life down to 1858.

(2) DR RICHARD HOBSON

Charles Waterton; His Home, Habits and Handiwork, by Richard Hobson, M.D. Cantab., Leeds, 1866. A whimsical production, but contains priceless "reminiscences of an intimate and most confiding personal association for nearly thirty years." In his eightieth year the Squire read Hobson's notes and endorsed all his facts.

(3) DR afterwards SIR NORMAN MOORE

Essays on Natural History, by Charles Waterton, Edited, with a Life of the Author, by Norman Moore, B.A., St. Catherine's College, Cambridge, 1871. The "Essays" are not quite complete, but a number of the Squire's letters are added. The "Life" is a reprint of the Squire's *Autobiography,* with a certain number of passages cut out and the addition of material supplied by the Squire about his schooldays, and a good account of the Squire's last days and death. The extracts from Moore's *Journal* are very valuable, but his enthusiastic statements about the Squire's infallibility as a naturalist are not supported by experts.

(4) REV J. G. WOOD

(a) *Wanderings in South America, etc.* Edited, with Biographical Introduction and Explanatory Index, by the Rev. J. G. Wood. With one hundred illustrations, 1880. The best edition of the *Wanderings.* The biographical introduction is founded on the autobiography and on Moore, but contains original reminiscences. It is ill-arranged, and sentimentalises the Squire on the lines of Thackeray's eccentric saint. Engravings quaint but interesting, especially those of the Squire's "dodges."

(b) *Out of Doors.* A Selection of Original Articles, by the Rev. J. G. Wood, M.A., F.L.S., 1895. Contains "The Home of a Naturalist," a puff of the Squire and the park, obviously written under the Squire's supervision and therefore before 1865.

(5) JOSEPH HATTON

Old Lamps for New, undated, but published in 1889. Contains "Stone Walls do not a Prison Make," reminiscences of H. D. Dixon ("the Druid") about the Squire and Walton Hall. This Dixon was an authority on cattle, and angered the Squire by refusing to praise a second-rate animal the Squire thought a prize beast.

(6) Mrs Pitt Byrne

Social Hours with Celebrities. This lady spent six weeks at Walton Hall in 1861, seeking copy for one of her social articles. She revisited the Hall in or about 1890, and found it greatly changed for the worse.

(7) *Memories of Waterton,* by Stonyhurst pupils, including Percy Fitz-gerald, quoted by Mr. Philip Gosse.

(8) *The Illustrated London News*

The number for August 24th, 1844, contained an article on the Squire and a full-length portrait. The number for June 17th, 1865, contained an illustrated article on the Squire's funeral and an account of his family.

(9) *Dictionary of National Biography*

"Charles Waterton," by Sir Norman Moore. A good, condensed biography containing much information in a short space. The best short account of Waterton.

(10) *Stonyhurst College Centenary Record 1894.*

(11) The Author of *Flemish Interiors*

This anonymous writer published *Gossip of This Century,* where he twice mentions Waterton and claims to have known him personally. He announces his intention of writing at length on the Squire in another book, but if this was ever published I have not found it. (See p. 192.)

(12) Edmund Selous

Introduction to the Everyman edition of the *Wanderings,* 1925. An estimate of Waterton by a naturalist of this century. The Index compares very unfavourably with Wood's. It contains in its very brief space such information as that a Jacamar is a Jacana, the spur-winged waterhen. It is nothing of the sort. Waterton's Jacamar belongs to the Galbulidae, a genus of common South American birds.

(13) J. Simson

Biographical Sketch of Waterton, 1880. I have been unable to find a copy of this very scarce work, but a report on the British Museum copy says that it contains no original biographical material, and points out some of the Squire's mistakes.

(14) Norman Douglas

Experiments, 1925. Contains an account of Waterton under the title, " A Mad Englishman." The student of Waterton will note that it contains the following errors: the explanation for the Squire's belief that curare might be a remedy for hydrophobia has been overlooked. (See *Essays,* Second Series, pp. xx–xxi.) The statement that Waterton "never wore hat or boots" is untrue. The barefoot entry into Rome in 1840 is dated before the climbing of St. Peter's in 1817–18, and both events are made to occur in the same year. The statement that the Squire never had an audience of the Pope overlooks the paragraph in Wood's edition of *Wanderings,* Introduction, p. 25. Mr Douglas says that Waterton simultaneously used as a pillow the wood block and the soles of his shoes—quite untrue. He never mentions the all-important fact that Walton was the first English bird sanctuary, but on the contrary describes it as full of devices for "catching and killing"!

(15) EDITH SITWELL

The English Eccentrics, 1933. Contains "Charles Waterton, the South American Wanderer," which begins by presenting the Squire as an absurd freak by bringing together, regardless of chronology, exaggerated versions of more obvious absurdities. He is then suddenly transformed into a great writer, a saint, a great gentleman; he was noble, brave, beloved, chivalrous, wise, loving, gay, and so forth. The student should note the following errors. The poisoning of the ass Wouralia in London in 1814 is hopelessly confused with the Nottingham experiments of 1840. (See Wood's *Wanderings,* pp. 151–2; *Essays,* First Series, pp. 304–6; Second Series, pp. xvi–xxi.) There is no evidence that the Squire rode on the revived donkey as asserted in this article. The story of the brood of malformed ducks is misunderstood and misreported. The Squire is stated to have fostered the duckling hatched with a reversed head, and to have felt for it the liveliest feelings of admiration, when in fact he never even saw it. (See Hobson, pp. 207–10.) The statement that the Squire loved all living things except man-milliners and rats is quite untrue, and overlooks, among other dislikes, closet naturalists in general, Protestant reformers, poachers, customs officers, passport officers, Mr. Lushington, Audubon, Rennie, Jameson, Swainson and many another. It is not true to say that the Squire captured the coulacanara to study its dental arrangements: it was to get a perfect undamaged specimen for his great collection. It was not Dr Hobson who persuaded the Squire "to fly" from a lower eminence, but some person unnamed, perhaps his confessor. The Protestant clergyman Wood is called "Father" Wood. The Nondescript is said to have been made from an enormous ape, when in fact it was made from a Red Howler monkey, whose body seldom exceeds three feet in length. By the way, there are no apes in the New World.

(16) PHILIP GOSSE

The Squire of Walton Hall, 1940. The only full-length book on the Squire since his contemporaries. The author has painstakingly collected everything he could find about Waterton, including unpublished letters and Norman Moore's journal. The book is largely made up of long quotations. (See below.)

(17) RICHARD ALDINGTON

In 1932 I wrote an essay on Waterton which appeared, of course anonymously, as a leader in *The Times Literary Supplement.* A few copies with my name were printed in 1934 for private circulation by Messrs William Heinemann. In 1935 the essay was again reprinted under my name in *Artifex, Sketches and Ideas* (London, Chatto and Windus; New York, Doubleday, Doran). Mr Philip Gosse has done me the honour of quoting almost verbatim as his own at least two passages from this article (one of 17 lines on his pp. 197–8, one of 23 lines on his pp. 278–9) in his book, *The Squire of Walton Hall.* The passages are reproduced without quotation marks, without any mention of my name anywhere in the book, and with no acknowledgment beyond a brief general one to the editor of *The Times Literary Supplement,* who did not write my essay.

In 1948 I published a long biographical essay on Waterton in *Four English Portraits,* issued by Messrs Evans Bros, London. It was through their generous encouragement that the present volume was undertaken.

(18) The remarks on Waterton by Brigadier-General Theodore Roosevelt are quoted from his foreword to Dr William Beebe's *Jungle Peace,* 1918.

(19) The Waterton family papers which Wood says Edmund Waterton intended to publish seem never to have appeared in print.

Postscript

Since this list was set up in type I have learned that the author of *Gossip of This Century* was a woman, the Mrs Pitt Byrne who wrote *Social Hours with Celebrities.*

Index